To Harry,

From the

Joe Glasser
Boston

Sell-Out to Stalin:
The Tragic Errors
of Churchill and Roosevelt

BY THE SAME AUTHOR

Des Géôles d'Anna Pauker aux prisons de Tito
Prix Silvio Pellico 1951
in French
Le Livre Contemporain, Paris (Epuisé)

Yalta si Crucificarea Romaniei
in Rumanian
Editione NAGARD
9 a Larga, Milano, Italy
Price 10 dollars

L'Europe de l'Est trahie et vendue
in French
La Pensée Universelle Editeurs
4, rue Charlemagne, Paris IVè.
Prix 89 FF.

Nicholas Baciu

SELL-OUT TO STALIN

The Tragic Errors of Churchill and Roosevelt

The Untold Story

VANTAGE PRESS
New York / Washington / Atlanta
Los Angeles / Chicago

The names of people and places in this volume have been maintained in their original orthography.

FIRST EDITION

Published by Vantage Press, Inc.
516 West 34th Street, New York, New York 10001

Manufactured in the United States of America
ISBN: 533-06096-6X

Library of Congress Catalog Card No.: 84-90004

In June 1945, General de Gaulle received Duff Cooper, the British ambassador to Paris, and told him, "We cannot make war with you, now. I realize it. But you have outraged France and betrayed the Occident. That cannot be forgotten."

—de Gaulle, *Memoir of War* (Vol. 3, p. 219)

Contents

Preface

Having escaped from the shipwreck of my native country, having experienced ten Communist prisons, I set out, in 1950, to share my experiences—in a book written in French, *Des Géôles de Ana Pauker aux prisons de Tito*—with the free Western world.

The book was destined to denounce, to this free world in which I had just arrived, the abuses of Russia in the invasion of my country by forced Communization; the liquidation of the intellectual elite of the country by intimidation, impoverishment, misery, and putting fetters on the minds of my countrymen.

I believed then, in 1950, as so many others did, that the Russians had committed abuses by military force in Eastern Europe in order to Communize and Russianize by betraying the good faith of the Americans and British; that the Russians had trampled on the solemn engagements made in the Atlantic Charter and the Declaration made in Liberated Europe at Yalta along with Churchill and Roosevelt; that the Russians had lied, had deceived, and had made themselves masters of Europe against the will of Roosevelt and Churchill.

That is what I thought in 1950. But for a long time, I have ceased to believe that, because, in the meantime, I have done much research and have discovered the truth.

But the same legends persist today, thirty-eight years after the end of the war. We hear also today that had Roosevelt lived, the destiny of the world would have been otherwise.

We also see how those admirers of that man of genius; that titan of the history of Great Britain and of world history—Winston Churchill—claim that their idol could not have prevented the Russians' becoming masters of Europe because of Roosevelt, who did not understand Churchill's plan to invade the Balkans in order to "cut" the Russian way into Europe; that Roosevelt bore all the responsibility.

ix

Was that so?

Churchill claimed—in the notorious interview with Stalin on 9 October 1944, in the Kremlin—that he had established spheres of influence "only for a period of three months." Is the truth not otherwise?

But we know now from ultrasecret documents only now declassified—in archives of London and Washington—what the tragic truth is. The secret documents, when analyzed, show how both Churchill and Roosevelt secretly decided—by themselves alone—the fate of the whole world.

The present volume, based on those secret documents, establishes the truth:

—That Eastern Europe was ceded voluntarily and consciously to Stalin.
—That the authors of this cession were Churchill and Roosevelt—the true forgers of the Iron Curtain.
—That, if mankind be today on the verge of a third world war, it is due only to the tragic faults of those two men.
—That neither the noble American people nor the great and glorious British people can be held responsible for the sale of Eastern Europe to Stalin. They had no idea of the arrangements. They did not approve them nor do they today.

That both President Roosevelt and Winston Churchill were in poor health during the course of the whole war has been established. We must ask ourselves whether their judgment was not impaired and influenced by the illnesses that afflicted them. All the more so when we know that both of them acted alone and in secret.

I have utilized these aforementioned documents to emphasize the case of Rumania and to analyze in depth the situation of that country, not because Rumania is my native land, but because the case of Rumania is typical; the same pattern of duplicity, cynicism, and treachery that was used against her has been applied also to the other countries of Eastern Europe.

During the war, Rumania was the cornerstone of the entire South European front. Had this been understood and had Rumania been given assistance the entire Hitler front would have collapsed, thus ending the war in 1943.

Besides, in 1943, only Rumania had started serious discussions to end the war, and we have access to an impressive amount of top-secret documents regarding these negotiations, especially in Stockholm and in Cairo. All these documents throw new light on many other events in other countries of Eastern Europe.

This is why an in-depth analysis of Rumania's case is so important.

*　*　*

In the course of the following pages, we shall see how Roosevelt, fascinated by the personality of Stalin, consented to all the latter's wishes.

Why was the war prolonged by two years when the satellites—especially Rumania—wanted to withdraw from it in 1943? Why could Admiral Canaris not have stopped Hitler and made a separate peace?

I have tried to reply as fully as possible to these questions.

In the light of certain secret documents from London and Washington, the Armistice treaties of Cairo, Stockholm and the Act of 23 August 1944, all appear differently from the way they had previously been perceived. All the Anglo-American protests against the installation of Communist governments in Eastern Europe were only deceptions and crocodile tears destined to hide the infamous concessions made to Stalin.

I must say at once that the so-called "Yalta Agreements" were not written treaties, secret and signed in February 1945, in the Crimea. No. By "Yalta," we must understand a whole, global understanding of secret, oral, or written agreements covering the entire period from 1941 to the Yalta Conference of February 1945.

Beginning in 1939, with Hitler, the claims of Stalin were becoming known to the Allies very gradually. The British were, in 1941, the first to know and to sanction—in 1942 by the Treaty of Mutual Assistance—these claims. The Treaty of Mutual Assistance was confirmed to Stalin in 1943 by American emissaries who gave Stalin Roosevelt's verbal—but categorical—promise at the Teheran Conference; the promise was to be sealed by secrecy until the American elections. It was confirmed first by triangular telegrams—Churchill–Roosevelt–Stalin—in May–June 1944, then by the agreements in Moscow between Churchill and Stalin in October 1944, and, finally, by Yalta itself, where the fate of Eastern Europe was not even discussed, because it had already been decided.

And so, we have to begin with the events of 1939 and follow them chronologically until 1948. In that year was an awakening of awareness among the American public as to how the situation might evolve in Eastern Europe. This lasted until 1954.

Let us proceed to the historical analysis of the events with humility and deference to the great leaders Roosevelt and Churchill and with the great respect we have and owe to their great and noble countries. But let us also analyze these events with the passion arising from having suffered for truth and justice and with the respect that we all owe to the historical truth.

1984   —N. B.

Table of Events

In order to help readers follow the events, especially in view of the great quantity of documents quoted intentionally by the author to support his affirmations, the following chronological table of the most important historical events is presented:

1939   Apr.:   Britain and France give solemn guarantees to Rumania.

       23 Aug.:   The Molotov-Ribbentrop nonaggression pact.

       1 Sept.:   Hitler attacks Poland.

       30 Nov.:   Russians attack Finland.

1940   June: The Russians occupy the Baltic countries.

       26 June: The Russians give an ultimatum to Rumania to cede Bessarabia and Bucovina.

       30 Aug.:   The Vienna Dictate: The Mutilation of Transylvania and the Dobrudja by Hitler.

       6 Sept.:   The Abdication of King Carol.

       11 Oct.:   German troops enter Rumania.

1941   22 June: Hitler attacks Russia. Rumania crosses the River Pruth.

       12 July: Signing of the Convention of Mutual Assistance between Britain and Russia in Moscow.

       6 Dec.:   Britain declares war on Rumania.

       7 Dec.:   The Japanese attack the Americans at Pearl Harbor.

       12 Dec.:   Marshal Antonescu declares war on the United States.

       16 Dec.:   Anthony Eden in Moscow. Stalin demands Bessarabia, Bucovina, and military bases in Rumania.

1942	May:	Anglo-Russian Treaty of Mutual Assistance.
		Russia's demands in Rumania and the Balkans.
1943	Jan.:	Roosevelt asks for "unconditional surrender."
	2 Feb.:	Surrender of the German armies at Stalingrad.
	5 Feb.:	Marshal Antonescu proposes to Mussolini common withdrawal from the war of Rumania and Italy.
	Sept.:	Rumanian armistice negotiations begin in Madrid.
	Oct.:	Attempts by Antonescu to conclude an armistice with the British at Lisbon.
	Oct.:	Conference of foreign ministers in Moscow.
	Nov.:	The Teheran Conference.
	Dec.:	Three British officers are parachuted into Rumania.
	Dec.:	Rumanian armistice discussions begin in Stockholm.
1944	17 Mar.:	Rumanian negotiations begin in Cairo.
	2 Apr.:	Solemn declaration on the part of Molotov.
	3 Apr.:	American bombardments begin in Rumania.
	12 Apr.:	Communication of the armistice conditions in Cairo.
	13 Apr.:	Communication of armistice conditions at Stockholm.
	31 May:	The Russians improve the armistice conditions offered at Stockholm to Marshal Antonescu.
	10 June:	Opposition Rumanian leader Maniu accepts the terms of the armistice offered in Cairo.
	12 June:	Roosevelt and Churchill agree to cede Rumania to the Russians (spheres of influence in the Balkans).
	17 June:	Maniu sends the "plan" for a reversed alliance to Cairo for approval.
	22 Aug.:	Marshal Antonescu seeks an armistice through the Turkish ambassador.
	22 Aug.:	Marshal Antonescu seeks an armistice through the Swedish minister.
	23 Aug.:	Arrest of Marshal Antonescu. Ceasing of hostilities.
	12 Sept.:	Signing of Rumania's unconditional surrender in Moscow.
	9 Oct.:	Churchill hands over Rumania and establishes spheres of influence in the Balkans.

1945	4–11 Feb.:	Yalta Conference.
	27 Feb.:	Vishinksy in Bucharest. Groza government, 6 March 1944.
	12 Apr.:	Death of Roosevelt.
	8 May:	Surrender of Germany.
	17 July:	Potsdam Conference.
	6 Aug.:	Atomic bomb drops on Hiroshima.
	15 Aug.:	Surrender of Japan.
	Dec.:	Conference of the three foreign ministers in Moscow.
	Dec.–Jan. '46:	Harriman and Kerr's mystifying mission to Bucharest.

1946	4 Feb.:	Britain and the United States recognize the Communist Groza government in Rumania.
	19 Nov.:	"Elections" in Rumania.
	1 Dec.:	Opening of Parliament without the presence of the Opposition.

1947	27 Jan.:	Signing of the Peace Treaties, in Paris.
	25 July:	Arrest of Iuliu Maniu, Mihalache, etc.
	25 July:	Dissolution of National Peasant Party.
	30 Dec.:	Abdication of King Michael I.

1948	April:	Berlin Blockade.
	May:	Arrest of Titel Petrescu and Dinu Bratianu, Opposition Rumanian leaders.
	4 July:	Exclusion of Marshal Tito from the Cominform.

1949	Feb.:	Triumph of Mao in China.
	23 Feb.:	Czechoslovakia becomes a Russian satellite.
	Aug.:	Russia explodes first atomic bomb.

| 1950 | June: | Korean War begins. |

| 1953 | Jan.: | General Eisenhower becomes president of the United States. |
| | 5 March: | Death of Stalin. |

Sell-Out to Stalin:
The Tragic Errors
of Churchill and Roosevelt

CHAPTER 1

Rumania, a Latin Country

Before touching on the events and important dates from 1939 onwards, we must say something about Rumania and the Rumanian people.

Settled by destiny in one of the most beautiful regions of Europe, with high mountains of up to 2,500 metres, clothed in superb forests of every kind; with hills, valleys, fields, lakes, rivers, and outlets to the Black Sea, Rumania was, in 1939, a country to be envied.

Rich in agricultural products, in oil, in minerals of every kind, she had always been a temptation to all her neighbours, to all conquerors.

A Latin people, with roots planted 4,000 years ago on the earth where she still stands, with a strong personality, the Rumanians, who were converted to Christianity six hundred years before the Russians, are profoundly religious, benign, and humane. They speak a Roman language, which is very close to the old Latin of their ancestors.

After the vicissitudes of history, from the barbarian invasions up to the grave trials of World War I, the Rumanian people at last regained their natural frontiers, the frontiers of their blood and language. They were at last united under the roof of Great Rumania.

The fulfilment of this historical right was made possible by the entry of little Rumania into the war in 1916, on 14 August, alongside the Allies: France, Britain, Russia, and, later, the United States.

Rumania entered the war at the most difficult moment for the Allies and forced the Germans to withdraw the forty divisions they had hurled against the small, but heroic Rumanian people. The Rumanian people fought heroically and resisted. The losses, both military and civilian, were frightful, but, alongside the Allies, they succeeded in realizing their millennial dream: the integration of all Rumanians in a single stage, in a single national home: Greater Rumania.

1

After centuries of struggle, sacrifice, suffering, and hope, the warm sun of national homecoming shone for the first time in the Rumanian sky, warming souls and promising better times.

After tragic losses of the First World War—a million men—in the struggle with the Allies for a common cause, Rumanians bandaged their wounds and set to work seriously.

The national consciousness that had been affirmed in the trenches was also affirmed in peacetime. Slowly, but surely, it forged new, organic laws that were more democratic, more just. A new constitution—with universal suffrage, with mandatory education, with grants of land to the peasants by the expropriations of the great landlords—was immediately voted. The democratic youth were serving their apprenticeship in a good, honest school. The inhabitants soon recovered their pride in every facet of life: culture, religion, science, and politics.

Rumania did not foresee a second world war and hoped only to live at peace with all her neighbours, with all nations.

But the curse that has followed this nation from birth—a curse that has lasted four thousand years—dealt her a fresh blow.

In 1939, the Rumanian people saw their national existence gravely threatened once more and were obliged to take up arms in order to continue their national existence on the map of the world.

Connected by blood, by language, and by culture with France and Italy, Rumania—a Latin island in a sea of Slavs—had to be liquidated, because she was an advance sentinel of Western Europe on the Eastern frontier. Her existence inconvenienced not only Russia, but also Bulgaria, Hungary, and Nazi Germany.

In 1939, Rumania was allied with France and Britain by treaties of mutual assistance that guaranteed independence and sovereignty to her frontiers.

On the local level, the Little Entente bound her by solemn treaties of friendship and mutual help to France, Czechoslovakia, and Yugoslavia. The *Balkan Pact* further bound her to Greece and Turkey.

The Treaty of Versailles guaranteed the existence of the Rumanian people and of Greater Rumania.

But, in 1939, European order crumbled like a house of cards under the unopposed brutality and military-political aggression of Hitler.

Within a few months, Rumania was left alone in the face of Nazi aggression, of Russian Imperialism, of the Hungarian and Bulgarian thirst for revenge.

2

The Rumanian people were alone, deserted, in danger of extinction.

The first victim of the Hitler–Stalin Pact of 23 August 1939, after Poland, was Rumania.

With France at a low ebb, with Britain struggling for survival and British guarantees withdrawn and useless, Rumania was alone, the prey of two brigands: Stalin and Hitler.

The result of the secret agreement—the annex to the pact between these two—was that Russia exercised the rights conferred on her by Hitler and gave an ultimatum to Rumania on 26 June 1940 to cede two of her ancestral territories: all of Bessarabia and the northern half of Bucovina. Hitler ordered her to conform, not to resist. She had to give them up.

In three days, more than three and a half million Rumanians had been swallowed up by Stalin, and more than 51,000 square kilometres of Rumanian territory had been seized.

After some weeks, Hitler—by the so-called Treaty of Vienna (Ribbentrop-Ciano talks)—was to take northwestern Transylvania from Rumania. She lost, once more, over two million Rumanians and 44,000 square kilometres of her territory, annexed to Hungary.

At the same time, as a result of this "arbitration," Rumania had to give up 400,000 Rumanians to Bulgaria and another slice of 7,000 square kilometres of territory from her mutilated country.

In a few months, the Treaty of Versailles was in ruins—due to the complicity of Hitler and Stalin.

The internal situation in Rumania in 1940 was also desperate. Led by a corrupt authoritarian king, Carol the Second, she was eaten up by contradictory currents, like the whole of Europe. Besides the historic democratic parties there was also a nationalist minority of the right, of course encouraged by Nazi Germany and by Fascist Italy.

As a result of the collapse after Hitler's "arbitration" in Vienna, and under the fist of Stalin since 26 June 1940, King Carol II could no longer remain on the throne. He abdicated at the beginning of September 1940, having appointed General Antonescu prime minister.

General Antonescu was one of the most distinguished Rumanian officers. Aide to General Presen in the High Command in World War I, he was admired and respected. He was also feared, because he was reputed to be a Spartan, disciplined, a great patriot, but authoritarian.

Having forced King Carol II to abdicate, General Antonescu assumed power alone, with a military government and technicians; without the historical Rumanian political parties; without a parliament.

Although at heart he was pro-French and pro-British (not only because of his fight alongside them in World War I, but also from his education in those countries), General Antonescu adhered, nonetheless, to the Tripartite Pact made with Hitler and Mussolini in the autumn of 1940.

At that time, like everyone else, General Antonescu thought that Germany would win, and especially that she would attack Soviet Russia.

Against the deep feelings of the country—which, in spirit, was in sympathy with her great Allies of World War I—General Antonescu took upon himself to change the historical situation and, alone, changed Rumania's alliance.

In the following months—after the occupation of the country by Hitler's armies by the so-called Instruction Units—General Antonescu began to occupy himself seriously with the Rumanian Army.

The whole country looked with horror towards the East, for they knew that the Russian peril had not passed and that it could become even more threatening.

The Rumanian people knew their history.

From Peter the Great to Stalin the Red, Russia had carried on the same policy of aggression and imperialism: under the Tsars, under the cloak of Pan-Slavism; under Stalin, beneath the mask of Communist ideology; Rumania looked eastward in terror. The theft of Bessarabia and Bucovina was only a beginning. She knew too well, because the Russian invasion of 26 June 1940 had been the twelfth invasion of her country.

SUFFERINGS UNDER RUSSIAN OCCUPATION

Rumania remembered with horror the years 1711, 1739, 1769, 1774, 1778, 1792, from 1806–1812; from 1826–1834; from 1853–1854; from 1848–1857; from 1877–1879; from 1916. Twelve invasions, including that of 1940. She looked eastward and shuddered because she was a Latin country, Christian and democratic. She knew what to expect from the East.

In this situation, Rumania entered the war against the Soviet Union declared on her by Hitler in June 1941, in order to defend her frontiers against further aggression by Russia and to liberate her brothers. It was a war of legitimate national defence, imposed on the Rumanian nation. A victim of Hitler, the Rumanian people were obliged to fight alongside him—their enemy in World War I. But what else could they do, when

4

the whole of Europe was in a state of collapse and they were left alone?

The Rumanian historical democratic parties were the National Peasant Party, led by the old and experienced Transylvanian democrat, Iuliu Maniu, whose achievement it was to regain Transylvania; and the National Liberal Party of Dinu Bratianu, whose ancestors were the architects of Great Rumania. Besides, there were the Iron Guard Party and the Socialist Party, under the leadership of a distinguished and romantic lawyer, Titel Petrescu. The Communist Party did not exist. They had not even a thousand members.

This was the so-called opposition of General Antonescu.

In the meantime I will mention some criticisms made by these parties of General Antonescu, some of them justified, others less so, in order to make the following analysis more complete.

1. General Antonescu proclaimed himself Leader of the State, dictator; he set aside the political parties and Parliament, suppressed the constitution, and the role of the king.

A government of national unity—formed of all the parties—so they say—could have avoided some of the mistakes made, being surrounded by mediocre and improvised collaborators.

2. United to the last man and the last Rumanian soul in the need to free their Rumanian brothers from the Russian yoke, and without questioning either the patriotism or the honour and the exceptional qualifications of General Antonescu, the Opposition did not reproach him for his declaration of war on Russia, but for his not halting the Rumanian troops on the Dniester after the occupation of Rumanian Bessarabia and Bucovina and instead continuing to fight on Russian territory.

The solution was not easy. From the military point of view, the enemy had to be pursued, conquered, and hindered from recouping. From the political point of view, Hitler had promised that the "Arbitration of Vienna" would be revised, and General Antonescu hoped to recover Transylvania, while the Hungarians fought alongside Hitler across the Dniester.

3. The proclamation by Antonescu, announced in his first days as governor of a Rumanian legionary state, was strange. Soon he saw his mistake and not only cancelled it but entered into direct conflict with the Iron Guard, keeping them at a distance all during the war.

4. He left it to Mihai Antonescu, his closest collaborator (foreign minister and later prime minister of Rumania), to speak of "the crusade against Communism" in his speeches.

Rumania was waging a just war to defend her nation and her people.

5

The Rumanians were not waging an ideological war, but simply defending their existence.

5. A tactical mistake was the declaration of war on the United States under pressure from Hitler. Rumania was heart and soul on the side of her great Allies and even if Britain had declared war on Rumania, General Antonescu even under pressure from Hitler—the Rumanian Opposition said—should not have agreed to declare war on America even though Rumania committed no warlike act against the United States.

6. The Opposition also accused him of not having accepted the conditions for an armistice in time, when Rumania could have been withdrawn from the war. They said that his fate (he fell under the bullets of a Communist firing-squad in 1946) and that of the country might have been different.

Would it? Would a different policy on the part of Antonescu have changed the destiny of Eastern Europe?

We shall see the reply later on, in the analysis of the secret documents, which answers this question to a great extent.

Examining these documents concerning Rumania, we examine also those concerning the whole of Eastern Europe—because Rumania's situation is specific. The same perfidy was used in every case.

Insincerity, bad faith, duplicity, and lies were used alike in Rumania and the whole of Eastern Europe.

CHAPTER 2

Franklin Delano Roosevelt— Dictator?

Before undertaking a serious examination of the political mistakes made by President Roosevelt at Yalta and during the course of the war, I will underline the sacrosanct character of the former president and the enormity of this almost impossible task of criticizing Roosevelt before the American public, whose freedom of opinion and spirit of criticism leads sometimes to licence and often to abuse.

But even today, thirty-six years after his death, Franklin Delano Roosevelt remains a titan, one of the greatest and most respected presidents of the United States.

Why? Why this unbounded admiration for the former president, in spite of all his political mistakes in the course of the war and at Yalta? Part of this admiration is undoubtedly due to his personality and his achievements in the first years in the White House, after his election. But part of it is also due to the fact that American public opinion was shielded from the knowledge of his great faults, in spite of all the "electoral" criticism of the Yalta policy. This criticism died out after his death or at the end of the campaign between the Democrats and Republicans in 1948.

One of the journalists covering the election in 1980 asked the candidate Ronald Reagan whom he admired most and whom he would choose as a model from among all the former presidents of the U.S.A. "Franklin Delano Roosevelt," replied the future president, although he was the candidate of the Republican Party—the party that had opposed Roosevelt and his policies, denouncing him ruthlessly in the years immediately after the war.

Did the subsequent president really believe this or was it simply an

7

"electoral" reply, knowing how much admiration, how much veneration the name of Roosevelt arouses even to-day?

That is why the subject is repellent, dangerous, and difficult. But it will be treated unhesitatingly in the following chapters; impartially, with all the courage and devotion that an objective criticism requires.

In order to understand the devotion of the American people to Franklin Roosevelt, we must remember that he took office in 1933 when the U.S. were passing through the most serious economic crisis in the course of their history: everything seemed to be collapsing and the institutions crumbling away, one by one.

Roosevelt, former governor of the State of New York, elected president with a large majority over the Republican, Herbert Hoover, brought a message of hope and confidence to a demoralized nation. In the first three years, after the great bank "crash" of 1929, the national income had fallen by more than half—from 87 billion dollars to 41 billion. Unemployment had risen from four million in 1930 to eight million in 1931, reaching the high figure of twelve million in 1932—more than a quarter of the work force of the entire United States. Some cities, e.g., Chicago, had more than half of their work force unemployed.

The memory of the "Great Depression" is more vivid even to-day than those of World Wars I or II. That was the real cataclysm for the American people.

But, by the so-called New Deal, President Roosevelt led them out of that crisis, introduced new social and judicial cadres, inspired them with courage, and gave them jobs and bread.

In what was known as "The Hundred Days," President Roosevelt introduced some fifteen programs, some of which changed the American banking system and radically reformed agriculture.

Some of these reforms fell into disuse while others remain and have become the basis of the entire American system: Social Security, minimum salaries, savings-books, trades unions, etc.

Surrounded by the "New Dealers," like General Hugh Johnson of NRA, Harry Hopkins of the Works Progress Administration, Henry Wallace in the Agriculture Department, and Harold Ickes, President Roosevelt assumed exceptional powers, truly dictatorial powers. He injected state control over a free economy, a liberal-capitalist one, rigorously and arbitrarily but this control, partly at least, brought immediate results. The crisis was swallowed up, and the American people regained confidence. Roosevelt had become not a hero, but a God—the God.

The entire nation was mobilized for work, as if in wartime. Immense public works were organized throughout the country. The dollar was no longer covered by gold. Of 330 monthly dollars' salary, a worker in the FERA of Harry Hopkins was content to receive only 82, but the Works Progress Administration (WPA) engaged over 21 million workers and spent over 10 billion dollars (the 1933 dollar). Like Hitler later on, in Germany, many of the important public works to be seen to-day are the work of those "New Dealers" under President Roosevelt: Triborough Bridge in New York, the barrage of the Grand Coulee Dam in the Columbia River, the canalization in Chicago; the installations and harbours, like that of Brownsville of Texas, as well as 70 percent of all the schools in the US (40,000), and 800,000 kilometers of high-roads.

The unions were organized in the industrial sectors, and the minimum salary established; the forty weekly working-hours; child labour was forbidden, and the Prohibition of alcohol was abolished.

President Roosevelt's New Deal created a substantial change in the lives of the American people, permanently.

Apart from the afore-mentioned programmes, Roosevelt introduced three great innovations in the philosophical basis of American public life:

The first clause of the Constitution, referring to the "general welfare," was to be interpreted as giving the government not only the right, but the *duty* to intervene in every aspect of the economy;

Secondly, that the government *must* ensure the right to a pension, to work, to a salary, to a home, and to health;

Thirdly, that the government has the duty to promote reasonable and equitable distribution not only of material goods, but also of political and statutory public power to the citizen. This aspect of his new philosophy created the first stage in the recognition of the rights of the Black people, of the Jews, and of other minorities to share in the governing of the United States.

Cleverly cultivating his popularity by his famous "fireside chats," broadcast over the entire American continent, President Roosevelt became, in fact, a dictator. Little did he care for the opinions of the Supreme Court of the United States, who had declared eleven of his new measures to be unconstitutional.

He counterattacked vigorously. He wanted to increase the number of nine High Court judges to fifteen in order to appoint his own supporters. The same happened with the Democratic Party, which he wished to purge of "the weeds," i.e., his personal adversaries.

Both attempts failed, but Roosevelt's popularity was intact.

He was chosen President of the U.S. for the fourth time—in thirteen years—and established a personal presidential regime, authoritarian, in keeping with his temperamental nature. Roosevelt believed in his own infallibility.

As with any human undertaking, Roosevelt had his critics, both when in office and later.

His economic programme was considered to be an improvization, lacking in ideology or any clear vision of the future. Professor William Leuchtenburg, in his work *Franklin D. Roosevelt and the New Deal*, remarks, for instance, that Roosevelt did not save America from the economic crisis, because in 1941 there were still six million unemployed. The crisis ended only on the outbreak of war when the entire work force was mobilized.

The man himself, though very likeable, was violently attacked. Even one of his admirers—John Gunther—in *Roosevelt in Retrospect*—accused him of insincerity, meanness in personal relations, two-facedness, of being amateurish and acting in haste, a hypocrite, vindictive, vengeful.

Nor did his private life escape criticism: There was some question of the nature of his relationship with his secretary, Lucy Mercer, throughout his lifetime. It is true that this criticism was made before the letters of the American journalist, Lorena Hickok, and especially those of the president's wife, Eleanor Roosevelt (published several years ago) became public knowledge. We see, between these two women, what may well have been a lesbian connection of more than twenty years.

Another incident in the private life of the Roosevelt couple should also be remarked, because it shows—even to a greater extent—the morbid condition of the former president as well as the dubious relationships of his wife, Eleanor.

A book that appeared recently in the United States, *Love, Eleanor: and Her Friends*,—whose author, Joseph P. Lash, was the hero in the purported incident that I will relate—casts a revealing light on Roosevelt, on his powers of judgment, and on the arbitrary nature of his governing as well as on the pro-Communist tendencies of the "First Lady."

The authenticity of this incident is not totally unquestionable, but it is based on authentic documents in the Pentagon; ultra-secret documents, which were "de-classified" on the basis of the American Freedom of Information Act and Privacy Act (See *U.S. News and World Report*, December 19, 1983.)

In 1943, an American army sergeant—Joseph P. Lash—head of the Communist Youth in his student years, in 1935, was allegedly seen in hotels in Chicago and Urbana, Illinois, with Eleanor Roosevelt. He, strong and handsome, was thirty-three years old; the wife of the president was fifty-nine.

As the U.S. was in the thick of the war in 1943, and as the FBI considered it strange that Eleanor Roosevelt was apparently meeting a notorious communist in hotel rooms, microphones were introduced in the rooms where the meetings took place. According to the report, the microphones revealed an amorous connection between the two. Colonel Forney of the Army Secret Service was supposed to have presented a recording of the incident to President Roosevelt in the White House in the presence of General Strong.

Allegedly, after the president had listened to the entire series of records—from which it seemed clear what his wife had been doing in the hotels with the ribald sergeant—he summoned General Arnold, head of the General Staff, and is said to have ordered him to send the sergeant at once to the Pacific front, as well as all those who had any first-hand knowledge of this incident. They were all supposed to be sent to the front line of battle against the Japanese and kept there until all were killed.

In view of this "ultra-secret" and "ultra-confidential" order discovered in the military documents in the Pentagon, is the question not justified as to whether Roosevelt was, in 1943, in complete command of his powers of discernment, or—as the doctors claimed—seriously attacked by very advanced arteriosclerosis? Otherwise, how can one explain how the Supreme Head of the Army could evidently give such an order, especially when it was a question of his own career and of the interests of his family?

But this incident explains even more clearly the pro-Communist sympathies of Eleanor Roosevelt—sympathies that she retained until her death.

Why do we bring up these aspects of the lives of Roosevelt and his wife? Because they can explain—especially in connection with the illness and incapacity of the president—many of his mistakes. That personal (lesbian?) connection of Eleanor Roosevelt was eventually able to influence the entire pro-Russian policy of the Democratic Party, which she

11

still controlled, especially after the death of the president. Because her friend (or lover!)—the journalist Lorena Hickok—had "progressive and pro-Russian leanings."

How strange was the fate of this Franklin Roosevelt! Born into a very wealthy, patrician family, he was destined to become a businessman or a playboy. But he entered politics and succeeded. He was twice governor of New York State, though paralysed in the limbs already in 1921 when he was struck by poliomyelitis. On crutches, and unable to stand unaided, he nonetheless succeeded in being elected president of the United States in 1932. What extraordinary strength of will he must have had in order to strive so desperately for power, and to succeed! A superhuman strength; diabolical, and according to certain doctors, morbid. But his disease will be discussed more fully later, being a subject that is extremely delicate and serious.

But let us return to the pre-war period and to Roosevelt's politics in that period.

His success in home affairs between 1933 and 1936 was unquestionable. Those were his good years when Congress hung on his words as on those of a god.

Between 1936 and 1938, Franklin Roosevelt had his failures with his unfruitful attempts to "pack" the Supreme Court of the U.S. and to "purge" his personal enemies in the Democratic Party. But these setbacks did little to overshadow his immense personal popularity or to quench his thirst for personal and absolute power.

At that time Hitler was ravaging Europe. After the annexation of the Ruhr and after the denunciation of the Treaty of Versailles, came the Anschluss with Austria in 1938. The cancer that killed Chamberlain caused the shameful Munich agreement with its baneful consequence—war.

In the U.S., public opinion, Congress, and even the government were isolationist—all except President Roosevelt.

Chosen as president for the third time, Roosevelt was, in 1940, master of America. His words and deeds were holy. He had become a legendary hero, above politics; above parties. He belonged to the entire nation.

This fact permitted Roosevelt to lead—step by step, day after day—the U.S. and the American people from total isolationism to active neutrality, then to limited commitment and eventually to war.

In 1939, when war broke out in Europe, the U.S. was totally un-

12

armed, without allies and without the possibility of acquiring any because the law forbade it. In record time and against the will of the majority of the people, Roosevelt changed the face of America completely. Because, long before Pearl Harbor, against the will of the isolationists (the majority of the American people), they were, in fact, at war with Hitler. The entire industry was working night and day, not only for America, but also for Britain. The American fleet ''borrowed'' an imposing number of British destroyers. Convoys of American ships crossed the Atlantic day and night to equip the British people with arms, munitions, and food. The American warships escorting the convoys had orders to attack Hitler's submarines or aeroplanes.

Step by step, day after day, Roosevelt became more deeply involved in World War II. Pearl Harbor was the final step. Wretchedly criticized, America was obliged to reply to the provocation. FDR was only waiting for this chance. His qualities as leader, as inspirer, permitted him to animate the nation to the last man, as with a magic wand.

A man who was paralysed, ill (as we shall see later), brought about this miracle. The entire nation, which had been against entering the war, were mobilized morally, economically, industrially, and militarily and fought a heroic war that they had not wanted. Heroically they were victorious, for this great and generous people deserved to win.

America entered the war unwillingly, waged it with courage and honour, and won it. But America lost the peace.

The great leader of the American people, President Roosevelt, became Commander-in-Chief of the American armies and knew how to fight, to inspire, and to conquer. He won the war for America. But also, by his tragic political mistakes, forfeited the superb, sublime results obtained on the field of battle by the heroic American people.

Why? Why did he lose the peace? Why, through his mistakes, did he cast the American people onto the threshold of a third world war, as we may see to-day?

Was Roosevelt naive? A romantic? A visionary led by the nose by Stalin? Was he ill, as has now been established, and did his once-agile brain fail to do duty in the last years of the war? Had his emaciated body, dragged along on crutches since 1921, become a burden? Had his titanic will also failed him? This must be the explanation.

Nevertheless, Roosevelt continued to govern, and to govern alone, as a real dictator; and together with Churchill and Stalin he shaped the fate of the whole world, for decades, for centuries to come.

Ill, incapable of looking clearly at problems, he withdrew more and more from Cordell Hull—his Secretary of State—and followed only his own whims. He had become isolated in his suffering with ill health. Fascinated by Stalin and his ''successes after the Revolution,'' he became, as we shall see, an easy prey in the hands of the tyrant in the Kremlin.

CHAPTER 3

Since 1941 Stalin Sought "Friendly Governments" on Russia's Western Frontiers

By 1941, Russia had her eye on her western frontier. As MacNeill writes, in his *America, Britain and Russia*, p. 535, "Already in the summer of 1941, Stalin sharply declared that he would not tolerate any 'enemy' on his western frontiers although he knew that if free elections were to be held in those countries, they would vote for governments hostile to Moscow."

In view of this situation—writes the British historian—Roosevelt had to make a choice between the independence and sovereignty of the Eastern European states and cooperation with the Soviet Union.

This is a new and categorical proof that Roosevelt as well as Churchill knew precisely, as far back as 1941, that Stalin wished to have absolute control over Eastern Europe.

Stalin's creation of the "satellite" territories was categorically announced by Ambassador Standley—as early as 1943—in a telegram in which he wrote to Washington: "In 1918, Western Europe tried to organize—to establish—a *cordon sanitaire* to protect it from Bolshevik influence. Is the Kremlin not going to establish a pro-Sovietic cordon now to protect her from Western influence?"

What more did the Americans need to know, apart from the utterances made by Molotov to Hitler in November 1940, in order to understand the expansionist ambitions of Stalin in which the former asked for military bases in Rumania and Bulgaria, a free hand in those countries, and military bases in Dardanelles? Or when the December 1941 Stalin proposed to the British to divide Europe between them, Stalin offering

15

the British military bases in Western Europe against Eastern Europe?

Even Ambassador Averell Harriman—this pro-Russian and cynical American aristocrat—pointed out to Washington Stalin's intentions for Eastern Europe: "The Russians will insist" he writes in this report (reproduced in the correspondence between Harriman and Roosevelt) "firmly and categorically on their 1941 frontiers. The Russians believe that the English have accepted this point of view and the fact that the Americans refuse to discuss this claim means—for the Russians—that they have no objection. The Russians will not be satisfied with territorial expansion only in Poland, but will insist on having a "friendly government" installed in Warsaw. They consider the Polish Government-in-Exile in London as inimical and wholly unacceptable. Above all else, the Soviets are determined not to have in Eastern Europe governments reminiscent of the old *cordon sanitaire*."

In their claims formulated in 1941 to the British and Americans, the Soviets were faithful to the eternal politics of the Tsars of Russia; to the Testament of Peter the Great, and faithful to themselves in the demands made on Hitler in 1939. But the German dictator thrust them aside and preferred war. The Allies accepted them, but in so doing, dug their future graves.

Thus, in the secret protocol of the German-Soviet Pact of 23 August 1939, Article 3 speaks of Rumania and says that "the interest of the Soviet Union in Bessarabia is recorded, and the total lack of the political interest of Germany in this region."

On the basis of this agreement, Bessarabia was stolen from Rumania in June 1940. Thus, Rumania became the first victim of the Hitler-Stalin Pact.

As regards Rumania, Russian effrontery went from strength to strength. In the interview between Molotov and Hitler on 12–13 November 1940, Molotov reproached the Germans for their guarantee of the new frontiers—so mutilated—of Rumania. Germany must realize—said Molotov—that that is a question of exclusively Russian interest.

On 12 November 1940, Hitler in his euphoria after his successes in Europe, proposed an agreement with Molotov to share the British Empire: "Germany should return to the West, and Russia to the East. Russia would find warm and free seas in Iran and the Persian Gulf and the Arabian Sea." Hitler was dreaming.

Molotov brought him back to earth: he spoke to him of Rumania, of Finland, of the Dardanelles, of military bases in Bulgaria, and a pact of non-aggression with that country.

On that date—12 November 1940—Ribbentrop, in turn, presented Molotov with a project of a treaty of alliance and two secret protocols to be signed by Italy and Japan. They planned spheres of influence. The secret protocols contained secret clauses with respective territorial aspirations. The Soviet Union was to have a free hand towards the southeast from her frontier to the Indian Ocean. The second secret protocol was to give her a free hand in the Dardanelles.

Molotov's reply was more than eloquent and showed the constancy of the politics of the Soviets. He demanded a serious discussion about Iran, guarantees for the Dardanelles, and raised the question of Bulgaria, Rumania, Hungary, Yugoslavia, and Greece, as well as Poland and the neutrality of the Scandinavian countries.

On his return to Moscow from Berlin, Molotov immediately summoned the German ambassador and transmitted the reply of the Soviet Union to Ribbentrop's proposals.

Here they are resumed:

Russia was ready to sign the Pact of the Four, with the following conditions:

1. Germany must at once withdraw her troops from Finland;
2. An exclusive guarantee of the Dardanelles by a pact of mutual assistance with Bulgaria, and land and naval bases along the Straits;
4. Soviet aspirations to be recognized in the regions south of Baku and Batum in the direction of Iran and the Persian Gulf;
4. Japan must renounce her rights to "petroleum and coal" in the north of the Sakhalin Islands.

CHURCHILL-ROOSEVELT FAR MORE GENEROUS THAN HITLER

Reading this to-day, one remains stupefied. Everything that was asked of Hitler and not granted—the latter preferring war—was obtained by the Russians from Roosevelt and Churchill. All, and even more, as we shall see when we analyse the Yalta Conference.

What naïveté and ignorance are reflected by these imperialistic Soviet demands on the American president who declared loud and long in 1943 that of one thing he is convinced: "that Stalin is not an imperialist."

Such an affirmation shows that Roosevelt was without political cul-

17

ture. He had read neither the history of Russia nor the Testament of Peter the Great, nor had he read Karl Marx or Lenin.

Because, if this man, who had become president of the most noble and most democratic country in the world, had known—even superficially—the history of Russia, he would easily have understood Russia's expansionist aims, which were entirely centred on the policies of expansion set out in the Testament of Peter the Great, using now Panslavism; now Communism to realize them.

Let us reproduce a synopsis of the main points of this Testament, as published by Theodor Codrescu on the 10 August 1892, who copied it from the French edition of February 1843, published in the newspaper *l'Echo Francais*:

1. Peter the Great, finding a stream, transformed it into a river, while his descendants must transform it into a wide ocean in order to fertilize the whole of Europe.
2. His descendants must keep Europe in a permanent state of war and profit by any suitable occasion to declare a war.
3. To profit to the maximum from the teachings of other nations, but to keep their own identity in spite of the presence of foreigners in Russia.
4. To sow discord in Poland.
5. To encroach as much as possible on the frontiers of Sweden.
6. To unite by marriage with German princesses.
7. To foster commercial relations with England.
8. *To extend unceasingly northwards to the shore of the Baltic and southwards to the Black Sea.*
9. To approach Constantinople and India as much as possible. Who will conquer them, will conquer *the whole world.*
10. To wage war continually against Turkey and Persia in order to conquer them and to reach the Persian Gulf.
11. To make of the Greeks, of Hungary, of Poland, etc., a Fifth Column of Russia.
12. After the conquest of Sweden, Persia, Poland, and Turkey, Russia should discuss the sharing out of the *world* with "the Courts of France and Austria." If the latter will refuse, they must be roused, one against the other, and then overthrown. This is possible and thus must Europe be destroyed.

   Drawn up in 1724 in Moscow and signed by Peter the Great.

That is what every politician ought to read before assuming the leadership of any foreign affairs. That is what a president of the United States should have known before offering himself as candidate to enter the White House in order to regulate the fate of the whole of mankind.

Had Roosevelt had this knowledge, he would have had a better understanding of the claims formulated by Stalin on the occasion of Anthony Eden's first visit to Moscow in December 1941. Let us hear what the former foreign secretary says in his book, *The Reckoning*, p. 290:

> The ideas of the Russians were very clearly defined and did not change during the three following years. Russia tried to obtain the most tangible guarantees for the security of her frontiers.
>
> Stalin proposed some Polish expansion westwards at the expense of Germany . . . Russia to take back her frontiers of 1941 with Finland and Rumania and to incorporate the Baltic States. The Curzon Line should be the frontier between Russia and Poland. Stalin demanded military bases in Finland and Poland and a guaranteed exit from the Baltic Ocean to the North Sea and the Atlantic.

These demands were insistently presented by Stalin for three days running. As Eden was not authorized to sign an agreement concerning the frontiers—but only military ones—Stalin postponed the signing until the resolution of the frontiers. Eden promised to discuss the question with his government and with the Americans. That was December 1941.

It should be borne in mind that from that date—December 1941—when the Russians were beaten and millions of their troops taken prisoner by the Germans, they were still demanding the territories occupied earlier in the year according to their agreement with Hitler, as well as zones of influence in the Balkans.

Stalin wished to form a "united front with the English," so as to ensure also Roosevelt's approval. This was also the wish of Churchill when he visited Moscow on 9 October 1944, as we shall see; i.e., a united Russo-British front.

We shall also see, later on, that in proportion as Russia recovered and her armies were reinforced, her claims became even greater; at every conference, she asked for more and more. She triumphed at Yalta where—although she was faced with the U.S. who had eleven million soldiers, with the most perfect equipment, the greatest air force and navy in the world—Stalin was able to obtain everything he wanted, and even more. But let us return to 1942.

19

CHAPTER 4

Once More, Stalin Demands Military Bases in Rumania after the War

Stalin's claims were clearly put forward to the British and Americans at the beginning of the war. They were insistently renewed on the second visit of Anthony Eden to Moscow at the beginning of 1942.

Just as Stalin demanded territorial concessions, military bases and zones of influence in Rumania from Hitler, so Stalin demanded *from the beginning*, from the British, territorial gains, military bases, and zones of influence in Eastern Europe, insisting that these be immediately registered on paper, in secret treaties (as he had done with the Germans).

The British were ready to agree to these concessions and to sign the secret treaties demanded by Stalin. But, as the Americans (or, more exactly, the State Department in the person of Cordell Hull) categorically opposed any discussion of these questions *before the victorious end of the war*, the British foreign secretary promised to place Stalin's demands before his government and to put pressure on the Americans.

This was in January 1942, before the Battle of Stalingrad, the Teheran and the Yalta Conferences.

As the memoirs of Cordell Hull are very eloquent, we will quote the respective passages:

"One of my greatest preoccupations and of those of the President during the first half of 1942, was that of Russia's territorial ambitions in Europe . . . and especially her insistence to convince the Western Allies to *guarantee these claims immediately* in writing" (Vol. II of the *Memoirs*, p. 1165).

It must be emphasized from the beginning—so as to better understand the errors made by Roosevelt concerning the Balkans—that the State Department, together with a "bi-partizan" commission formed of the Democrats and the Republicans, had prepared a plan to regulate the peace, based on the Atlantic Charter—a plan that excluded any territorial annexations and zones of influence.

Cordell Hull had made this quite clear to Eden before his visit to Moscow, in a telegram of 5 December 1941, sent to his ambassador, Winant.

Rejecting the British arguments in favour of signing agreements on territorial changes and zones of influence, Cordell Hull explains in his *Memoirs* in Vol. II, p. 1166:

> Concerning the policies of post-war problems, we have emphasized that *these were clearly defined in the Atlantic Charter* which represents both the point of view of Great Britain and of that of the Soviet Union (who also signed this Charter later on).
>
> We have concluded [continues Cordell Hull], that it would be utterly shameful if any one of the three Governments should express a desire to enter into negotiations—or arrangements—concerning post-war problems.
>
> No arrangement, no agreement must be signed during the war referring to any individual country, thus endangering a Peace Conference which must ensure a just and long-lasting peace for everyone.
>
> "*Above all* [writes Cordell Hull], *there must not be any secret agreement.*"

Why was the State Department so suspicious of Anthony Eden's visit to Moscow, and why did they insist that the latter should *not sign any secret agreement with Stalin*?

> Because [writes Cordell Hull], it was clear to us that, in Moscow, Eden would be confronted with specific territorial demands by the Russians. *Stalin had formulated them categorically in his first meeting with Eden.* He had demanded that England arrange *immediately* to agree to the reestablishment of the Russian frontiers as they were before Hitler's attack on 22nd June 1941. In concrete terms, the Baltic States—Estonia, Latvia, and Lithuania—parts of Finland, Poland and Rumania, must be incorporated in the Soviet Union. Stalin demanded in 1941 that the Polish frontier must follow the Curzon Line which had become the Hitler-Stalin Line in 1939.

Rumania must give Russia certain facilities for bases; In exchange she would receive certain Hungarian territories.

In order to convince Eden to accept these post-war arrangements, Stalin proposed that Britain have certain military bases in France and Western Europe. (The division of Europe into two had been in Stalin's mind already since 1941, and was clearly outlined to Great Britain.)

After Cordell Hull's warning, Anthony Eden signed no agreements on his second visit in January 1942, but he promised Stalin to discuss his proposals with his own government and to convince the Americans.

As Cordell Hull knew he would be put under pressure by Churchill and Eden to sign such agreements with Stalin, he gave a report to President Roosevelt on the 4 February 1942, maintaining rigidly his own opposition and that of the State Department to any discussion whatever regarding territorial changes or zones of influence during the war, and warning the president of the U.S. not to approve any such agreements, while to Churchill and Eden he wrote:

"If Great Britain and America by any secret agreement were to abandon the principle of refusing to sign any territorial changes in time of war and until the Peace Conference, they would (be blackmailed in the future, notes the author) run into difficulties in future and would be unable to resist Russian pressure regarding frontiers, territories and zones of influence."

And this—"*every time the Soviet Government would be in a favourable position.*"

What admirable judgment! What impeccable logic! What vision of a true statesman!

"There is no doubt," writes the secretary of state in his secret report of 4 February 1942, to President Roosevelt, that the Soviet government has "tremendous ambitions with regard to Europe . . . enormous, fantastic ambitions and the moment will come when the United States and Great Britain will have to declare, categorically, that they can *not* accept them, at least before the Peace Conference. Therefore, it is better to adopt a clear, firm stance now than to hesitate and thus avoid taking up such a position."

Cordell Hull advised this firm position, although he was expecting blackmail and pressure from Stalin on the American government.

"He"—Stalin—"could refuse to co-operate with Great Britain and the United States, or to threaten to make a separate peace with Hitler.

22

He will put on pressure through the British and American Communist Parties'' (how well aware was Cordell Hull of the existence and potential betrayal of the Fifth Column!—author) ''but,'' insisted Cordell Hull, ''if we allow ourselves to give way to such pressure, Stalin will be encouraged to adopt the same tactics and in future, to obtain more, and more important concessions and claims.''

In that report of 4 February 1942, the State Department speaks of the demoralizing effect that such territorial agreements and zones of influence would have on the small nations who *oppose Communism* and on the world in general, on seeing the moral and juridical principles on which American politics were based, solidified in the Atlantic Charter, abandoned.

THE ATLANTIC CHARTER

Here we must leave this report for the moment and the *Memoirs* of Cordell Hull, in order to familiarize the reader with the so-called Atlantic Charter, signed on 12 August 1941 by Roosevelt and Churchill, and, later on, by Stalin, who adhered to it.

The drafting of this charter was inspired by the English *Magna Carta*, by the American Constitution, by the Declaration of Human Rights, by the Wilsonian principles. It evolved from the generosity of soul and spirit of the American people, this people free of persecution, from the struggle for individual liberty, for equality, for justice, and for the right of people to self-determination.

It is a superb document, full of human nobleness but which was besmirched by Roosevelt (who even pretended before his death that he had not signed it) and Churchill, not to mention Stalin whom no-one asked to respect this Charter because no-one trusted him, apart from Roosevelt (personally), Churchill, and the Communist Comrades who had infiltrated the White House.

These are some of the clauses of the Atlantic Charter, signed by Roosevelt and Churchill:

Firstly: neither the U.S.A. nor Great Britain seek any territorial extension or zones of influence.

Secondly: they do not wish to see *any territorial changes which are not expressly sought by the respective peoples*.

Thirdly: they respect the right of all peoples to choose their own form of government under which they wish to live; and they wish to see—re-established after the war—the sovereign rights and their own governments of those who were dispossessed by force.

Clause six of the Charter speaks of a just peace, in which all nations would live in security within their own frontiers, so that every citizen could live without fear in peace.

Clause eight advocates the abandonment of resorting to force, by opening wide the doors of the United Nations after the war.

That is the basis; those the principles on which American politics were built by the Department of State in the time of Cordell Hull, so long as he was at the head of American foreign affairs. Unfortunately, as we shall see, Roosevelt mocked both Cordell Hull and the Atlantic Charter and the moral principles of the entire American nation, giving to Stalin all that the latter had asked from Churchill—both territories and zones of influence.

THE ANGLO-RUSSIAN TREATY OF ALLIANCE OF APRIL 1942

In February 1942 Cordell Hull, the American secretary of state, became ill and was unable to resume his post until the 20th of April.

In the meantime, Stalin's pressure on the British was increasing. He wanted, at once, to sign a treaty of alliance in which his territorial claims should be included, together with the approval of the Allies.

Moreover, on the occasion of a visit to Washington, Anthony Eden informed President Roosevelt of these claims, sent to him by Maisky, the Russian ambassador in London. The following are the reactions of Roosevelt to these Russian demands:

The Baltic States: Roosevelt, for obviously electoral motives (there being a great number of American refugees from those countries) would like . . . a plebiscite.

Poland: There is no longer any question of the sovereignty and independence of Poland, for which country Britain entered the war, nor of the Atlantic Charter. Roosevelt spoke with Eden about changes of territory, of population. He added that only the *Big Three would decide what Poland and the other small countries would, or would not, have*; he saw no point in discussing the latter at the Peace Conference.

Bessarabia: President Roosevelt agreed with Eden that the Soviets had the right to win back this province *because it had been a Russian province for the greater part of its history.*

What an absurdity. The oldest Rumanian land, which belonged to Rumanians and their Daco-Thraco-Roman ancestors for four thousand years, to be a Russian land. They robbed it from Rumania in 1812.

How ignorant of history was President Roosevelt.

Roosevelt never heard of the rape of Bessarabia in 1812 by the Russians; of its retrocession by various treaties back to Rumania; of the condemnation of this Russian "rapt" (annexation) by Karl Marx himself, in a letter to Engels and in an article in the *Herald Tribune* as far back as 1863. Listen how disposes—the author—the father of the Atlantic Charter—of ancestral Bessarabia, the oldest Rumanian land of four thousand years.

Finland: In addition to the "adjustments" of the frontier in 1940, President Roosevelt and Eden were in agreement to let the Russians have Hangoe (but of course this arrangement had to be kept secret for American election reasons: many American electors are of Finnish origin).

Yugoslavia: The president wished to create two states: Croatian and Serbian. Eden did not approve.

Czechoslovakia, Rumania, Bulgaria, Turkey, and Greece: Regarding these countries, the president and Eden did not expect to have frontier problems.

Austria and Hungary: The president and Eden were in agreement that these should be *independent*. (Therefore, the other satellite states, dependent.) Eden believed that Stalin wished to "punish" the Hungarians and to give part of their territory to Rumania. (Did not Stalin—knowing of the "independence" of Hungary, desired by Eden and Roosevelt—somehow wish to ensure a greater buffer territory by giving Transylvania back to Rumania?)

Every scholar of European history knows that Transylvania belonged to Rumania—and their ancestors—four thousand years ago, like Bessarabia, and that the Hungarians annexed it. The Transylvanian population is, in the greatest majority, Rumanian.

ANGLO-RUSSIAN COMRADESHIP

In March 1942, as Herbert Feis, in his excellent book (*Roosevelt, Churchill and Stalin*) says, Stalin considered that the Anglo-Soviet Alliance was no concern of the Americans, being a question only among

25

themselves. In other words, the affairs of Europe were exclusively the concern of the British and the Russians, who were ready to concede zones of influence mutually.

In this state of mind, Stalin persuaded Churchill to sign the agreement immediately, including his territorial claims. For this purpose, Molotov was sent to London on 20 May 1942.

In the course of the negotiations, the Americans—in the person of Cordell Hull, now back in his office in the State Department—opposed, again, and with vigour, any treaty involving territorial changes or concessions. In the end, his opinion was accepted, but naturally, not without a struggle. Stalin wished to have a secret treaty relating to Rumania and Finland, but in the end was satisfied with a clause by which Great Britain recognized "Russia's special interests" in those countries.

Cordell Hull could not achieve more. The treaty was signed in that way, without any specific Russian territorial claims in detail. But the door had been left wide open by the British for zones of influence.

THE CONFERENCE OF FOREIGN MINISTERS
IN MOSCOW IN 1943

At the conference of the ministers of the three Allies, held in Moscow in October 1943, Anthony Eden returned to the offensive and again raised, indirectly, the problem of *zones of influence*.

On page 218 of his book *Roosevelt, Churchill, Stalin*, Herbert Feis—after having pointed out that the Three had undertaken not to make any separate peace and to keep each other informed of any enemy attempt to make one—speaks of the case of Rumania, which wanted to break away from Germany and to side with the Allies.

Secret agents, of the government in collusion with leaders of the Rumanian parties, appeared in Cairo and elsewhere and tried to sound the British government about the conditions of an armistice, reported Eden on 25 October 1943, to Stalin and Molotov, in the presence of Cordell Hull.

Anthony Eden asked Molotov what he thought should be done. The latter replied that the only condition for Rumania's exit from the war must be *Unconditional Capitulation*, and that it would be useless to discuss the matter further with these agents, for they had no solution to offer. Eden agreed with this remark and added that his government:

26

"believes that the Soviet Government has the right to decide any question concerning *Rumania, Hungary, and Finland*, because only their (the Russian) Army is engaged in war with them."

That was the origin of the zones of influence. This made Stalin the master of Eastern Europe.

After having accepted the Soviet demands to mutilate Rumania by the rape of Bessarabia (there had not yet been any question of Bucovina) and other countries of their territories, the British put forward also the idea of zones of influence, offered in October 1943 in Moscow—for all Eastern Europe.

In the course of this discussion—evidently under the influence of Cordell Hull—the British government replied to the "secret agents" of Cairo that the only formula *is the unconditional capitulation of Rumania.*

A month later, the existence of this sounding for a Rumanian peace was confirmed by Churchill: "How would Rumania react to Turkey's entry into the war?" (said he in Nov. 1943 in Teheran). "They were already putting out genuine peace feelers for *unconditional surrender*" (Churchill, *The Second World War*, Vol. V, p. 353).

It would be very interesting to know who were these Rumanian emissaries who were offering unconditional capitulation in 1943. (Because the Rumanian government and the opposition leaders didn't want unconditional surrender, but a just and noble armistice with guarantees for their independence and sovereignty.)

From the above, the following conclusions concerning Eastern Europe should be noted:

1. In 1939, by the Ribbentrop Pact, Russia already was promised Bessarabia from Rumania.
2. In April 1940, Molotov had asked Hitler for a zone of influence in Rumania and was refused.
3. Since 1941, Stalin sought recognition of Russia's territorial claims in Rumania, the Balkans, Baltic States, and Finland and since then, Churchill was ready to recognize them, as was also Roosevelt.
4. The State Department, in the person of Cordell Hull, was against any territorial agreements during the course of the war, also against any zones of influence.

They believed in a peace organization—the United Nations—which would guarantee the security of the Soviet Union, without any necessity of yielding up territories for military purposes or zones of influence.

5. The suggestion of zones of influence was the idea of both Churchill and Eden, at least in October 1943.

6. In autumn 1943, the Rumanian "secret agents" in Cairo and elsewhere had been informed that Rumania could only withdraw from the war *by unconditional surrender*.

This was more than a tragedy, it was one of the biggest mistakes of the war.

"Unconditional surrender" prolonged the war, as will be seen, for over two years.

With the exit of Rumania, Italy, and other Axis satellites, in 1943, as was planned, Germany would have collapsed, easily and surely. Rumania was the turntable to all military and strategical positions of the Southeastern European front.

CHAPTER 5

Roosevelt Offers Eastern Europe to Stalin in 1943

There are still many naïve people who speak of "Russia's bad faith," of her violation of the Yalta agreements, of the abuse of Eastern Europe by her armies, of Churchill's efforts to bar Russia's path into Europe, and of landing (invasion) in the Balkans towards that end.

Why go on believing these tales? I will reproduce, first of all, a sensational document in which it can be seen how Roosevelt, personally—and on 20 February 1943—promised Stalin a free hand in Eastern Europe.

This is an ultra-secret document addressed to Zabrousky and Weiss—two personalities of importance in the Zionist Movement, who went to Moscow to see Stalin.

This letter—certainly intentionally circulated by the latter—fell into the hands of General Franco and was utilized by his foreign minister, General Jordana, in the famous discourse in Barcelona in April 1943. It was a desperate cry against the promises of Roosevelt, which would have meant the Communization of Europe.

This extraordinary letter was first published on 7 February 1951 in the *Figaro*, where the *Memoirs* of Jose Marie Doussinague, director of the Spanish Foreign Ministry, were being published.

It must be emphasized that these two heads of the Zionist Movement went to Moscow—most certainly to convince Stalin to agree to the creation of a homeland for the unhappy Jewish people, expelled from their country and exiled throughout the world for so many centuries. In order to create a state of Israel, the Jews needed not only the consent and cooperation of Stalin to establish it in Palestine, but also his sanction and concurrence to allow the Jews in Russia to emigrate to the new state.

Roosevelt certainly wished to aid this grave and important mission, otherwise there can be no other explanation of this extraordinary letter. Roosevelt had direct means of communication with Stalin: Averell Harriman in Moscow; Harry Hopkins, who was there every month; Gromyko in Washington. Why did he approach Zabrousky and Weiss "to mediate between him and Stalin about the differences of opinion which have arisen between them?" Was that the business of private individuals? Certainly not. The explanation must be sought in Roosevelt's desire to see them succeed in their mission and to convince Stalin to create the state of Israel. The letter was one of introduction of these two for good luck. It is unbelievable, but true, that complete silence reigned over this document, which was so decisive in the politics of Roosevelt. Not a single historian discussed it. It was a real conspiracy of silence. Here is the letter in its entirety:

White House—Washington
20 February 1943

Dear Mr. Zabrousky

As I said in my conversation with you and Mr. Weiss, I was profoundly moved by the fact that the National Council of Young Israel had had the extreme amiability to offer itself as intermediary between me and our common friend, Stalin, at such a delicate time in which any danger of friction in the heart of the United Nations—created at the price of so much sacrifice—would have had fatal consequences for everyone and, especially, for the Soviet Union.

In consequence it is in your interest and in ours to lessen any asperity with Litvinov—which would be difficult—who, to my grief, had to warn that those who come in contact with Uncle Sam will have to face unpleasantness, a warning viable both for foreign affairs as well as for home affairs. Soviet claims, when it is a question of Communist activity in the U.S.A., are doubly intolerable.

Timoshenko proved to be more reasonable in his short, but profitable, stay here and I should like a new interview with the Marshal to constitute a quick step towards an exchange of views with Stalin, an exchange which I consider extremely urgent when I think of the benefits which result from the meeting between Stalin and Churchill.

30

The United States and Great Britain are disposed—without any kind of moral reservation—to give absolute equality of vote to the U.S.S.R. in the future organization of the world after the war. She will be a member—as the British Prime Minister communicated at Adana when presenting his draft project—of the leading group at the heart of the Council of Europe and of the Council of Asia. By these means the inter-Continental expansion of the U.S.S.R. will be justified, as well as the giant struggle against Fascism, which will deserve the eulogy of historians.

We wish to see these Continental Councils (I speak in the name of my country and of the grandiose British Empire) composed of all independent States with a fair proportional representation of course.

Also, dear Mr. Zabrousky, you may assure Stalin that the U.S.S.R. will be present in the Directorate of those Councils (Europe and Asia), on an equal footing and with the right to an equal vote with the United States and England and that she will form part of the high Tribunal which will have to be created to resolve the divergencies between nations; that she will intervene also in the selection and preparation of the international forces; of the arming and the command of these forces which, under the orders of the Continental Council, will act in the interior of every State with the aim that the norms so cleverly elaborated for the maintenance of peace, in the spirit of the old League of Nations, may not be violated anew; these institutions which regulate relations between States and their armies will be able to impose decisions and ensure that they are obeyed. In these conditions, benefitting by such a high position in the tetrarchy of the Universe, Stalin ought to be content and never again renew his demands which create insoluble problems (nonetheless, the secretariat is destined for France with the right to *a consultative and not deliberative vote, as a reward for her resistance*, but also as a *punishment* for her earlier vacillations). Therefore, the American Continent will remain outside any Soviet propaganda and under the exclusive influence of the United States, as I promised our continental Allies; *France will have to stay in the English orbit*, having, however, a large autonomy and right in the Secretariat of the tetrarchy. *Under the protection of England*, Portugal, Spain, Italy and Greece will evolve towards modern civilization which will draw them out of their traditional lethargy. In

31

addition, this will give the U.S.S.R. an additional harbour in the Mediterranean. *We yield to their wishes regarding Finland and the Baltic. In general, we will ask Poland to adopt a reasonable attitude based on understanding and compromise. Stalin will be left with a wide field of expansion in the small countries of Eastern Europe.* Naturally, we must consider the rights of Yugoslavia and Czechoslovakia—two loyal nations—without leaving out the total recuperation of the territories snatched temporarily from Great Russia.

After the dismemberment of the Reich and when certain zones have been joined to other States, thus creating new nationalities, the German peril will no longer exist, either for the U.S.S.R. or for Europe and the whole world.

Regarding Turkey, Stalin would have to understand the necessary assurances which Churchill had given to President Inonu, in both his name and mine. Stalin must be assured of the harbour which will be given to him in the Mediterranean.

As regards Asia, we are in agreement with his demands barring any ulterior complications. About Africa—what to do? It will be necessary to give something to France in order to compensate her for her losses in Asia and, also, something to Egypt, as promised to the Waldists. It will certainly be necessary to compensate Portugal and Spain for what they have given up and in order to reach a better world equilibrium. The United States will put her right foot forward as conqueror and will reclaim, inevitably, some vital points for their zone. That means to do justice. And lastly, we must give Brazil the little colonial expansion promised to her.

Please inform Stalin, dear Mr. Zabrousky, that, for the general good and for the rapid destruction of the Reich that *all these are only a general outline to be further studied*. But we must give in to them regarding the colonization of Africa, while they must cease their propaganda in America so as to end their interference in the working-class.

Transmit also the assurance of my full understanding; of my sympathy and my desire to ease the solution of those problems. Towards that end, the interview which I propose would show a practical interest.

As I have said, I read with the greatest pleasure, the general terms of the interview in which I have learned of your decision to offer me—in the name of the *National Council*—a copy of that most sacred treasure of Israel—a copy of the Torah. This letter is a proof that I welcome it. I reply to your loyalty with the fullest confidence.

Please convey to the important organization over which you preside an expression of my gratitude, as well as the fact that I remember with pleasure the banquet offered on the occasion of its 31st anniversary.

I wish you the greatest success.

Franklin D. Roosevelt

ROOSEVELT AND STALIN ARE BOTH "ZIONISTS"

We have a short, but eloquent note from the Yalta Conference concerning the visit of those two Zionists to Moscow. Passing from one subject to another, Roosevelt addresses Stalin:

"I am a Zionist. But you, Marshal?"

"On principle, yes, I too am a Zionist," replied Stalin with indifferent calm. "But in practice it is difficult. I have tried to organize a national home for the Jews, but they were unable to become acclimatized. They all returned to their former homes."

The Jewish State Stalin was speaking about is located in the Far Eastern region called *Birobidjian*. This region is located along the Amour river, which separates China from the USSR, and where fighting took place between the frontier guards.

Birobidjian is a region bigger than Belgium. The Constitution made by Stalin on 29 August 1936, in its Article 87, mentions an "autonomous Jews region" (Republic).

It goes without saying that the founding of the "autonomous region" had strategic aims. In fact, this "Jewish State" had nothing of a national Jewish state: no national Jewish laws, no Yiddish language, no Jewish culture, religion, privileges, not even an "abécédaire": elementary reading book, in their mother tongue: Yiddish.

Stalin's "Jews' State" was nothing more than another imposture, and tragic farce of Stalin.

One can therefore understand that Russian Jews did not rush to be colonized over there, under such conditions, and that even today, the Jewish population of this region is only about 7 percent of the whole population of Birobidjian.

33

But Stalin kept his word and agreed to the creation of the State of Israel. He helped not only to found it, but allowed Jews from Eastern Europe and Russia to emigrate there.

Truman recognized the State of Israel at once after the proclamation of independence, and the Soviet recognition followed immediately after that.

In the light of these documents, it is not to be wondered at, that, at Teheran, in 1943, there was not much discussion of Eastern Europe. The hand was already played. After Churchill, Roosevelt—by the letter quoted—had conveyed to Stalin his consent to the subjugation of Eastern Europe.

ROOSEVELT OFFERS THE BALTIC STATES AND POLAND TO STALIN IN NOVEMBER 1943, AT TEHERAN

But the cynicism of this president who, even to-day, is considered to have been one of the greatest presidents of the United States, was only equalled by his electoral cynicism. At Teheran, Roosevelt forgot about the Atlantic Charter, the Constitution of the United States, and the Great Charter of the Declaration of Human Rights. Guest of the Russian Embassy—i.e., prisoner of Stalin—Roosevelt accepted the demands for territories and zones of influence in Eastern Europe, without discussion. All he asked in return from Stalin was the latter's help in his campaign for the 1944 elections "when he would again present his candidature." He made an agreement with Stalin, asking the latter to lie to the American people and to hide the truth from them about their plans *until after the elections*.

In the proceedings of the meetings between Roosevelt and Stalin at Teheran, kept by Charles Bohlen, who served as interpreter, we read the following discussion between the two:

> Roosevelt said further, that there are many Lithuanians, Latvians and Estonians in the U.S.A. If he himself [Roosevelt] agreed that these States form part of Russia and if it is certain that the American Government would not go to war to prevent re-occupation by the Russians, American public opinion, at least, might wish to hold a referendum and a right to self-determination. Regarding this,

34

Roosevelt expressed his personal conviction that the inhabitants of the Baltic States would vote with pleasure, in any future plebiscite, for incorporation into the Soviet Union.

And further—without any embarrassment—the president of the greatest, most powerful, most honest and generous people, asks Stalin to be his electoral agent:

"Roosevelt now became more direct" (probably because Stalin did not understand the election procedure in the U.S.A.) "and said to Stalin that he (Stalin) would be of great help to him in the elections if he would make a public declaration about free elections in the annexed territories."

The conclusion of this discussion between Stalin and Roosevelt at Teheran is drawn by the American, John Lewis Gaddis, in his book: *U.S.A. and the Cold War*, p. 139:

> The President clearly stated that the U.S.A. would not oppose the territorial changes proposed by Stalin, but that Stalin must not expect public acceptance of those territorial changes *until after the electoral campaign of 1944*. Any promise of free elections or plebiscite, which Stalin might make, would be appreciated if such changes were acceptable to the American people. [In other words, to compel this honest, upright, and generous nation to agree to the territorial thefts and zones of influence demanded by Stalin. Author's note.]
>
> Roosevelt said nothing about a free choice for the peoples of Eastern Europe and it is clear that Stalin left this discussion, convinced that his chief worry would be how to put this question of annexations and zones of influence to the American people in a more favourable light and *how to avoid, at all costs, any assurance that he would adhere to the principles of the Atlantic Charter.*

So here, dear readers, is the source of "free elections" in Rumania in 1946, when Harriman, Kerr, and Vishinsky came to Bucharest to "convince" Iuliu Maniu, Dinu Bratianu, and Titel Petrescu to form a "national" government and take part in the elections.

But I will return later to those elections as well as to those who travelled from Moscow to Bucharest to commit this crime against the Rumanian nation, as they had done also against the Poles.

Also, in the course of the talks in Teheran, Roosevelt agreed to the mutilation of Poland with the elections in mind.

"The Presidential Elections" began Roosevelt, "will be held in 1944," and though he would not wish to be a candidate, he might well become one "if the war was not to end before that." The president—continues Bohlen, Roosevelt's interpreter, in his report—reminded Stalin that there are six or seven million Americans of Polish origin in the U.S.A. and so, as "a practical man," he does not wish to lose their votes.

"He agrees personally with Stalin that the Russo-Polish frontier should be moved to the west and the Poles should get territorial compensation from Germany. *He hopes however, that Stalin will understand that, for political reasons, he cannot make any such arrangement publicly at present.* Having heard this, Stalin replied, assuring him that he had understood" (Charles Bohlen, to James C. Dunn, 1943, Hull, Mss. Box 52).

At that time, i.e., when the Supreme Commander of the American army was selling Poland to Stalin, the heroes of the Polish divisions were fighting side by side with the admirable American divisions at Monte Cassino on the Italian front in a life and death struggle for a better and more just world, as had been promised in the Atlantic Charter.

Brave Polish soldiers were dying for the glory and independence of their nation; betrayed and sold, just as they had died in the war for Britain.

CHAPTER 6

Germany Loses the War by Betrayal at Stalingrad

In the meantime, on the Eastern Front, the destiny of the war began to change. The Rumanian troops, who were fighting with those of Germany, Hungary, and Italy before Stalingrad, were suffering heavy losses. Without heavy modern artillery, without anti-tank guns, without means of signalling, the Fourth Rumanian Army was obliged to operate on a wide front from the Engeni Heights to the Kalmuck Steppes. On 19 October 1942, in an extraordinary offensive, the Red Armies penetrated the Rumanian positions. The attempt of the First Rumanian Armoured Division to come to their aid failed, owing to a stupid radio failure.

So the Battle of Stalingrad had begun. This was the beginning of the end. How was it possible for such a sudden dramatic change from permitting the German Army to advance on the Russian lines? An onslaught that caused tens of thousands of Rumanians to be taken prisoner, thus causing the Rumanian government, in the person of Marshal Antonescu, to realize that the war was lost.

To answer this question, we will reproduce an article published in *E.N.R.* of 1 February 1976 where the answer appears:

But the most dramatic case of lack of vigilance which changed the face of the world was that of Germany.

The German armies were advancing with breath-taking speed towards Moscow in 1941. An exceptionally hard winter with the thermometer at $-50°C$ had paralysed the tanks of the elite Panzer Divisions of General Guderian. Hitler's unbelievable mistake in postponing the attack on Russia for six weeks in order to assist

Mussolini in his disastrous campaign in Albania, was certainly a terrible blow, as was also his stubbornness in refusing to withdraw his troops from the approach to Moscow "for hibernation."

The army maintained—and some people still do—that "Corporal" Hitler did not obey the generals, that he was a beginner, unfit. Raymond Cartier, in his book *Les dessous de la guerre Hitlerienne*, which is based on the Nuremberg Trials, upholds the opposite opinion: Hitler was a military genius, an extraordinary strategist. *He alone* made the plans for Sedan, for Warsaw, for the Ardennes, for Russia. But there was a "but" . . . which Raymond Cartier does not reveal, probably in order to spare the susceptibilities of the Russians.

It was not the plans that failed, nor the pitiless winter that conquered the German armies on the Eastern Front.

In 1941, the Germano-Rumanian Armies advanced into Russia at a breathtaking speed. Within five days they had taken 200,000 prisoners.

During the next weeks, the next months, the Russians armies surrendered by whole units, by hundreds of thousands, by millions.

The whole Russian front was ready to collapse.

And all of a sudden, great Russian forces appeared and counterattacked. From whence did they come? From Siberia, Mongolia, Manchuria, that is, all the armies of the eastern frontiers of the Soviet Union. One hundred and eighty divisions, fresh, well-equipped, were brought from the frontier of the eventual theatre of military operations with Japan and hurled against the Germano-Rumanian armies.

How was it possible for Stalin to withdraw all the Russian armies and leave the Japanese a free hand to enter the Soviet Union if they had wished to attack the Russian Army in the back and create a tentacle, a giant pincer with the armies of Hitler?

The famous Russian spy, Richard Sorge, correspondent of the *Frankfurter Zeitung* in Tokyo, was the reply to that amazing question.

The historical truth is that *this German journalist was the real conqueror of the German Armies by leaking* out information to Stalin, out of ideological conviction.

Richard Sorge was the conqueror of Stalingrad, of Berlin—not Stalin, not Marshal Zukov, not the Soviet armies.

This journalist—former member of the German Communist Party; of Russian origin—was accredited to Japan. He enjoyed the complete confidence of the German ambassador and of Hitler's military attaché. He even had access to the safe and knew the cipher. He sent word to Stalin that the Germans would attack on 21 June 1941, but Stalin did not believe it. But, as Sorge foresaw, Stalin's confidence increased. From now on, he took note of all information sent, especially by radio from Tokyo, by Sorge.

And, in 1941 in a restricted and ultra-secret meeting in Tokyo, under the presidency of the Emperor, *it was decided that Japan would not attack Russia under any circumstances.*

This ultra-secret decision found its way into the hands of Sorge, by the betrayal of his accomplice Ozaki Hozumi, and he sent it *immediately to Stalin*, through his clandestine transmitter. This time Stalin believed it.

That is why Stalin withdrew the entire army from the Mongolian and Manchurian fronts (not even leaving frontier guards) and hurled them against Hitler.

It is true that Japan had signed a Treaty of Neutrality with Russia in April 1941. But it is no less true that the USSR had—which was normal—the entire eastern front equipped with troops, not knowing what Japan would do, especially in view of the lightning advance of the German armies.

Obviously, it was not in Russia's interest to divulge this truth. The crushing of the German Army ought to have been the work of Stalin, not of treachery.

But the truth seeped through slowly. The Secret Service of General MacArthur succeeded in reconstructing the entire dossier of Richard Sorge and his Japanese accomplice, Ozaki Hozumi, the counsellor of Prince Konoye, who had been three times prime minister of Japan.

It was established, without any doubt, that Richard Sorge informed Stalin of the imminent attack on Pearl Harbour, but that the latter had not breathed a word of it to the Americans.

The report of the ultra-secret meeting, held by the *Imperial Council* on 2 July 1941, was sent to Stalin by Richard Sorge on 15 October 1941. And this report recorded the decision to attack Indo-China and *not to attack Russia under any circumstances.*

That Richard Sorge betrayed—or spied—is not surprising. That he recruited Ozaki Hozumi, the intimate collaborator of Prince Konoye—and therefore of the Emperor himself—is extraordinary, but understandable.

But that this Sorge, born in Baku, in Russia, of a Russian mother, was a member of the German *Communist Party*, could become a member of Hitler's Party and, *without being screened*, was sent to Tokyo as a *Nazi* journalist *accredited* to the Hitlerist Embassy in Tokyo is *unbelievable; unimaginable* for its lack of vigilance.

When he was enrolled in the Hitlerist Party in 1933, no one asked what this devoted Nazi had been doing in Moscow between 1924 and 1927. If anyone had asked, he would have found that Sorge was a member and employee of the *Komintern* in Moscow and had attended there the school of espionage.

If his past had been raked up, it would have been discovered that when Sorge was praising Hitler in the *Frankfurter Zeitung*, he was attending, for instance, the World Congress of the Komintern, in 1935, in Moscow.

How was it possible that the National Socialist Party had not checked him? Or the secret services of Admiral Canaris, or of Himmler or Heydrich? Or the people of the German Embassy in Tokyo?

That is why I speak in this article of vigilance. The West—Germany, Great Britain, and the United States—not to mention France—allowed themselves to be deceived, sold, betrayed, both in time of peace and in time of war. Under the mask of democratic liberties, the most abject treason was being carried out in the heart of the Western democrats. And not out of interest but from "political convictions," i.e., Communist. The Western democrats forgot that freedom and democracy defend themselves every day from the well-organized actions of the Fifth Column, both in wartime and in time of peace.

It ought to be remembered too that together with Sorge's activities, an equally great betrayal was taking place under Hitler's nose in his headquarters. A number of ten officers of the General Staff, of high rank, made a pledge to destroy Nazism, even at the cost of the military defeat of Germany. As specialists they remained on the General Staff during the whole course of the war.

Their link with the Russians was Rudolf Roessler, a German journalist, installed as a bookseller in Lucerne. His military conspirators in the Fuhrer's headquarters had endowed him with a radio-receiver, the same as that supplied to all the large German units. When an order was sent out from Hitler's headquarters, Rudolf Roessler received it at the same time. He transmitted it at once to the Russians through the team, in Lausanne and Geneva, of Alexander Rado. In this way, especially after the autumn of 1942, the Russians knew exactly the day, time, and place of the units that would attack them.

Through these two great German betrayals, the Russian victory of Stalingrad was made possible, and allowed Stalin to win the war and to put forward his claims at the conferences of Teheran and Yalta.

CHAPTER 7

The Astounding Evidence
of Cardinal Spellman

After he had agreed to give Stalin zones of influence in Eastern Europe, on 20 February, in writing, President Roosevelt informed Cardinal Spellman—head of the Catholic Church in the United States—of his intentions, one evening in the White House.

This was to clear the ground, the more so because the revered Cardinal was a declared anti-Communist and had to be neutralized. In addition, Cardinal Spellman was, in a way, a personal representative of the president in many of his wartime missions; he had travelled a great deal and seen many interesting places and people. It is said that it was he who was responsible for the overthrow of Mussolini.

The discussion took place after the Roosevelt-Churchill talks in Quebec, in August 1943, three months before the conference in Teheran and a year and a half before the Yalta Conference, in February 1945.

Winston Churchill was in Washington. Cardinal Spellman had a discussion lasting one-and-a-half hours with Roosevelt, which he immediately wrote down and it was reproduced in his *Memoirs* published, unfortunately, only in 1962, nearly twenty years later.

The Cardinal's notes are astounding, frightening. From them can be seen how President Roosevelt—head of the most democratic state in the world—who held the fate of the whole of mankind in *his hands alone*, was a very sick man almost two years *before* the end of the war. They reveal the boundless admiration that Roosevelt had for Stalin and how *the whole* of Europe must be subjected to him. That was a policy and an abberration of a very sick man.

Definitely, Roosevelt was fascinated by Stalin. We must keep in mind that it was he who had recognized Stalin's Soviet Union in 1933, thus avoiding her collapse.

42

We must also remember that in 1936–1938, when Stalin liquidated ten million Russian peasants and famine was spreading like fire through the whole of Russia, because of these mass killings, it was Roosevelt who sent Stalin millions of tons of American grain, and helped in this way, the Communist regime to remain in power.

In the light of these revelations, it is not surprising that Roosevelt agreed—as we shall see later—to accept Churchill's wishes to give the Balkans to Russia and this *without the knowledge and without consultation of his own foreign minister*—Secretary of State Cordell Hull—who for four years had been categorically opposing the creation of any zones of influence.

Also, in the light of those revelations of Cardinal Spellman, we see how the agreements over these territorial cessions and creations of zones of influence were kept *secret*, both from the American government and from Congress, as well as from the American people themselves. Roosevelt hid his intentions from them, deceived them, as we shall see in his speech after his "triumphal" return from Yalta.

But let Cardinal Spellman's *Memoirs* speak for themselves:

> He was planning to make an Agreement between The Four Great Powers. As a consequence, the world would be divided in spheres of influence: China was to have the extreme East; the United States, the Pacific; *Great Britain and Russia, Europe and Africa. But as England's interests are primarily in her Colonies, it could be taken for granted that Russia would predominate in Europe.*
>
> He—Roosevelt—hoped that, though all this could be wishful thinking, (i.e., that he was deceiving himself) that Russian intervention would not be too harsh.

This is why the Russians were constantly asking to have zones of influence also in *Africa*: because Roosevelt granted this to them. Churchill was in complete agreement. It cannot be conceived that Roosevelt would have confided to Cardinal Spellman on 3 September 1943, when Churchill was in Washington where he had come after the Quebec Conference. Had Churchill not agreed, Roosevelt would not have expressed this joint opinion. Thus are explained the telegrams of May and June 1944, which will be treated later in a special chapter, as well as the infamous night of 9 October 1944, in Moscow, when Churchill (in agreement with Roosevelt on both occasions) tried to force the hand of the State Department to confront Cordell Hull with a *fait accompli* regarding the Balkans.

43

His desire is [continue the *Memoirs* of Cardinal Spellman, p. 223] to convince Stalin, which is scarcely probable, not to extend his territory further than a certain line. He would certainly receive Finland, the Baltic States, half of Eastern Poland and Bessarabia. There is no use in opposing Stalin, for he has the power to take them in any case. So it is better for him [Roosevelt] to offer them himself gracefully; smiling! "Further," continued Roosevelt, "the population of Eastern Poland wish (hark!) to *become Russian*. And it is not yet sure whether Stalin will be satisfied with these Polish frontiers."

So it is possible that the Communist regimes will be extended, but what can we do? Perhaps France would escape if she were to have a Government like that of Leon Blum (Popular Front with the Communists.)

To my direct question, [writes Cardinal Spellman] as to whether Austria, Hungary and Croatia [Catholic countries that were of particular interest to the Prelate. Author's Note] will become a kind of Russian Protectorate, the reply was categoric: *Yes*. And he—President Roosevelt—added with admiration: we must not forget the magnificent economic achievements of Russia, the extraordinary, magnificent economic progress. [Though, even to-day, sixty-five years later, there is not enough bread to feed the population. Author's Note]. Her financial situation is stable. *It is natural that the European Countries should undergo deep transformations to adapt themselves to the Russians*; but he hopes that after ten or twenty years *of European influence, Russia will become less barbarous*.

In any case, the U.S.A. and England cannot fight with Russia. He hopes that through a forced friendship, they will reach a true and lasting relationship. The European peoples will have to, purely and simply—bear; support Russian domination in the hope that in ten or twenty years they will be ready to live better with the Russians. Litvinof had told him—and he himself hopes—that the Russians will adopt 40% of the capitalist world and capitalism will keep only 60% of that system. So an understanding is possible.

Those are some notes of Cardinal Spellman.

Could any mental aberration be greater? Not only did Roosevelt show that he was totally ignorant of the history of Europe, of Russia, but of knowledge of Communist ideology and its repressive systems. Certainly part of that ignorance was voluntary, intentional, in order to convince the Prelate that all would be well in ten or twenty years.

However, after this discussion of 3 September 1943, Cardinal Spellman was aware of Roosevelt's bad health and intentions. He ought to have given the alarm, especially as he was in doubt as to the president's sanity. But the Cardinal was silent. His silence lasted twenty years. This is why I have written in ending an article on that silence in Nov. 1978 on the occasion of the election of the new Pope, John Paul II, from which I will quote a few extracts in Chapter 27.

As regards the alarming flaws of the sick President Roosevelt—that the people robbed by the Russians should assist "those barbarians to become civilised," in ten or twenty years and to live together as brothers, I invite readers to read part of an "open letter," which I sent to the great writer, Alexander Solzhenitsyn. It gives the reply to President Roosevelt and gives a posthumous blow to his observations regarding "the civilizing of his Russian barbarians" by the enslaved people.

Very esteemed Master,

I take the liberty to write you this letter, not only to present my respectful homage and my very humble thanks for all that you stand for as well as for your actions for the defence and dignity of Man, and for his existence, but also to submit to you a suggestion, perhaps a project.

The idea came to me on reading your last work: *The Gulag Archipelago*. In this book you have not only outlined the suffering and the tragedy of Man, deprived of nationality and the idea of fatherland.

In *The Gulag Archipelago* you have indicted a whole system; a whole regime and its representatives, who have directed Russia since 1917 until to-day. In this book, as well as in all the others you have written, as well as in your whole attitude, you have condemned the Marxist foundation (with its excesses) of this regime as well as the expansionist, territorial politics of those who embody it.

From this point of view, *The Gulag Archipelago* remains not only the picture of your sufferings and those of the Russian people; this work constitutes a dossier of overwhelming accusation for this whole period which began in 1917. Your work has become a historical monument belonging to the literary, cultural and juridical life of the Russian people, and also to the history of Mankind, becoming an integral part of universal history.

In this context, I respectfully allow myself to believe that your work can be enlarged. *The Gulag Archipelago* of the Soviet Union could be completed by a *Supplement* of this Archipelago of peoples subjugated by the rulers of the Kremlin, especially of those neighbouring peoples of Eastern Europe: *The Gulag Archipelago of the Subjugated Countries*.

Because, as you know, the inhuman regime of the Soviet rulers is not limited to Russia and the Russian people. It was initiated, directed and applied with diabolical passion by the rulers in all the countries occupied by the Soviet Army. They introduced the same regime into all these countries as in the U.S.S.R. with all its excesses and all the sufferings inflicted on the Russian people.

The laws of these countries were replaced by Soviet laws; the application of these laws was controlled by so-called Soviet "Counsellors," thus affecting and changing every aspect of human life in these lands.

In penal matters, for instance, the "surveillance" of citizens, their "arrest" the "law-suits," "the carrying out of punishments" inflicted, all took place exactly as in the Soviet Union, as well as by their direct representatives in those lands. In other words, the rulers of the Kremlin inflicted on the peoples of Eastern Europe the same sufferings as on the Russian People. The hangmen and their methods were the same.

Personally, I am one of the victims of the Soviet Occupation of my very dear country—Rumania. I have been an exile for twenty-five years after having passed (for a shorter period and under a less severe regime than yours) through ten Communist prisons. As a result, I have experience of the regime and of its prisons. I did my duty towards my country and to myself to the best of my modest means and wrote about both of them in *Des Géôles de Anna Pauker, aux prisons de Tito*.

For that reason I respectfully allow myself to believe that the sufferings inflicted by rulers of the U.S.S.R. not only on the Russian people, but also on the peoples subjugated by the U.S.S.R., constitute an *entirety* and that the history of that suffering and the tragedy inflicted on all these peoples by the same terrible and inhuman hand, *ought to constitute a comprehensive whole* and that the *Gulag Archipelago* of the Soviet Union—the hell of Solzhen-

46

itsyn—ought to be completed. The outline of this gloomy past of the history of Mankind must, I believe include those peoples of Eastern Europe who shared the same painful and unjust destiny as the Russian people with the purpose of compiling a large Encyclopaedia of that epoch.

Being one of those who have always admired the human qualities of the Russian people; their contribution to learning; to science and to the universal arts; being also among those who suffered terribly because of the leaders of yesterday and today, I would be happy to see the tragedy of my people and those others subjugated by the U.S.S.R. after the Second World War, written under the inspiration and counsel of a Russian—of yourself, the most loyal; most valorous of that people.

Such a gesture would not only disclose for history the inhuman treatment by the Russian rulers of these peoples, but would cement the friendship which these peoples would wish to cultivate for the Russian people. Written on your initiative, published together with your own work, it is clear that the *Gulag Archipelago of the Satellites* would have a wider circulation: your own and that tragedy would become known to millions of people who would read your books and also learn, from the voice of greatest authority—your own—that the system of terror imposed by the leaders of the Kremlin is the same both within and without the frontiers of the U.S.S.R. In this way, being warned, they could ponder on the fate awaiting them. For, even today, after fifty years of Communism, and in spite of all the evidence, books, and the millions of refugees living in exile, there are many who still imagine that if their country should have a Communist Government, it would be different from that of the Soviet Union. They do not yet understand that the Kremlin rulers have long arms which are unscrupulous and which manoeuvre the same system everywhere.

Many are the books which have described the tragedy of the peoples in the grasp of the Soviets. Writers of talent or simply witnesses describe their own experiences or those of their friends or family. Each does his duty towards his country and his people. There are books written with great talent and power of evocation which only sincerity and truth could have inspired.

But all these books have only touched the hem of the tragedy;

47

an encyclopaedia; a comprehensive account, in order to prove and brand the crimes perpetrated by the rulers of Moscow towards the peoples of Eastern Europe, has still to be written.

A survey like your own; a veritable historical, juridical, general and complete one has not yet been made and I permit myself to believe that this should be done by the writers of those countries, under your supervision and published under your High Patronage, together with your *Gulag Archipelago*.

Obviously, each of those peoples possess writers of talent; of profundity, who have already produced work of this kind.

But it would be useless to expect of them to be a *Solzhenitsyn* because he is unique. Because he was sent by God to fulfil a mission which transcends the bounds of his country—Russia—and of the Russian people. The respect and admiration felt by the whole world are not directed only to the genius and courage of the great Russian writer and citizen, but also *to the man* who belongs to the whole Universe through his ability and suffering; his faith; his dignity and his courage to defend the human being.

That is what permits me to believe that my suggestion might be accepted.

I think that this ''supplement'' to the *Gulag Archipelago* could be written either by one or by several writers of each country, each dealing with some part of the material to be used in the entire project.

For each of these countries, material exists in abundance. Numerous books, articles and testimonies have been published. Some survivors of this ''Satellite Gulag,''—of whom some have spent twenty years in prison—are today living in the West. Therefore, this material could easily be compiled.

You would be astonished, very esteemed Master, to see, by this comparative study, how this repressive system, this operation of destruction of peoples and individuals, has been transferred from that in force in the U.S.S.R.; as if a single malevolent magic wand had directed everything. It is enough to quote the simultaneous and identical trials in Bucharest, in Budapest, in Prague, in Warsaw or in Sofia, and the presence of Soviet ''advisers'' for the initiation, instruction and procedure of them in those countries, in order to ascertain that they are identical with those of Stalin and Vishinsky.

It is quite possible that such a work would have the assent and even the secret support (for the necessary material) from the actual Communist rulers of those countries. In my opinion, they have every interest to splinter the past terror of their country. They have every interest to show that their role and that of their Party was that of one single executant and that those truly responsible were the Kremlin leaders, etc. etc.

A GREAT RUSSIAN PATRIOT BUT ANTI-IMPERIALIST AND ANTI-EXPANSIONIST

With the greatest of courage, Alexander Solzhenitzin in his superb "Letter to the leaders in the Kremlin," written in Moscow, on September 5, 1973, while he was still in his fatherland, gave his wise, human and clever political answer, both to President Roosevelt's hallucinations, and to Stalin's sickened mind, concerning their territorial annexations, and their imperialistic domination.

"We have enough strength, intelligence, and heart to build our own house; why should we preoccupy ourselves with the whole planet? (p. 27).

"There remains for us only one road to follow and the sooner it will be marked out, the more salutary it will be for us (p. 28): let us devote ourselves to our *internal* development and expansion and not *external.*

"*Naturally, this change of objective must mean the renunciation of our tutelage over Eastern Europe.* Also, there must be no question of our holding by force any of the *countries on our boundaries.*"

Further on, on page 35 of his letter the great writer concludes: "How can our country dare to invent and plan international objectives and affairs so long as our own people remain in such a state of misery and so long as we are considered as her sons?"

Why have the Occident, and the American Administration not paid more attention to this great prophet? Why do they fail to see the truth where it is?

CHAPTER 8

"Those Sick Men Who Govern Us"

This is the title of a very interesting book, which, on reading it, fills one with fear. The authors are Messrs. Accoce and Rentchnick.

It is unbelievable, astounding, to discover that nearly all the great politicians in the course of—and after—World War II were incapacitated by serious illness that affected their powers of judgment by affecting the brain. Most of these men had dictatorial powers, which enabled them to make their own decisions in an atomic age when it is enough to press a button to blow up the whole planet.

Before passing on to the cases of Franklin Delano Roosevelt and Winston Churchill, let us glance at a few undisputed medical cases among these great personalities, according to this book:

1. Neville Chamberlain, the famous British prime minister—who signed the shameful and tragic agreement with Hitler at Munich in 1938—had been suffering for about four years from stomach cancer, which affected his whole personality. He was against war, a partisan of peace and disarmament; prime minister and senile for about four years, an easy prey to a Hitler without scruples, fierce and aggressive. Germany was armed to the teeth, while Britain was completely disarmed, owing to Neville Chamberlain.

The British premier lived in his own imaginary world, incapacitated by arteriosclerosis as well as cancer—which had been kept secret—which was torturing him.

Thus, certain historians explain—e.g., MacLeod, in his book *Neville Chamberlain*—the sending of the telegram to Hitler asking to be received at once in Munich. This telegram, which involved the fate of the whole world, was sent privately by Chamberlain, in his own name, *without the knowledge or approval either of the Cabinet, or of Parliament and without*

50

even having consulted Lord Halifax, his foreign minister. Can anyone doubt that the illnesses from which he was suffering did not affect this decision or his determination to remain in power until 1940?

2. General Gamelin, supreme commander of the French Armed Forces in 1940, was completely suffering from a split personality, as Pertinax shows in *Les Fossoyeurs.* Why? Because of syphilis contracted long before 1930, when he was treated in the military hospital in *Val de Grace,* in Paris,

This senile man—because of his glorious past—became supreme head of the French armies that had to face Hitler. No one suggested that he should have a check-up, as any ordinary soldier.

3. Benito Mussolini—like General Gamelin—suffered from neuro-syphilis, contracted long before his flight to Geneva in 1908, where he was treated in the University Polytechnic of Dermatology, as can be discovered in the files of that hospital. (V. G. Hilbert: *Benito Mussolini).* Treatment based on mercury and arsenic can have serious secondary effects on the brain and the whole organism.

4. Adolf Hitler suffered from Parkinson's Disease. According to Dr. Crinis, director of the Psychiatric Clinic in Berlin, this is a certainty. His personal physician, Morell, says that his first heart attack in 1941 was followed by a permanent blood pressure of 200/140, while from 1942, he suffered severe headaches with frequent loss of memory. Added to this was his obsession that he would die of cancer, as his mother had done. All this led to his fits of madness and frightful errors of judgment. If the odious way in which he exterminated the Jews can be explained by his dementia, Hitler's errors of judgment can only be attributed to the illness from which he was suffering.

With all his megalomania, with all his claim to the superiority of the German race, one cannot admit that a normal man could have made two such terrible mistakes: (a) to seek a lasting friendship and political understanding with Great Britain and at the same time to carry out a policy to liquidate the Jews and Masons. However ill-informed, Hitler must have known how great is the influence of the Jews and Masons in the formation of British politics, and been aware of the international solidarity that exists between them, and of their powerful influence in the United States. For his policy of seeking friendship with Britain, he ought to have known that he must ally himself with the Jews and Masons. Was it not his Parkinson's Disease that prevented him from making clear judgments? (b) But his immense, inexplicable error with regard to the

Russian people? This people, especially the Ukrainians, who were only waiting to be freed from the tyranny of Stalin and of Communism, could have been Hitler's most faithful allies, instead of becoming his deadly enemies.

In the first two months of the war, whole armies surrendered to the Germans who were received as liberators. But Hitler—instead of proclaiming the freedom of this subjugated people, called them his satraps and exploited and terrorized them. Instead of wooing them, he only forced them back into Stalin's ranks, by his absurd policy.

It was only in 1944, in Prague, that a congress was held, under General Vlasov, to proclaim the independence of the Soviet Republics, i.e., after Hitler had lost the war.

How could he have made this mistake? Was it not due to his Parkinson's Disease?

5. Stalin? He too suffered from arteriosclerosis. Within five months he had three heart attacks, after Yalta, in 1945. Professor Vyasnikov—who, together with seven other doctors made an autopsy after his death on 9 March 1953—speaks of "the disease of Alvarez," as in the case of Lenin. But that disease—small, but repeated attacks in the brain cells—profoundly affects the human brain and unbalances the personality. But neither Stalin, nor the others I have mentioned, gave up the reins of power. Stalin continued to rule for eight years after the first attack. During that period, we saw the liquidation of the *bourgeoisie* in the satellite countries, the Berlin Blockade, and the Korean War.

Certainly Stalin was mentally ill. He had all the characteristics of this illness: suspicion, sadism, intolerance of any criticism, thirst for revenge; these, together with his megalomania, are irrefutable proofs.

This disease increased in proportion to the advance of his arteriosclerosis. Milovan Djilas, in *Conversations with Stalin*, speaks of Stalin's "tragic and terrible senility" in January 1948. Djilas was surprised at the decline of the tyrant in the two previous years, since 1946.

But all the events of the Cold War began at that time—after 1948: the Berlin Blockade, the Korean War, the "Doctors' Plot," the ex-communication of Tito, the liquidation of the historical parties in Eastern Europe, etc.

Stalin's predecessor—Vladimir Ilitch Oulianov, *alias* Lenin, who died at the age of fifty-four, had, like Stalin, an autopsy. The result: the brain in a grave crisis of arteriosclerosis. The imprints of the four cerebral attacks suffered by Lenin were clearly visible on the two hemispheres of his brain. A complete softening of the brain with rare periods of lucidity. This softening did not occur at once, but gradually, step by step, over a long period of time, during which this sick man ruled over Russia.

Before passing on to the case of President Roosevelt, I will mention the cases of President Eisenhower and President John Kennedy.

6. The great General Eisenhower was sixty-two when, in 1952, he was elected president of the U.S.A. On 16 April 1953, he had a first stroke with frightful stomach pains. The doctors diagnosed Chron's Disease, i.e., a thickening of the mucous of the intestines and, what was more serious, very high blood pressure. This led to a heart-attack on 25 September 1955, followed by another on 7 July 1956. General Eisenhower, supreme commander of the Allied Armies in Europe, would have withdrawn from command any officer or general who had been unfortunate enough to have suffered a heart-attack or high blood pressure. He would have considered him incapable of command without risk to the army.

But as regards himself, President Eisenhower did not hesitate to stand again for election and presented his candidature again in 1956.

In 1957, on 25 November, Eisenhower had a grave stroke. Until the end of his second mandate, the great American hero suffered three more heart attacks and after his term of office, suffered four more. The tenacity and heroism of this man is incredible in view of the assault of so much illness. He resisted heroically and refused to retire. His duty was to govern because "for that I have been chosen."

7. The case of President John Kennedy is even more eloquent. He was ill before having been elected president at the age of forty-three. He suffered, according to Dr. Rentchnick, of Addison's Disease, characterized by progressive anaemia. Experts say that this disease causes cerebral upsets with schizophrenic tendencies and hallucinations. Treatment—according to the doctors—must be psychiatric, as well as medical.

But this disease was hidden from the American people before his election, as well as during his presidency. As in the case of Roosevelt, the entire dossier of John Kennedy was kept secret from his family. No autopsy was made.

As in the cases quoted above—which I do not wish to analyze (which would be outside the scope of this book and of my competence) but in the light of the politics of these men—I ask myself only whether their judgment was not influenced by the illnesses from which they suffered or by the effects—direct or secondary—of the medicines with which they were treated?

In vain did two leaders of the Democratic Party—John Connally and Mrs. India Edwards—try to draw the attention of their party to the fact that John Kennedy was suffering from Addison's Disease and would be unable to fulfill his role of president as required. The Democratic Convention by-passed the objection of the former governor of Texas, as well as that of the president of the women Democrats, and designated John Kennedy, who was elected.

Once installed in the White House, Kennedy swam in the pool twice daily and took two very hot baths lasting for thirty minutes every day. When was there any time left for him to deal with affairs of state, when so much time was spent in bed? He seemed permanently tired.

His dilettantism, his lack of political experience were surely responsible for his enormous mistakes during his period in office. But did not Addison's Disease play an important part too in these mistakes? Let us review them quickly:

1. The tragic, disastrous landing in the Bay of Pigs in Cuba. Arranged by amateurs, abandoned by the Americans, all the Cuban exiles were taken prisoners on landing. The U.S. lost all the credit that it might have enjoyed from behind the Iron Curtain and in the whole world.

2. The meeting in Vienna on 3 July 1961 with Khrushchev was also a disaster. The Ukrainian peasant, a go-between sharp-witted, soon realized the lack of experience of John Kennedy. He asked openly—and documents of the meeting prove it—that he (Kennedy) should allow Communism to prosper both in Russia and in all the countries where people are "freeing themselves," because that is the destiny of history. Do you imagine that John Kennedy put the *Moujik* in his place on hearing him talk of historical destiny, human liberty, and right of self-determination? No. Instead, he complained of Fidel Castro who was making intrigues in South America. He asked Khrushchev what he would do if a pro-American Government should be elected in Poland and began to instigate their neighbours—Communists—to form a "democratic policy." Khrushchev replied that certainly, he would intervene in Poland to prevent such a thing. As you see, not only did Kennedy recognize the spheres of influence estab-

54

lished by Churchill and Roosevelt with Stalin, but also the right of the Russians to crush any attempt at liberalization, or change of regime in those unhappy countries. In that way, Kennedy became the author of the Breznev Doctrine, or at least, gave it his blessing.

3. The Berlin Wall and the creation of the two Germanies were also the work of Kennedy, who remained passive and accepted the Wall, and the division of Germany in two.

4. The Vietnam War was also the work of Kennedy, who sent no fewer than 20,000 American officers and men to Vietnam. It was neither Nixon nor the Republican Party who began that war, but John Kennedy and his Democratic Party.

5. The missile crisis in Cuba. Many believed, and still do, that the withdrawal of these missiles was the success of Kennedy and a defeat for Khrushchev. The truth is otherwise and must be established. It must be emphasized from the start that the Kennedy administration was irresponsible and guilty of the fact that they did not supervise the movements of the Russians in Cuba, allowing them to bring and install those missiles, aimed towards America. This had been done months before, and Senator Keating and Senator Dole drew Kennedy's attention to it publicly, weeks before the crisis. For electoral reasons, the latter neglected to take any steps, and the world was on the threshold of an atomic war. Did Khrushchev withdraw those missiles? And at what price? First, that the Americans should withdraw theirs from Turkey, and then to promise *never to invade Cuba nor try to overthrow Fidel Castro.*

The consequence? Castro, knowing himself to be free of invasion, sent his armies to Africa, and agitators into Central and South America, knowing that as a result of the Kennedy-Khrushchev agreement, he would never be invaded.

That is why I consider Kennedy to have been responsible for a disastrous policy both for the United States and for the Free World.

After his assassination, he became a martyr and entered legend and the imagination of the world as a great president.

And that because John Kennedy had become a legend before entering history. History, surely, would have considered him to have been a disastrous president and it would not be surprising

55

if the explanation were to have been Addison's Disease, of which he suffered.

Before completing this chapter, we must remember the name of the great and illustrious General de Gaulle. I do it with a sad heart, for this giant of French and of universal history knew how to withdraw in time from the political arena, so as not to fall victim—he too—to the inevitable ravages of old age.

Nonetheless, the great general had a moment of human weakness in May 1968, as former President Pompidou says. When Paris was in full revolution, the general set out, with his family, to Germany, to General Massu without saying anything to the prime minister. The latter succeeded in convincing him to return, which de Gaulle did. The great general was eighty years old; eighty years of struggle, which consumes the human frame even more.

This is why a formula must be found to subject politicians to a thorough medical examination before assuming power, and, in time of government, an obligatory retirement at a certain age—perhaps 70—must be considered.

A medical consultation, regular, thorough and most of all, objective, ought to be instituted for political leaders. For they are men, like all of us, and may be attacked by diseases that affect their judgment, their will, and their powers of perception.

As we see further, in the cases of Roosevelt and Churchill—those giants of universal history—no such rules were respected. Both governed while seriously ill and decided—both of them—the fate of the planet, alone and in a dictatorial manner.

CHAPTER 9

A Sick Man in the White House and a Dying Man at Yalta

The end of the war began to come into sight. The peace had to be discussed and organized. A political conference was to follow the military conference at Teheran in November 1943. In July 1944, President Roosevelt proposed such a "summit" conference to Stalin, suggesting, through his ambassador—Averell Harriman—Athens, Salonica, Cyprus, Constantinople, or Scotland as the venue. Stalin beat about the bush for eight months to propose, in the end, Odessa, or Yalta. Roosevelt agreed and the conference was arranged at Yalta for the 4 February 1945. In the meantime, Stalin had occupied half of Europe and came to the conference with a victor's laurels. For him, the war was as if over, while the Allies were suffering a grave German counter-offensive in the Ardennes whose result was as yet uncertain.

Stalin had obliged the invalid president of the most powerful country in the world, to travel halfway round the world—from Washington to Yalta—to negotiate with him! He obliged the great hero of the American people—Franklin Delano Roosevelt—to cross the Atlantic and the Mediterranean by ship and plane, to come to his house in Yalta—sick as he was!

On 3 February, on a day of terrible frost, twenty-five aeroplanes landed on the aerodrome at Saki, with the 750 persons who composed the two delegations—American and British. At ten minutes past twelve, the president's plane touched down in front of the hangar.

Marine Lieutenant Norris Houghton, in his book *That Was Yalta*, tells us how President Roosevelt was taken *in the arms* of one of his security agents—Mike Reilly—who brought him from the plane to a jeep,

57

specially fitted up for an invalid like Roosevelt and in that he reviewed the Soviet Guard of Honour.

Then Harry Hopkins—the true *alter ego* of President Roosevelt and number-two man in America—was brought from the plane *on a stretcher*. Harry Hopkins was suffering from stomach cancer. He had been operated on in 1936.

Roosevelt died sixty-six days after Yalta. Ten months after Yalta, Harry Hopkins died too. One of a cerebral attack, the other of generalized cancer. In order of importance, at Yalta, telephone number one was reserved for Roosevelt; number two for Harry Hopkins, while number four was reserved for Alger Hiss—Roosevelt's adviser, member of the American Communist Party (therefore Stalin's agent).

That was the representation of the United States at the conference that was to decide the peace of the world "for a hundred years," and the fate of mankind. During the voyage on the cruiser *Quincey*, President Roosevelt did not leave his cabin at all, but rested on his bed, looking at his stamp album. The dossiers, which had been prepared over four years by that exceptional statesman, Cordell Hull, were entrusted to Alger Hiss. Roosevelt did not even look at them. Roosevelt was ill and dying. There were only sixty days left.

Churchill was aware of this. He remarked to Lord Moran: "He no longer has the physique for his great mental power." Lord Moran tells us in his book, *The Struggle for Survival*, about Roosevelt at Yalta:

> To a doctor [he had been Churchill's personal physician since 1940], President Roosevelt appears to be ill—very ill. He has all the symptoms of cerebral arteriosclerosis in such an advanced state that I give him no longer than a few months to live. Before our departure for Yalta, Dr. Roger Lee of Boston wrote me that Roosevelt had had cardiac insufficiency eight months ago.

During the meetings in Yalta, Roosevelt was making superhuman efforts to follow the proceedings. He was apathetic, dozing, as Churchill noted. When documents were handed to him for his approval, he did not even look at them. He was absent. They were examined from time to time by Harry Hopkins who had come to the conference on a stretcher. After three days at the conference, Roosevelt felt ill. His blood pressure rose to 300/170.

On the fifth day, after a *tête-à-tête* of thirty minutes, in his apartment

58

with Stalin, he offered the latter control of the railway in Manchuria, the Sakhalin Islands, and the Kuriles, etc.,—that is, he opened the door to the whole of Asia to Stalin. Churchill was not present, only his (Roosevelt's) ambassador, Averell Harriman and his interpreter, Charles Bohlen. Churchill knew nothing of the interview, nor did Stettinius, his Secretary of State. An ultra-secret treaty was signed and given to Churchill to endorse. He signed it without any discussion.

At the banquet given next day, Churchill raised his glass to "peace for a hundred years," while Roosevelt—the height of irony—raised *his* glass to "respect of the rights of the small nations!"

On the sixth day of the conference, Roosevelt was tired, irritable, indifferent. He felt that the end was drawing near and said he wanted to return to America. With difficulty, he remained until the conference ended on 11 February.

And once more, Mike Reilly took him in his arms like a sick child, put him on his invalid's jeep to review the Guard and again, in Reilly's arms, entered the plane. He set out on his last journey for Warm Springs in Georgia, where he died on 12 April 1945, after twelve years in the White House. On the plane and on the ship, he was accompanied by Harry Hopkins—his faithful companion throughout his life in his political struggles—on a stretcher.

The physical decline of the president, even at the time of the first conference in Quebec, did not escape the notice of Lord Moran—Churchill's doctor—who noted in his diary:

> So far as I am concerned [he wrote on page 179], I am asking myself to what degree his ill health, his powers of judgment and perception, have become impaired; or his will to examine a problem thoroughly before he enters into discussion with us.

> It seems to me that since I saw him last, he has lost 14–15 kilograms, so that one could thrust one's fist between his collar and his neck. I do not believe that a man of his age can lose weight to such an extent without a good reason.

> I believe that we must attribute the physical and mental behaviour of the President at Teheran—when he met Stalin—to this deterioration.

At Teheran the president stayed in the Russian Embassy where Stalin arranged his interviews at 10 P.M. when the sick president had need of rest. On arrival there, Stalin arranged their first interview *à deux* on 28 November 1943.

Next day Churchill invited the president to lunch, *but Roosevelt refused.* Instead, he accepted an invitation to lunch with Stalin. This caused Field Marshal Brook to say: "This Conference has ended before it began. Stalin has the President in his pocket."

According to Roosevelt's own physician—Admiral MacIntire—his patient was only overcome "by too much work and *his age.*"

But this was not the opinion of Cardinal Spellman, who says on page 246 of his *Memoirs,* that a year before Yalta, he observed "signs of irresponsibility" in the president.

Also—more than a year before Yalta—Cordell Hull observed, after the Quebec Conference in October 1943:

> When Roosevelt returned to Washington from Quebec, he did not realize the devastating nature of the report of 15th September 1943 which he had approved by an OK and signed.

The report in question was nothing more or less than the infamous Morgenthau Plan to transform Germany into a country of shepherds.

Some days later, Stimson, the Secretary of War, read out the report to Roosevelt.

> When he had heard it [says Stimson] the President replied that he was flabbergasted at the idea of such a thing and especially that he had approved and signed it.

Mrs. Ralph Truman, who was present on 20 January 1945 at Roosevelt's inauguration in the White House, describes her impressions:

> Mr. Roosevelt came out to the southern verandah at the White House to take the oath. Everyone, including myself, was "horribly shocked"; stupefied at what we saw. It was obvious that he was a very sick man. After the inauguration, when I came home, I said to my husband—General Truman—that I don't give the President more than three months to live.
>
> (*Plain Speaking*, p. 207, Truman.)

In turn, Harry Truman, gives also his impressions of the inauguration:

> He [Roosevelt] was standing in the cold, his hands trembling. He could hardly speak. I remember how Frances [Secretary of Labour in the Cabinet] wept when she saw what had become of him and hid herself so that the President would not notice. It was a very, very sad sight.

And that dying man left for Yalta after a few days, to confront the greatest tyrant in the history of the world, to decide the destiny of the world for centuries to come. No one tried to prevent his going: neither his family, nor his doctors, nor Congress, nor the American government. Why? Because for them Roosevelt was God.

With regard to the unquestionable illnesses of both President Roosevelt and Harry Hopkins, it is natural to ask ourselves the following questions: Was Roosevelt in full possession of his power of judgment at Yalta? Was Roosevelt conscious? Did he know exactly what he was doing at the Yalta Conference?

Or was he, as Harry Hopkins, stricken by illness, and therefore diminished in his capacity to make the best and gravest decisions?

Had Stalin taken advantage of this failing of the intellectual faculties of President Roosevelt at Yalta? Or was the die cast long before this conference?

Had Stalin taken advantage of the fact that he had, close to the president, and as his most important personal counselor, Alger Hiss, member of the American Communist party, who could influence the very sick president in favour of Stalin?

Or, maybe the influence of Alger Hiss at Yalta was minimal, owing to the overwhelming admiration Roosevelt felt for Stalin; and maybe the arrangements with him were carried out long before Yalta?

Consequently, as a last and most important question, what malady was Roosevelt suffering from? And since when?

Let us now examine the information and material I was able to find, and let us try to answer these questions, because if we can answer them, we can easily answer all the others.

What illness was Roosevelt suffering from?

As I have said previously, as in the case of John Kennedy, no post-mortem was done on Roosevelt. Similarly to John Kennedy, all his medical files disappeared.

In any event, in 1970, Dr. H. G. Bruenn published in the *Annals of Internal Medicine* his personal clinical notes, in the capacity of someone who had examined the president in March 1944. The diagnosis of Dr. H. G. Bruenn is categorical and without appeal: ROOSEVELT SUFFERED FOR MANY YEARS FROM ARTERIOSCLEROSIS. He had as well hypertension (high blood pressure): 185–105.

An electrocardiogram done by Dr. Bruenn revealed that the president suffered also from heart failure of the left ventricule.

In May 1944 (please keep in mind this important date), another X ray showed the president's gall bladder full of stones.

On 5 August 1944, President Roosevelt suffered a mild heart attack; his blood pressure climbed to 260–150. This man, who fought with such superhuman courage for his life, arousing the admiration of the world, was left by his doctors, his family, and the American Congress, to go to Yalta to face Stalin and to decide with him of the fate of the world.

Another doctor, an English one, from the British Delegation commenting in March 1944 upon the president's state of health wrote: "For us it was crystal clear that President Roosevelt was in the terminal stage of his illness. We at Yalta were stunned when we saw that President Roosevelt, a dying man, came to such a Conference when his place was obviously in a clinic or in a hospital. In his deteriorated state of health, his decision to go on such an adventure at Yalta, was a great mistake and poor judgment on the part of President Roosevelt. His decision to go to Yalta cannot but be attributed to his high spirit of sacrifice and responsibility."

I ask myself whether this "high spirit of sacrifice and responsibility" mentioned by the English doctor, should not, on the contrary, have compelled the ailing President to avoid going to Yalta in his diminished physical and mental conditions? Another doctor, Dr. Rentchnick, in his book discussing Roosevelt's illness, concluded that Roosevelt had been suffering long before March 1944 of the so-called maladie d'Alvarez; the same malady diagnosed in Woodrow Wilson, Churchill, and Stalin.

As I have stressed before, the Alvarez sickness consists of a series of "small strokes," in other words, small attacks (vascular) in the brain. The malady is called by some doctors senility.

The illness has many characteristics, such as: vertigo, poor movement coordination, stuttering, permanent fatigue, loss of memory, somnolence, irascibility, and an altered writing.

Many doctors can trace the evolution of the Alvarez malady by examining the alterations of their patient's handwriting and assessing thereby the deterioration of their minds.

In our case, Dr. W. G. Eliasberg in his book, *How Long Was Roosevelt Ill Before His Death?* wrote in 1953: "Long before Yalta, the handwriting of Roosevelt's was terrible; it was almost like the handwriting of a man suffering from Parkinson's disease, or of a sick man, victim of circulatory troubles in the brain."

And Doctor W. G. Eliasberg concluded: "We can ask ourselves whether President Roosevelt would not have been better off not to go to Yalta? And whether Churchill and Stalin did not take advantage of a sick man; a sick President."

This is the answer to the question: What kind of illness was Roosevelt suffering from? The Alvarez illness. Very advanced, and grave senility due to lack of circulation in the brain, causing its deterioration.

Since when had Roosevelt been ill? Very long—before March 1944.

Even his best friend and alter ego, Harry Hopkins, criticized Roosevelt's behaviour at the Teheran Conference in November 1943, telling Churchill and Lord Moran that: "Roosevelt was 'inept' and incapable. The Russians put to him a lot of questions and he gave very bad answers."

But this is not the answer to our question: Since when had President Roosevelt been ill?

As I pointed out before, and as I shall stress further on, President Roosevelt acted—in his physical condition—ALONE, AT ALL THE IMPORTANT BIG CONFERENCES. At Teheran, instead of staying in the American Embassy, he stayed in the Russian Embassy. And his Secretary of State was absent. He was in Washington. The same thing happened in the Casablanca Conference, when Cordell Hull was also absent.

Furthermore, even during the Second Quebec Conference, with Churchill, on September 15, 1944, neither his Secretary of State nor his War Secretary were invited.

Roosevelt told Cordell Hull that only military problems would be discussed; therefore, he did not need him. But he failed to invite Stimson, his War Secretary, either.

It happened that the Quebec Conference was considered extremely important, and the ailing president was all alone.

At Quebec, for instance, the military zones to be occupied in Germany were established, giving birth to the problem of the lack of access to isolated Berlin by the American and the British Forces. One of the strangest mistakes made during the war.

Maybe the presence of the Secretary of State and the Secretary of War would have prevented such a fateful mistake from occurring?

Their presence may even have prevented the approval by Roosevelt and Churchill of the Morgenthau Plan, which Roosevelt later denied having either read or approved. But the president was alone, and he was very ill.

In order to understand how serious was Roosevelt's illness, and the extent to which his judgment was impaired, it is enough to add another extraordinary fact, and unbelievable one:

At the end of 1944, the big American spy, Donovan, Chief of the CIA, was able to buy 1500 Soviet documents of unparalleled importance, as well as both the military and diplomatic Russian codes. Those would have allowed the USA to know Stalin's intentions, and thus, to adjust American policy accordingly. On learning about it, Roosevelt ordered Stettinius to hand the documents back at once to the Russians, including both secret codes, to make sure the Russians could alter them.

Is this the reaction of the president of the United States? The reaction of a normal military Commander-in-Chief, defending his country? Or is it the reaction of a sick man, overwhelmed by Stalin, and unable to understand where the interests of his own country lay?

CHAPTER 10

Since When Had Churchill Been Ill?

With regard to the health of this titan of universal history and one of the most respected and most admired political figures of Great Britain, we have today, a complete record left by his personal physician—Lord Moran—who cared for him from 1940 until his death in 1965, at the age of ninety-one.

Charles Wilson, Lord Moran, was appointed personal physician to Churchill by the British Cabinet in 1940 when the latter was appointed prime minister at the age of sixty-six. It was a clever decision on the part of the government, considering the war situation and the exceptional quality of the prime minister.

From the time of his appointment, during the whole war and for the rest of his life, Lord Moran followed Winston Churchill, step by step, day and night, like a shadow. He kept a diary where, every day, he noted his impressions and important facts in the life of his illustrious client and friend. A year after Churchill's death, Lord Moran published his diary, entitled *The Struggle for Survival: Winston Churchill.*

Two important facts stand out clearly from this journal: the precarious state of Churchill's health and that it was kept hidden from the British people.

Apparently of robust constitution, Churchill did not have the problems of physical debility of Roosevelt, who was paralyzed in both legs at the age of thirty-nine, as a result of an attack of poliomyelitis.

Even at the age of sixty-six, Churchill's physique of vigorous aspect inspired strength and will. These qualities, along with his oratorical prowess and unquestionable genius, helped him to mobilize the British people both materially and morally, and lead them to victory on the battlefield.

Churchill was a giant. A giant who appreciated the good life, whisky, and Havana cigars. He enjoyed all three to the full.

Churchill took two baths daily; one in the morning and the second after his afternoon rest—a rest that he took religiously wherever he may have been or in whatever circumstances.

As an illustration of this, Churchill tells how, on the eve of the landing in Normandy, General Eisenhower asked him, after his—Eisenhower's—report, what he thought of it. Churchill replied that he could not give an opinion because he had been sleeping during Eisenhower's report.

Probably this custom of resting had had a salutary effect on the life of this extraordinary man. He recovered quickly from the overwhelming task of being prime minister, especially in war time. He had to be a giant, a superman, to resist without feeling the strain or collapsing.

But Churchill was also just a man like all others. With all his robustness and iron will, he was also subject to our common biological laws, especially as his physical, moral, and intellectual efforts were extraordinary.

Winston Churchill had a first attack of angina on 27 December 1941, when he was at the White House. It was three weeks after Pearl Harbour; the United States had entered the war and Churchill was sixty-eight years old.

Lord Moran, his physician, cleverly concealed this first attack: "the Prime Minister needed two days rest after the fatigue of the journey." Furthermore to allay any suspicion—Churchill continued to drink whisky and to smoke his Havana cigars and take his two baths daily.

Thus, no one learned of this first attack.

Before coming to the next attack, it is my duty to speak of the crises of depression about which Churchill and Lord Moran spoke. Churchill called these crises his "black dogs."

At such times, Churchill was melancholy and depressed. Dr. Rentchnick, speaking of them, writes that they were characterized by "maniaco-depressions," some of which became a psychosis with fits of confusion, which constituted a serious illness. Churchill recovered from them quickly, but they were always noticeable.

This doctor attributes these crises to three causes: he was born prematurely at seven months, he was deprived of parental affection, and brought up by a nanny. He stuttered a little, which gave him a feeling of inferiority. He was humiliated in World War I by the Dardanelles affair in 1917, which also left a feeling of inferiority.

Without allowing myself to discuss the arguments of Dr. Rentchnick,

I emphasize only that he wrote these opinions in 1976, and since then new books have appeared, which show them in another light.

Thus, Ted Morgan published a volume of 600 pages about Winston Churchill, titled *Churchill: Young Man in a Hurry*, in which he attacked all the faults of the great statesman with brutality and diabolical cruelty.

In his book, Ted Morgan affirms—and shows—that Randolph Churchill—Winston's father—was a syphilitic and that he died of that disease, that in his whole fatal career he showed a mental irritability bordering on madness, that he showed "disdain" for his son Winston, which no doubt influenced the future Prime Minister.

This book, published by Simon and Schuster in New York, appeared in February 1982, therefore after the medical comments of Dr. Rentchnick.

In the light of the contents of this book, it is now certain that Churchill had a family taint. Could his crises of depression—his "black dogs," as he called them—have been hereditary?

Sometimes, Churchill's behaviour made one question very seriously the state of his mind? And whether he was not overcome by his "black dog days," an old complaint of his.

As an example, Elliot Roosevelt, the son of the president, described an encounter with Winston Churchill in 1941, when he was invited to stay for a week-end at Chequers, the residence of the prime minister.

"The next day," writes Elliot Roosevelt, "as I was leaving, the butler told me Mr. Churchill wished to say good-bye to me. I knocked on his door, and entered.

"Churchill was dictating to his male secretary, with a large cigar in his mouth, and he startled me out of my socks.

"HE WAS ABSOLUTELY STARKERS MARCHING UP AND DOWN THE ROOM."

This was the prime minister of Great Britain (the British Empire), who wanted to say good-bye, stark naked, to the son of the president of the United States.

This seems to be no incident, rather a strange way Churchill had of dictating in the morning, stark naked to his secretaries.

Mr. Donald Wayne, in a letter to the editor of *N.H.T.*, writes about another case he heard of from Max Perkins, of Scribner's, which was Churchill's publishers: "On a trip to New York, as Winston Churchill needed a secretary for some corrections, Mr. Perkins offered his own secretary, a quiet, modest woman named Irma Wyckoff.

"She duly found Churchill sitting naked atop his hotel bed, smoking a cigar.

"Miss Wyckoff took his dictation and galley corrections gamely for two days, but her composure flagged and she departed on the second day so visibly shaken that a Churchill aide, accompanying her to the door, was moved to try to comfort her: 'Don't worry, Miss,' the aide said. 'He doesn't notice you.' "

Did Churchill always dictate his mail completely naked, in the morning, to his secretaries? Or only on his "black dog days"?

In any case, his behaviour is open to questioning.

Not all people, and not at all times, were politicians allowed to rule without undergoing some kind of physical and mental tests.

The ancient Egyptians used to pass the so-called HEB-SED JUBILEE.

It was a ceremony during which every Pharaoh, after thirty years of rule, had to submit to a physical and mental examination, in the presence of high-ranking priests and the court, in order to prove that he was still fit to rule.

These Egyptians thought—before the Third Dynasty—that a Pharaoh could not rule more than thirty years, so he was generally killed, or forced to resign.

After the Third Dynasty period, the Pharaoh had to pass the Heb-Sed test after thirty years to be able to continue ruling.

Whether this was symbolic or not, the principle is full of wisdom.

Why haven't the democracies followed such a wise example?

But let us return to the health of Winston Churchill so that we may follow it, step by step, in the political events created and lived by him.

Churchill's health had deteriorated since October 1942. Anthony Eden mentions in his diary a remark made by Max, one of his government colleagues, to the effect that he was "worried about Churchill's health," which he found to be broken and that "he is no longer the same man." The same remark was made by another colleague—Bredan—on the same day: Winston was "very low in health."

Of course! For Winston had been suffering since childhood from his "black dogs," which showed up sporadically and which, undoubtedly, had become aggravated with time and because of the war, which this exceptional man of genius bore—like Atlas—on his shoulders.

Lord Halifax also noted in his diary in 1942, the political pirouetting of Churchill before Stalin and Communism; his indecision and hesitations, as well as the inconsistency of his attitudes on that question:

I cannot help being impressed by the radical change in Winston Churchill regarding Russia. When Anthony Eden proposed that he come to an understanding and collaborate with Stalin, Churchill called Eden a dog and a pig; now he tries to insist that Roosevelt help him to form a friendship with Stalin.

On 30 January 1943, on his return from the conference at Casablanca, Winston Churchill had a serious attack of "pneumonia."
After the Teheran Conference in November 1943, Lord Moran notes:

Churchill was tired, exhausted, broken. *More and more often he has lapses of memory*. Churchill is aware of, and more and more preoccupied by his physical condition. His blood pressure has risen steeply.

In this state, was his illness at Carthage on 30 January 1943, only pneumonia? Was it not an attack of arteriosclerosis, of senility, as Anthony Eden and Lord Moran seemed to think? This is a disease that comes gradually. Did Churchill suffer from it in 1941? Referring to the "pneumonia" in Carthage, Lord Moran notes on page 153:

So far the heart has not been mentioned in the bulletins, but it seems safe now to make a reference to the gravity of the illness.

The illustrious patient had been treated with "digitalis" for "pneumonia" and stayed in bed for two weeks at the height of the war. Was it not a stroke?
When we read Lord Moran further, on page 406, when he recorded the attack in June 1953, we find an important indication regarding that:

When I saw the Prime Minister today, he seemed played out, *as he was at Cairo before the Carthage illness*. I thought his speech was slurred and a little indistinct. Twice I had to ask him to repeat what he had said.

During the visit to Moscow, Lord Moran also gives us his impressions about what Churchill achieved there:

69

As far as I can tell, the P.M.'s plan is prospering. Stalin seems to meet him halfway. *It may be that our stock has gone up or simply that Stalin is getting his own way in everything.*

Do the reassuring words of Stalin mean anything to the P.M.? Does he trust Stalin? The trouble is that when the P.M. gets an idea into his head, he lets his imagination play round it and will not bother to fit in with the facts. At any rate he still makes his plans in the faith that Stalin's word is his bond.

There are relapses, to be sure, when the P.M. discovers that he is getting nothing out of Stalin.

Besides, he wants nothing but Stalin's friendship. I said to him this morning that Russia would have things all her own way in Europe after the war. He answered, as if he were only half interested: "Oh! I don't think so. When this fellow goes, you don't know what will happen. There may be a lot of trouble."

Also in Moscow, in October 1944, when Churchill gave away Eastern Europe to Stalin, Lord Moran notes in his diary:

He—Churchill—seems to be broken; tortured by two lines of action: one day he pleads with Roosevelt to form a common front against Communism, while next day, he hurries to gain the friendship of Stalin. Sometimes these obsessions succeed each other with bewildering rapidity.

In 1945, his physician says:

I did not at once tumble to the truth: Winston was sliding almost imperceptibly into old age. [page 785, to add on page 787] But a stroke is, after all, only the outward sign of a hardening of the arteries in the head, *which had been going on for a long time.*

Since when? Since when did Churchill suffer from arteriosclerosis, and to what degree did it influence his actions and decisions?

Let us follow now, in chronological order, the evolution of the health of this extraordinary man, in the twenty-four years that follows his first heart attack, on 27 December 1941, in Washington.

On 24 August 1949, Churchill had his first stroke in Monte Carlo.

In 1950, after another stroke, he lost his speech.

In 1951, on 27 October, he returned to power as prime minister.

On 21 February 1952, after two years in office, Churchill had a second cerebral attack. But he remained in office.

On 26 June 1952, he had a third attack and stayed in Bermuda, remaining completely infirm; he lost the sequence of his words, mixed up his dates, places, and time. But he did not resign.

Moreover, he insisted on trying to convince General Eisenhower, president of the U.S.A., to visit Stalin together. It was an obsession. Eisenhower refused. But Churchill remained prime minister in that mental condition. He resigned only on 6 April 1955 at the age of eighty.

He retired to Chartwell where he had only a few hours of lucidity daily. The rest of the time he slept or gazed into space.

On 26 October, he suffered another attack and again lost his speech and memory.

In October 1959, he had a fifth attack accompanied, this time, by a kind of epilepsy.

On 17 November 1959, Churchill had a sixth attack.

He survived for another six years and died in 1965 at the age of ninety-one. The titan remained a titan in the face of life and death.

But in the global perspective of Great Britain's history?

But in the face of universal history?

But in the view of the peoples of Eastern Europe enslaved by Stalin? The historians of tomorrow will have to judge him. The historians of today—as in the case of Roosevelt—cannot do it. It is too soon. Legend and history are mingled.

The enormous mistakes of Roosevelt and Churchill will have to be judged objectively, coldly, impartially. Taking stock—by and large—of these mistakes, these historians will inevitably ask the question: to what extent did their physical condition influence their politics?

Personally, I consider Churchill to be the more guilty of the tragedy of the peoples behind the Iron Curtain. Roosevelt was not versed in world history; ignorant of the meaning of Communism and Marxism. He was a dangerous dreamer; a romantic. He was ill and in his illness, he was fascinated by Stalin. He knew nothing of the virulence of Russian imperialism or of the mortal danger of Communist ideology.

But this was not the case with Churchill. He knew both the Russians and the Communists well. He had fought them in 1918–19 when he looked on Stalin as an "assassin and tyrant." He knew what the 120 million people behind the Iron Curtain could expect from Stalin. Churchill knew what he was doing and did not hesitate to do it. Therefore, his sins are grave—deadly—against all the peoples of Eastern Europe.

Churchill—together with Roosevelt—put the chains of slavery on the feet of these peoples.

CHAPTER 11

Unconditional Surrender

It is without question that President Roosevelt's greatest mistake during the war was his use of the term "unconditional surrender."

This mistake prolonged the war by two years, with all that it meant in loss of life and destruction. It upset completely the equilibrium of forces in Europe and in the world. It hindered a peace dictated by the Anglo-American powers, but one that was just and wise and would have kept Europe intact, with a conquered Germany but a reintegrated pro-Western world.

Without the clause about unconditional surrender, Stalin would not have had either the Balkans or Europe at his feet, while Russia would not have been able to threaten world domination today or tomorrow. We were not then on the threshold of a third world war.

How could such an enormous political and military misjudgment have been made? However incredible it may seem, this fatal mistake was made by *Roosevelt alone, without consultation with anyone.*

Roosevelt announced the principle of unconditional surrender at Casablanca, in January 1943, *at a press conference.* That was how his own Secretary of State heard of it for the first time. Cordell Hull states that both he and Churchill were stupefied.

Cordell Hull, secretary of state—the most capable, loyal, and most generous ever to have been appointed by the American people, had been Roosevelt's minister from 1933. In spite of that, Roosevelt had not taken him either to Quebec, Casablanca, Cairo, or Teheran. Eden, Molotov, and Churchill were always present with Stalin. How many mistakes could Hull have prevented had he been present to preserve the sick president from making them!

Cordell Hull was opposed to the condition of unconditional surren-

73

der. So were Eisenhower and the army in general. This led, inevitably, to the solidification of national unity when all Europe was in disarray and to the renewed morale of the army just when it was beginning to break up.

Without having a long-term political objective in view, the American Army was forced to fight for military victory only. Their only role and aim was to conquer the enemy and punish him; thus, total victory whose only objective was peace, devoid of any political considerations for the morrow.

The idea of unconditional surrender had entered Roosevelt's head when, as a schoolboy, he read of the unconditional surrender demanded by the American General Grant during the American Civil War. But Grant himself ordered General Ruckner, who commanded Fort Donelson, to send the officers and soldiers home after the capitulation. But that was a Civil War between brothers, and the generosity of General Grant was normal. How could Roosevelt have made such a comparison with the situation of today and be inspired by it?

Realizing the frightful mistake made by Roosevelt at Casablanca, Cordell Hull tried to mend it, as far as possible. But he was unable to achieve much, in spite of all the intervention of Eisenhower, of Admiral Leahy, of the British government, as well as of the Russians who, in the meantime, had seen the aberration of such a clause. Roosevelt stuck to his guns, stubbornly. He would listen to no one.

Leaving Roosevelt aside for the moment, Cordell Hull sent a memorandum to Harriman in Moscow on 25 January 1944, asking him to inform Molotov that the American government preferred to consider the situation of each country separately, from case to case, without renouncing, or clarifying publicly the clause of unconditional surrender.

Anthony Eden, too, in a telegram of 17 March, 1944, also demands its rejection.

> It may be necessary to apply the principle of unconditional surrender in the cases of Germany and Japan, but we will obtain better results in the small countries of the Axis if we expressly and openly renounce it—or even tacitly.

Cordell Hull, in agreement with the British point of view, presented President Roosevelt with a new memorandum, on 25 March 1944 in which he recommends "flexibility" regarding the satellite countries in the armistice negotiations.

THE CORNERSTONE OF
THE SOUTH-EASTERN EUROPEAN FRONT

It must be remembered that in those crucial months, Rumania tried to get out of the war and sign an armistice, but not one of unconditional surrender. Marshal Antonescu had talks in Stockholm, through Mr. Nano, with Mme. Kolontay. Marshal Antonescu, Rumanian dictator, with Iuliu Maniu, the leader of the Rumanian opposition, also negotiated through Prince Barbu Stirbey, with the ambassadors of the three Great Powers in Cairo. They wanted to sign armistices, but not unconditional surrender.

While the State Department awaited Roosevelt's reply, Gromyko—the Soviet ambassador in Washington—visited Cordell Hull and told him that the Soviet government agreed with Eden's proposal to modify the principle of unconditional surrender with regard to the satellite countries.

As in the meantime Roosevelt had again rejected the proposal of Cordell Hull, the latter returned once more to this subject. On April 3, when Bucharest was being bombarded mercilessly by the American Air Force, with the aim of demoralizing the population and the Rumanian nation, Cordell Hull, for the fourth time, asked the president, who was ill in bed, to abandon the aim of unconditional surrender with regard to Rumania and Hungary at the same time, as both the Soviet and British governments saw *military advantages* in that capitulation.

The president again alone and against all refused to abandon the principle in itself. So, on 11 April 1944, he replied in the negative to the British and Russians.

In the meantime, the Russians communicated their conditions for an "armistice" for Rumania to Stirbey on April 12, 1944.

As Russo-British pressure continued for a change in that clause of "Unconditional Surrender" the three governments made a declaration on 12 May 1944 (while Rumania was negotiating her armistice), which, in fact, said nothing and which, in the end, was equivalent to unconditional surrender:

> Hungary, Rumania, Bulgaria and Finland still have it in their power to withdraw from the war—by ceasing to collaborate with the Germans and by resisting the Nazi Forces by every possible means,—to shorten the War in Europe; to reduce their own sacrifices and to contribute to the Allied Victory.

75

It was a vague declaration without any precision; without any guarantee.

Without the unconditional surrender clause of Roosevelt, the Axis satellites could have withdrawn from the war in the spring of 1943 when Marshal Antonescu proposed to *Mussolini to withdraw from the fighting*, together with all the *satellites in a single and well co-ordinated movement*.

Mussolini was in agreement with that proposal—on principle—but postponed this decision, because of the unconditional surrender clause. He asked for time to reflect on it. This cost him his life.

It is, therefore, clear that if the principle of unconditional surrender had been abandoned, the war would have ended in 1943, at least with regard to the satellite countries; and certainly also to Germany soon afterwards.

What a political and military mistake—and unforgivable—was such a clause of unconditional surrender! This stubbornness of President Roosevelt; wasn't it due to his advanced illness?

IN 1943, ADMIRAL CANARIS HAD ALREADY ASKED THE AMERICANS FOR HELP TO OVERTHROW HITLER AND TO END THE WAR

The negative and tragic clause of "unconditional surrender," with its consequences of extending war in Europe for almost two years, must be kept permanently in mind when discussing the merits of Churchill and Roosevelt for achieving victory.

This is true now, more than ever, when we know, without any doubt, that Admiral Canaris was directly in touch with Allen Dulles, in Switzerland, during the war.

Indeed, in the course of his testimony, given before an American Congressional Committee, kept secret until now, Allen Dulles testified not only about his permanent contact with Wilhelm Canaris, Chief of the Abwehr Intelligence during the war, but he testified that about 10 percent of the entire Abwehr had turned against Hitler.

Why weren't these people helped to overthrow Hitler? and make an armistice, and peace with Germany, at least by 1943, when the Generals' conspiracy asked for help?

Why was the war unnecessarily prolonged for almost two years? Unconditional surrender? To make Stalin master of the world?

Who is responsible? Not Roosevelt and Churchill? And why? And how did they fail to seize such an opportunity, and exploit it? Where lies the explanation? The history of tomorrow—today it is too early—must come out with a definite and clear answer.

The "unconditional surrender" clause was aggravated to the utmost point of absurdity and folly by the Morgenthau Plan, approved by Roosevelt and Churchill, which planned to annihilate and destroy the entire German industry—industry so necessary—indispensable—to the whole of the European continent's very existence. To convert this highly industrialized country into an agricultural one, what a folly!

This thinking was consistent with Roosevelt's plan for treating the Germans: "To have only soup for breakfast, soup for lunch, and soup for dinner, and this for a very long time" (*Speaking Frankly*, page 182, by James Byrnes).

In February of 1944, the German General Karl Wolff, Commander-in-Chief of all fifty-five armies in Italy, went to Zurich and met the American statesman Allen Dulles, to discuss an eventual surrender of the German Army in Italy.

He was told that there was only one way: "Unconditional surrender."

On March 15, 1944, British General Airey and American General Lemnitzer went to Switzerland and met again with General Karl Wolff. On instructions from Roosevelt and Stalin, both generals put forward the same "unconditional surrender" clause, which precluded any negotiations.

What a mistake. The surrender of the German armies in Italy, especially if this would have been coordinated with the "volte-face" of Rumania, who wanted to make it at the time, would have opened widely, and unopposed, the advance of the Allied Armies into Vienna, Elba, and ·Berlin. It would have paved the way to the surrender of Hitler, and would have definitely kept out the Russians from Central Europe, if not from all Eastern Europe. But the Roosevelt-Churchill team played fair with Stalin. He was informed of the negotiations, which subsequently broke down, and World War II was prolonged for another fourteen months.

77

CHAPTER 12

Rumania's Efforts to Withdraw from the War

I want to stress from the beginning that, entering into a thorough investigation of the Rumanian tragedy, it is not only due to the author's deep attachment and ties of blood (kinship) with his native land and people, but it is based upon very serious military and political grounds. And examining them, we shall see the tragic errors made by Roosevelt and Churchill.

Indeed, Rumania's geographical position, easily seen on a map by everyone, made her the soft belly of Hitler's Europe. By her geographical position, Rumania was the turntable of the entire Southeastern European battlefront.

Hitler understood the importance of the strategic position of Rumania, in spite of his criminal pact of non-aggression, made with Stalin in 1939, in which, in its secret protocols, he gave Stalin Rumanian territories, and zones of influence. When he decided to go to war against Russia, Hitler immediately occupied Rumania militarily. He wanted to ensure his control this way, upon all of Eastern Europe.

There are other serious considerations for which Rumania was so important and was therefore, the keystone of an early end to World War II.

Indeed, from the economic point of view, with her petroleum and her important agricultural products, she represented great assets for Hitler in waging war, and it was essential to deprive him of them.

Through her network of communication, as one can see on the map, Rumania was a keystone of the entire German Southeastern European battlefront.

What enormous consequences would follow from cutting, by a Rumanian armistice, all those communications.

It must also be borne in mind that at the beginning of the war, before her mutilation by Hitler and Stalin, Rumania had 18 million inhabitants and still, by 1943, she had the largest population in Eastern Europe, after Poland.

From the military point of view, the Rumanian army was by far the most important in Eastern Europe, in 1943. Despite all the heavy losses incurred, the Rumanian Army represented a considerable power because Marshall Antonescu did all he could to keep most of it in Rumania, and not on the battlefront. General Wilson, the military chief of the Allied Forces in the Middle East, and the Chief of Staff in Washington, realised the importance of the Rumanian Army, and advised, as you will see, an early armistice, not unconditional surrender, with Rumania.

I would add that the Rumanian Army was a heroic and disciplined one.

Politically, and by affection and affinities, the Rumanian people had their deepest roots with those of its great allies, the British, the French, and the Americans, with whom Rumania fought and won World War I.

Before 1940, when Rumania was left all alone, and the British and the French were denying the solemn guarantee they had given her, Rumania was bound to live or to die with the great Allies.

By political and military treaties, Rumania was bound to Yugoslavia and Czechoslovakia, through the "Little Alliance." Furthermore, with Greece and Turkey, all together they tried to balance the German-Hungarian power.

Add to all this the alliance of kinship ties, and the warm feelings uniting Rumania to the country of her ancestors, Italy, and one can see what an extraordinary impact Rumanian withdrawal would have had from the Axis; a *volte-face* in 1943 would have changed the whole military and political situation.

What an extraordinary opportunity, militarily and politically, for a wise and skilful leader, to take advantage of Rumania's desire, through its government of Marshall Antonescu and the leader of the Opposition, Iuliu Maniu, in 1943, to try to break away, with Italy and other satellites, and to make an armistice with the Allies, *not* an unconditional surrender.

However, owing to the unconditional surrender clause, proclaimed by Roosevelt, nobody dared do anything but obey.

We shall see further the efforts displayed by Rumania to get away from Hitler, but she was not heard, understood, or helped.

Rumania could have won the war for the Allies in 1943, stopping the massacre of millions of people, but she was forced to carry on fighting until 23 August 1944, because she could not be granted an armistice, but only an unconditional surrender.

What was valid for Rumania was valid for Italy, as well as Hungary and Finland.

Let us examine in detail the Rumanian efforts and initiative.

As a soldier and strategist of great worth Rumanian Marshal Antonescu realized, after Stalingrad, that the war was lost. He was deceived, as were many other doubtless, about the solidity of the Anglo-Russian American Alliance. Like Iului Maniu and Dinu Bratianu, the leaders of the Rumanian democratic opposition, the Marshal believed in a landing in the Balkans of the Allies and in the eventual entering of Turkey into the war. But that did not prevent him, as in 1943, from attempting to withdraw from the war.

I will run quickly now over the different attempts (and you will see that there were many) even before the discussions in Stockholm and Cairo, which were the most important for Rumania.

As Anthony Eden wrote earlier, at the Conference of Foreign Ministers in October 1943 first, and then Churchill, at the Teheran Conference in November 1943, both spoke of the peace feelers put out by the Rumanian emissaries who were seeking an armistice.

The most spectacular attempt was that of Mihai Antonescu, made on 15 January 1943, as Bova Scoppa, former Italian minister in Bucharest says in his book, *Colloqui con due dittatori*. Through Mihai Antonescu, as intermediary—and of course with the unquestionable consent of Marshal Antonescu—he proposed to Count Ciano that together they should take the initiative to withdraw Rumania, Italy, Hungary, and the other Axis countries from the war.

Count Ciano agreed. Mussolini did not. On 1 June 1943, a new initiative was taken by Mihai Antonescu. Mussolini was now inclined to accept. He invited Mihai Antonescu to Rome. Declaring himself in agreement, in principle, with Antonescu's idea, Mussolini asked for a little time. On 1 July 1943, Mussolini asked him again to wait for two more months.

Antonescu's third attempt was made after the fall of Mussolini, through Guariglia. He replied that Italy was negotiating unconditional surrender alone at Lisbon and the affair was left at that.

Also in the course of 1943, the following steps were taken towards a Rumanian Armistice, according to the documents that I have been able to consult in London and Washington.

In October 1943, Victor Cadere, the Rumanian minister in Lisbon, spoke to the British ambassador in Lisbon. This step was of course taken in the name of Antonescu's government, which was seeking an armistice.

Also in Lisbon, another Rumanian personality Pangal, was negotiating in the name of Mihai Antonescu.

Apart from Rome, Rumanian Armistice soundings were being made by the Vatican. In Stockholm, George Duca made contact in the name of the Rumanian Opposition (Maniu and Bratianu) with the British and American ministers there.

The Rumanian vice-consul in Istanbul was also involved. He proposed to overthrow Marshal Antonescu, with the support of the generals—so he said—Nicolescu and Potopeanu. The same proposal was made again by the vice-consul in February 1944 to the British government.

In Switzerland, Grigore Gafencu also had talks both in the name of the Rumanian Government and of the Opposition. Also in Switzerland the spokesmen of Tatarescu—a former Rumanian Prime Minister—were negotiating in favour of King Carol II, whom the Russians wanted to make use of, as we shall see later.

Prince Nicolae of Rumania too was playing his part on the sunny snowbound slopes at Saint Moritz, in discussions with the Russian emissary, Vladimir Socaliu.

Let us not forget, among this throng, Princess Bibescu of Rumania, who was also agitating in the name of Mihai Antonescu.

The most serious attempt at an armistice was, however, made at Madrid when Mihai Antonescu made contact, through an emissary, with Hayes, the ambassador of the United States. Iuliu Maniu the opposition leader was also informed of this meeting.

To the American ambassador's request that Mihai Antonescu sign a declaration of unconditional surrender, in the name of Rumania, leaving it to be published and put into effect by the Allies after the military conjuncture, Mihai Antonescu agreed to this, laying down only the condition of either an Anglo-American landing in the Balkans, or of Turkey's entry into the war. Towards this end, he offered to entrust this document to the Turkish government. This government refused to accept the document and the affair was left unsolved.

A detail should be noted: that Iuliu Maniu had suggested sending a friend of his, Sabin Manuila—who knew the American ambassador in Madrid—to take part in the discussions there in the name of the Rumanian Opposition.

Regarding the talks in Cairo, it is worth noting that Iuliu Maniu had already communicated, by secret radio on 9 November 1943, that he wished to send a delegate to the negotiations.

The reply he received (document FO 371/43992 and R 294/G) was that the emissary must *address himself to all three of the Allies*—not only the Anglo-Americans—in order *to be authorized to sign an unconditional surrender*.

This is clear, precise. It is also confirmed from the English document number R. 11506/111/6. Therefore the Rumanian opposition leader, Maniu, knew from then on that he must approach *all three*—therefore, including the Russians—and that there was no longer any question of an armistice, but only of unconditional surrender. This communication was made after the Conference of Foreign Ministers in October 1943, in Moscow, when Eden raised the question of sending Rumanian "peace feelers" for an armistice.

In June 1944, apart from the talks in Cairo and Stockholm, we find an entire series of consultations—official, officious, or private, for an exit of Rumania from the war and a *volte-face*. We will enumerate them before going any further.

A most important official attempt was made on 14 February 1944, in Lisbon by Victor Cadere. He had come from Bucharest and had at once informed the British ambassador in Portugal that the Rumanian government were ready to send an emissary immediately, authorized to sign an *unconditional surrender to all three Allies*, on condition that once the German troops had been driven off Rumanian territory, the Russians would withdraw from the country.

Of course this message (document FO 571/43992) was sent at once—to *Moscow*—to the Soviet government as well as to that of America.

Strange to say, Molotov's reply of 16 February 1944 to the British government said that the action taken by Rumanian Victore Cadere was premature. This surprised Churchill, who, in a secret note (number R

2467) addressed to Anthony Eden, remarked that on 10 January 1944, already Dekanosov had agreed to authorize Novikov to negotiate with Rumania in Cairo.

The explanation of this extraordinary refusal to the offer to surrender unconditionally and addressed to all three, can only be explained by the Russian desire to negotiate directly with Marshal Antonescu, as they had begun to do in Stockholm. From then onwards, the Russians reproached the Rumanians continually because the latter had not made direct representations to them, alone.

Note: the advice given by Viorel Tilea—former Rumanian minister in London and still living there at the time—to Iuliu Maniu, can be seen in the summary in document FO 371/43992 of 25 January 1944.

Maniu had telegraphed to Tilea that "Rumania was on the side of the Anglo-Americans, but if the latter will not land in Rumania and if only Russian troops enter the country, the Rumanians would fight to the death."

Tilea replied that Maniu was deceiving himself, that a desperate resistance on the Dniester would mean suicide, that in his opinion the only solution would be to overthrow the government, surrender to the Russians in the hope that the Anglo-Americans would be able to convince the Russians to be more humane and generous.

On 23 January 1943, a memorandum of fourteen pages, written in French by Mr. F. Nano, Rumanian minister in Stockholm, was sent through the Belgian ambassador, Prince de Croy, to the British. This caused a veritable diplomatic storm because it had been addressed only to the British, and the Belgian government was obliged to explain in a memorandum of 24 February and to disavow the ambassador.

On 17 April 1944, Grigore Gafencu, the former Rumanian Secretary of State—who, from Berne, was keeping in constant touch with Maniu and Benes—met the British ambassador and on the part of Antonescu, discussed the question of surrender. He was told that the matter should be addressed to all three. He made another approach on 22 April 1944.

Marshal Antonescu personally—through his military attaché in Ankara—sought to find out what military aid he might expect from the Allies if he were to withdraw from the War.

On March 30 1944, Scarlat Grigoriu, secretary of the Rumanian Legation in Madrid, discussed the possibility of a "Rumanian Government in Exile" with Mr. Truello—an American diplomat—formed of Rumanians from Portugal. He suggested Victore Cadere, Mihai Antoniade, George Antoniade, Nicolae Dianu, and, of course, himself. Pangal was to be excluded from the government of Scarlat Gregoriu, for some unknown reason.

Discussions took place also in the spring of 1944, in Ankara and Instanbul between C. Bursan and Gigurtu, a former prime minister, and Anglo-Americans.

Now we come to another desperate attempt in Madrid with a member of the American Legation on 24 June 1947. This was an official and collective step taken by Mr. Grigoriu and Brutus Coste of the Rumanian Legation in Madrid as well as by Mr. Barbul of the cabinet of Prime Minister Antonescu, from Bucharest.

In an official discussion, these three men informed the Americans that, from June 6, 1944, the Rumanians had lost all hope of seeing a landing in the Balkans (a landing had been made in Normandy, in France). They understood therefore that the surrender of Rumania would have to be made to the Russians. But they wanted to know "for their own in-formation"—so as to prepare the ground—what role would be played by the Anglo-Americans in this surrender and whether they would be present—or only in theory. This was because the Rumanians were afraid that they would be left to the discretion of the Russians.

At the same time, those three Rumanians informed the Americans of the steps taken by the Russians at Stockholm and Berne, as well as those taken by the Rumanian and Russian military attachés at Ankara with a view to an armistice.

On being presented to the State Department, this message met with a negative reception. No answer was to be given to the Rumanian gov-ernment. Unofficially, they could be told that they must accept the terms of the so-called "armistice" offered by the Big Three at Cairo on 12 April 1944.

The Secretary of the Rumanian Legation received this reply on 30 June 1944, when it was immediately forwarded to Bucharest. On that occasion, Rumanians informed the Americans that, at Stockholm, Ru-mania—by treating directly with the Russians—had obtained better con-ditions for the armistice than those offered at Cairo, by all three allies.

All this can be found in document number F.O. 371/44004 in the State Archives, in London.

CHAPTER 13

Three British Officers
Parachute into Rumania

In December 1943, three Britain officers were parachuted into Rumania: Lieutenant-Colonel de Chastellain, former Director of the Unirea Oil Company in Bucharest; Major Ivor Porter, and Captain Metzianu.

This action was taken to make direct contact with the government and with Iuliu Maniu the leader of Rumanian opposition. They were equipped with radio and special ciphers.

By mistake, the pilot dropped them far from the farm where they were awaited, and they were arrested by the Rumanian police. Of course they were not treated as prisoners of war but as important guests. The government and Maniu made use of Colonel de Chastellain's radio and cipher-code to send messages to Cairo. It is said that Marshal Antonescu himself had a long interview one night secretly with the British colonel. And this can easily be understood.

But, by a leak on the part of the press—as in the case of Prince Stirbey's visit to Cairo—later it became known. The foreign press even wrote that those three officers were bearers of a project for a "treaty" with Rumania. However, in Rumania they were welcome; extremely useful to the government, and many people thought that this was the prelude to a British landing in the Balkans.

Their presence in Rumania, when found out by the Russians from the press, stirred up a violent row between them and the British. In a letter of a violent and extraordinary vulgarity, Molotov reprimanded Churchill directly.

This affair happened after the secret Anglo-American negotiations in Switzerland regarding the surrender of the Nazi armies in Italy, where the latter considered that they had been betrayed.

Churchill replied to Molotov in even more violent terms, using in his first version, the expression "stupid fool." The expression was later "softened" by Anthony Eden. But even if the words "madman" and "beast" had been "boiled down," the letter of 2 May (number 1328), was no less violent.

Churchill explained to Molotov that the objective of the parachute incident was to improve means of communication with Rumania, without any ulterior motive.

The British prime minister assured Molotov that in the Rumanian question they (the British) were trying to work with him and with Stalin. Churchill said he was surprised that Molotov could, for a single moment, imagine that he (Churchill) had any secret with Rumania or that he was trying to intrigue against the Russians there.

In paragraph five of his letter, Churchill insists that he considers the Russians to be masters of their policy in Rumania on the basis of the terms of surrender. In other words that the Russians "have the last word."

The letter was dated 2 May 1944, i.e., before the agreement with Roosevelt about zones of influence, so Churchill was anticipating seriously.

After the explanations given by the British ambassador in Moscow, the storm died down. But the Antonescu government and the Opposition went on using the services of Colonel de Chastellain for all their messages with the Military Command and with the emissaries in Cairo.

It must be emphasized, in order to understand more easily the question of the negotiations in Cairo and to follow them, that the commission formed by the three Allies in Cairo also had *direct radio contact with Colonel de Chastellain*, as can be seen clearly from the telegram from Lord Moyne (number 981) of 17 April 1944. From its contents, it can be seen that he was communicating messages direct to Marshal Antonescu. The document quoted, speaks of the armistice conditions communicated through de Chastellain to Antonescu, and Lord Moyne asks that they be revealed also to Maniu.

Apart from the radio from that so-called prison of the British colonel, Iuliu Maniu—certainly with Antonescu's consent—had also his personal radio transmitter.

Also, the link between Bucharest and Cairo for Marshal Antonescu and Maniu was maintained by diplomatic courier *via* Ankara (Alexander Cretzeanu). The departmental head of the Coding Department of the Foreign Ministry was Nicolescu Buzesti, son-in-law of Prince Stirbey and cousin by marriage, of Cretzeanu who, in turn, was a grandson of the prince. In the last phase of the discussions and before 23 August 1944, Niculescu Buzesti too had a radio post in the forest of Baneasa, by which he communicated with Cretzeanu. He was each day with the King, to inform and advise him.

We will return to the means of communication because they were of vital importance, the more so because Colonel de Chastellain's radio post, as well as that of Maniu, ceased on 5 August 1944.

On May 23, Prince Stirbey complained of bad radio connections with Maniu. Lord Moyne asked Novikov, the Russian ambassador, whether he could not do something to improve them. The latter did not reply.

Also in an ultra-secret telegram from Lord Moyne from Cairo to London on 29 June 1944, we find that Mr. Constantin Visoianu the second Rumanian emissary also complains that the radio set "Reginald" has not been repaired and also the fact that, through Ankara (Alexander Cretzianu), messages came very slowly. He proposed that a new operator be infiltrated into Bucharest.

It should be remarked also that all the messages sent to Cairo for those two Rumanian representatives in Cairo had been censored by the Russians and the Americans before being sent on. Visoianu complains of this procedure also on 14 June. Russia rejected the complaints . . . explaining that this way they themselves could receive communications more quickly.

I emphasize that Niculescu Buzesti did not communicate directly with Cairo, but only with Ankara. Cretzeanu forwarded to Cairo.

After this introduction, I will now approach the question of the armistice negotiations—first at Stockholm and then in Cairo. I do this, not because I wish to reopen this painful subject, in order to stir up the controversy that has again split the Rumanian exiles in two. I consider that after thirty-eight years, passions should have cooled and the subject approached in its historical aspect; that it may be analysed coldly in the light of the Secret Service documents recently declassified after thirty or thirty-five years. This extraordinary and most important material must not be allowed to get lost. For the history of the Rumanian people, it must be learned and preserved. That is the aim of this chapter: to deal not only with the armistice negotiations, but also the Act of 23 August 1944 and its consequences.

Far be it from me to accuse anyone or cast any aspersions. I will only go so far as not to draw any definite conclusions, for the last word belongs to the Rumanian people. They will judge tomorrow. So I will not hide facts. They speak for themselves and say a great deal.

This chapter would not be complete—nor this book—if I were not to emphasize the important part played by Mr. Rica Georgescu in sending messages between Maniu and the Allies from 1940, right up to the armistice.

Director-General of the Romana-Americana Standard Oil Company, Mr. Rica Georgescu was one of the leading members of the National Peasant Party and an intimate and well-trusted friend of Iuliu Maniu.

Having organised since the autumn of 1941 a network of radio transmissions to the Allies, he was arrested by Antonescu, but was not brought to trial. Iuliu Maniu, in person, told the Marshal that if Mr. Rica Georgescu were to be tried, he himself would be a witness for the defense and say that Rumania needs to keep up her connection with the Allies—always her friends—who had helped her in the forming of Great Rumania. And so, she has need of radio. Antonescu understood. Mr. Rica Georgescu did not go on trial, nor was he handed over to the Germans who demanded him insistently.

Imprisoned for four years in the jail of Malmaison, he communicated, he transmitted messages in code from Maniu to Cairo, and surely also messages from the government. As I have not access to the Rumanian Archives, I limit myself to the consideration of only the Anglo-American declassified documents, which I regret being unable to compare with those of Rumania.

Freed on 23 August 1944, Mr. Rica Georgescu was appointed Minister of Oil on the express wish of Iuliu Maniu—as a long article in the paper *Dreptatea* said—on 14 May 1946, in order to honour "his courage; suffering; patriotism and competence."

CHAPTER 14

Churchill and Spheres of Influence in the Balkans

Readers will remember that the State Department in Washington was against any territorial arrangements before the Peace Conference and *hostile to the creation of any zones of influence.*

For four years, Cordell Hull had been working on a political plan to be applied *after the war.* A non-partisan committee was composed of Democrats and Republicans working on that plan, which foresaw the right of self-determination and which was based on the Atlantic Charter, and on the Declaration of Human Rights. The plan envisaged a global system for the maintenance of peace, in which the small nations were to be protected in their independence and sovereignty by a world security system. It was, for the most part, a plan to create the United Nations.

Because of this well-defined policy of the State Department and of the American Congress, Cordell Hull rejected Eden's proposal at the Conference of the Foreign Ministers of the three Allies in Moscow in 1943 to create spheres of influence in the Balkans and in Europe in general.

But this did not discourage Churchill from achieving this aim nor from reaching an understanding with Stalin behind the back of Cordell Hull. Holding to the forms of parliamentary democracy, Churchill asked Eden, on 4 May 1944, to prepare an urgent report for the Cabinet and for the imperial conference on:

> The basic problems which exist between Britain and the Soviet Union and which are now developing in Italy, Rumania, Bulgaria and Yugoslavia and above all, in Greece. The hub of the question [said Churchill] is *whether we have to accept the Communization*

89

of the Balkans and of Italy. Mr. Curtin spoke of this problem this morning, but my opinion is that we must reach a definitive conclusion about it.

In conformity with this demand, Anthony Eden prepared his *TOP SECRET* report (WP (44) 304) of 9 June, which became accessible to the public in 1972. Eden's report was accompanied by a personal letter in which he begged his colleagues in the War Cabinet not to draw hasty conclusions that "irreconcilable interests" would arise between the British and Russians in the Balkans; and especially as this would lead to a conflict. But Eden recommended ability and prudence.

We must not hesitate to make known our special interests in the *Eastern Mediterranean*, i.e., in Greece and Turkey, and also in other parts of the Balkans.

The report of these pages with twelve headings analyses the situation in the Balkan countries, as in Point 7, which speaks of Rumania:

In Rumania, after having annexed the territories which they desire, the Russians will ask for *"A Government friendly to the Soviet Union"* over which they will have a *considerable measure of control*. As regards Communism in Rumania, it is non-existent and anti-Russian feelings are predominant. But if Rumania refuses the Soviet conditions (N.B. *not the Allied*) the result in the end will be even harsher conditions and they will be obliged to have a Government under complete Soviet subjection.

Conclusion:

Let us concentrate our influence in Greece and Turkey and base it on Turco-Greek friendship as a fundamental element in our policy in Southeastern Europe and in the Eastern Mediterranean. At the same time, let us avoid direct competition with Russia in her influence in Yugoslavia, Albania, *Rumania* and Bulgaria; let us try on every possible occasion to spread British influence in those countries.

But why did Anthony Eden "pipe down," even before his government colleagues? Because, without waiting for their consent, he had

90

already come to an understanding with the Russians. Now he awaited only the blessing of America and of the British Cabinet.

This understanding—*proposed by Eden*—is not in any doubt. It can be seen clearly in three documents.

The first is on page 73 of Winston Churchill's sixth volume on *World War Two*:

> On the 18 May 1944, the Soviet Ambassador in London came to the Foreign Office to discuss a suggestion made by Mr. Eden, i.e., that *Rumanian* affairs—temporarily and in connection with the war—should be the preoccupation chiefly of the Soviet Union, leaving to us the question of Greece. Russia is ready to accept this suggestion but wishes to know whether we have consulted the Americans.

Therefore, before 18 May, Eden had offered Rumania to the Russians. He proposed this, to be more exact, on 5 May 1944, when he received the Soviet ambassador—Gousev—in London.

In other words, the British offer to hand over Rumania as a zone of influence to the Russians was made more than a month *before the Top Secret Report* made by Eden on 7 June 1944, to be discussed and approved by his colleagues in the War Cabinet.

On 18 May, three weeks before the report, the Russians had *accepted*, but they wished to know whether the Americans were aware of it and whether they too agreed.

These data are absolutely reliable and unquestionable. They result also from the telegram sent by Churchill to Stalin on 11 July 1944, in which he says:

> A few weeks ago, Eden suggested to your Ambassador that Russia must play the leading part in Rumania and Great Britain the lead in Greece.

Confirmation of the date of 5 May of Eden's proposal and the Russian acceptance of 18 May, results even more clearly from a memorandum presented by Andrei Gromyko, the Russian ambassador in Washington to Cordell Hull, Secretary of State, on 1 July 1944 when the Russians wished to be certain of the agreement of the U.S.A.

Why did the Russians suspect that the British agreed with them without American consent?

Very simply: for the United States State Department had been opposing for three years the idea of zones of influence and categorically and for all time. Not only at the meeting of the foreign ministers in Moscow, in 1943, but under all circumstances.

On 21 March 1944, Cordell Hull had repeated the disapproval of the State Department of these zones:

> "Given that the provisos of the Declarations of the four great nations will come into force, *there is no longer any need for spheres of influence*; of allies; of balance of power; etc."

That was the official policy advocated by the State Department, in agreement with the American Senate through the bi-partisan Advisory Committee on Post-War Planning and Foreign Policy.

This was well known both by the Russians and the British.

But this did not prevent Churchill from trying to overthrow it; by a diabolical perseverance, by a great cynicism, and by deceiving the State Department, but in this, Churchill had the complicity of Roosevelt, as I will point out.

But let us take the facts in their chronological order.

On 30 May 1944, Lord Halifax, British ambassador in Washington, called on the Department of State to ask Cordell Hull what the American government thought of an arrangement between the British and Russians in which the Russians would have "controlling influence," "the last word," in Rumania, while Britain would have the same role in Greece. He added that difficulties had arisen between the British and the Russians over the Balkans, especially Rumania.

Cordell Hull *replied categorically* to the British question, informing Halifax, once more, and openly that he was against any kind of division of Europe or part of it into spheres of influence, as was opposed also at the conference in Moscow.

In view of the refusal of the Department of State, Churchill next day addressed himself *directly* to President Roosevelt, over the head of Cordell Hull. Why? Because he knew that the president was in agreement with him and was only awaiting some formula in order to overcome the objections of the State Department.

On 31 May, therefore, Churchill sent a telegram to Roosevelt in which—the height of perfidy—he says in line four that he had asked Halifax (on 31 May, after the latter had already been there on 30 May) to discuss the question with the State Department. The president pretended to be unaware of Cordell Hull's refusal.

In that telegram, Churchill admits that they (the British) had proposed that the Russians play the leading part in Rumania and they, themselves, in Greece.

> Such an arrangement [says the telegram] is the natural evolution of the military situation because Rumania falls within the sphere of the Russian Armies and Greece within the Allied Command of General Wilson in the Mediterranean. I hope, [continued Churchill] that you will give your blessing to this proposal! [And that this caesarean operation can be performed against the State Department, Churchill resorts to the perfidious formula] three months for the validity of the arrangement:
>
> "Of course we do not want to carve up the Balkans into spheres of influence and it must be specified clearly in our arrangement that it applies only to wartime and does not affect the rights of any of the Great Powers at the Peace Conference."

This telegram of 31 May 1944 was sent by Roosevelt to the State Department to be studied and judged.

In his *Memoirs*, p. 1453, Cordell Hull tells that the State Department—following a conference of the chief collaborators—were *unanimously* agreed:

> that we could not lend our support to any such agreement and, in fact, should do what we could to discourage it. While we could understand Britain's natural desire to strengthen herself in the Mediterranean (Greece) . . . we felt that any *such arrangement as that proposed, no matter how temporary, would inevitably conduce to the establishment of the zones of influence which we have been stoutly fighting.*

What prophetic foresight had this great statesman and what a tragedy that Roosevelt stabbed him in the back—as well as the Department of State!

While Cordell Hull was editing his reply to the telegram of 31 May from Churchill, the latter returned to the attack (he was very pressed to sell Rumania and the Balkans) and, on 8 June, Halifax went again to see Cordell Hull and to plead, for the Russians to "play this hand," i.e., to have a free hand in Rumania. Lord Halifax mentions also for the first time, in this report, Bulgaria and Yugoslavia. The height of effrontery—he reminds the Americans of "Monroe Doctrine," i.e., not to interfere in the affairs of Europe as they do not interfere in those of South America.

Not even this message convinced Cordell Hull. He opposed this categorically and convinced Roosevelt to do the same.

On June 10, 1944, the president telegraphed to Churchill his opposition, identifying himself with the arguments of the State Department, i.e., that any arrangement—even temporary, would lead to the fatal division of the Balkans into spheres of influence, however much Churchill insists that it is limited to military questions. In the same telegram, Roosevelt proposes the foundation of a Commission of Supervision of the Balkans, which would eventually resolve the misunderstandings, and "*to forestall the creation of exclusive zones of influence.*"

In view of such a categoric refusal, anyone would have given up. Anyone, but not Churchill. Why? Because he had become obliged to the Russians and had to deliver the goods; to hand Eastern Europe to the Russians on a tray. As well, he knew, as he says in his second message to Halifax, that he would try again:

> "I have every reason to believe that President Roosevelt is in complete agreement with me as regards the arrangement with Greece."

Why was Churchill so convinced that Roosevelt agreed with him, when the whole policy of the State Department and of the American Senate, over a period of four years, was one of opposition to the creation of zones of influence? Why was Churchill sure that Roosevelt thought differently from Cordell Hull and the American Senate? Why? Because he had come to an understanding with Roosevelt about zones of influence in Quebec, in 1943. Roosevelt told the same thing on 20 September 1943, to Cardinal Spellman. Churchill knew that Roosevelt had promised Eastern Europe to Stalin in a letter sent to Weiss and Zabrousky, as we have seen. Roosevelt also proposed (orally) to give Stalin Poland at the Teheran Conference, in November 1943, on condition not to reveal this before the presidential elections of November 1944.·

Churchill was certainly aware of all this. That is why he "had reasons to be convinced that Roosevelt was in agreement with him."

By misfortune, the Secretary of State went off for a few days rest.

CORDELL HULL STABBED IN THE BACK BY
HIS OWN PRESIDENT

In his absence and without the knowledge of the State Department, the Senate, and the American people, President Roosevelt agreed to accept Churchill's proposals.

Two days after Cordell Hull's departure on holiday, Churchill telegraphed again directly to Roosevelt on 11 June 1944.

This time, in a longer telegram, Churchill speaks of the armistice conditions drawn up on 12 April, as well as of the possibility of a *coup d'etat* in Rumania with a realignment of the Rumanian Army.

> It seems, [he says] that the Russians are on the point of invading Rumania in great force and that we will help Rumania to regain Transylvania if Rumania will play our game, which is possible; considering all this, it would be a good thing to allow the Russians to take the lead, knowing that neither you nor we have a single soldier there and they will do whatever they please.

In order to give President Roosevelt even more arguments to justify his (Roosevelt's) approval, Churchill adds, perfidiously: "The Rumanian Army has caused many casualties among the Russian troops, and they entered the war against Russia with great enthusiasm."

So that this explanation could be accepted by the State Department, the Senate, and the American people, Churchill proposed to Roosevelt: "I suggest that the arrangement regarding Rumania, Bulgaria, Yugoslavia, and Greece should have a trial period of three months, after which it will be reviewed by the Three Great Powers."

Roosevelt replied on 12 June 1944, *accepting Churchill's proposal*, adding (so as not to offend his own Secretary of State), "We must be careful to insist that we will not create any spheres of influence after the war."

Churchill replied the same day that he was "deeply grateful."

The result was that an Iron Curtain was drawn across the eastern frontier, Eastern Europe and of Rumania, and night fell over these peoples.

I should add—as to emphasize even more, the authoritarian dictatorial character of President Roosevelt—as well as his duplicity, even towards his closest collaborators—that, on giving his agreement on 12

June, he informed neither the State Department, Cordell Hull, nor the Senate about the agreement reached.

Cordell Hull—returning to Washington from his holiday and unaware of the telegraphic assent given by his president to Churchill—sent the memorandum to the British Embassy as it had been approved by the president on 9 June, and in which he had rejected the idea of spheres of influence and had proposed the creation of a Commission of the Three Great Powers for the Balkans.

Even more, knowing nothing of Roosevelt's approval, given on 12 June, the secretary of state drew up a new report for Roosevelt on 17 June (five days after the latter had given his assent), in which he drew the latter's attention to the true intentions of Churchill.

> "I draw your attention to the fact that Mr. Churchill, quite openly, means to apply his proposals in the whole Balkan region, mentioning also Bulgaria and Yugoslavia, as well as Rumania and Greece, making an analogy with our situation in South America."

(The Monroe Doctrine, which established exclusively American influence in that region, or more precisely, excludes foreign interference in South America. Author's Note).

"This position is extremely dangerous," concludes Cordell Hull in his report of 17 June. But the matter had already been settled, behind his back, by his own president on 12 June. What shame! What tragedy!

The height of ridicule was that Cordell Hull did not discover this until 26 June and—the height of irony—only from the British ambassador in Cairo. The latter, having spoken with the American ambassador, Lincoln MacVeagh, informed him of the telegram to the president of 12 June 1944.

Surprised, and not believing his eyes, Cordell Hull wrote to President Roosevelt, including a copy of Ambassador MacVeagh's telegram and asking whether it was true that in his—Cordell Hull's—absence, the entire policy of the U.S.A. had been altered.

Roosevelt did not reply but, like an archivist, sent copies of the exchange of telegrams with Churchill to the State Department Archives. Why didn't Cordell Hull resign after such appalling goings on? Probably, out of a sentiment of patriotism because it was wartime and he wanted to prevent other policy changes.

The Russians, in turn, sounded the Americans on 1 July, through Gromyko. He confirmed Roosevelt's suggestion of a three-month period, considering it was wartime. But in his reply, Cordell Hull emphasized that the American government was unhappy about this kind of agreement, which, by its nature, could lead to a division of some Balkan regions into spheres of influence.

President Roosevelt approved this report too. Unfortunately from the opinion of some doctors, it appears that the president no longer knew at that time, what he was doing, what he was approving, and what not.

The following is an extract from Cordell Hull's report, which had been approved by Roosevelt in the question of *spheres of influence*:

It would be very wrong to make any arrangement which would depart from the principle adopted by the three Governments, by which they categorically rejected the idea of Spheres of Influence. Consequently, the American Government hopes that the steps they will take will in no way prejudice the policy of collaboration of the Allied Governments and no individual, independent steps will be taken. Because any arrangement which would suggest such spheres of influence could only do harm and work against the establishment and efficient functioning of a *wide and general system of security in which all countries will share and will have their place*.

We have added, [continues Cordell Hull] that a period of three months will permit the British and Soviet Governments to decide whether such an arrangement is practical and efficacious; and to be applied only in time of war, without affecting the rights and responsibilities of the three principal Powers during the period of establishing peace, as well as afterwards; and this holds good for the whole of Europe.

[And Cordell Hull continues] In conclusion, we presume that the arrangement between them (the Russians and the British) will not clash with the interests of the American Government or of any other Government associated with the three great Allies.

That is why Cordell Hull remained in the State Department after Roosevelt's telegram of 12 June 1944: to try to save the situation and prevent the disaster becoming definitive. He fought on and hoped. It was his last attempt to obstruct the cession of Rumania and of Eastern Europe to the Russians. It was his last effort to prevent Churchill doing this. But, he did not succeed. Churchill went to Moscow and the arrangement of three months became permanent on 9 October 1944, against the will and knowledge of Cordell Hull, but with the knowledge and consent of Roosevelt.

This memorandum of the State Department was handed to the Russians on 15 July 1944 and was formally endorsed by Roosevelt.

In the meantime—on 11 July 1944—Churchill telegraphed to Stalin to bring him up to date with the arrangement and with Roosevelt's approval for the period of three months.

> A few weeks ago, Eden proposed to the Soviet Ambassador that Russia take the leading part in the affairs of Rumania, while England do the same in Greece. That was to avoid an unpleasant triangular exchange of telegrams. When Molotov suggested that this should be transmitted to Eden and the Americans, I did so and the President agreed to let us give it a trial period of three months. Those three months—July, August and September—could be very important months. In spite of that, I see that you foresee certain difficulties. Why not let that plan be tried for three months?

With all this diabolical insistence of Churchill's, Stalin did not want such an arrangement, because he wanted it to last indefinitely and with official American approval—not their opposition.

So, after Cordell Hull's memorandum of 15 July 1944, Stalin replied immediately to Churchill on the same day:

> As regards the question of Rumania and Greece, it is clear to me that the American Government are in some way doubtful about this question. Therefore, it would be better to return to it after we have received a reply from the Americans to our questions. And once I have had this reply, I will not hesitate to write you further on this matter.

The matter was left at that stage from 15 July 1944, until the visit of Churchill and Eden to Moscow.

CONCLUSIONS REACHED

In order to help readers to follow the events in this labyrinth of documents quoted, I will draw preliminary conclusions, i.e.,

1. In spite of the categorical refusal of the Department of State—respective of Cordell Hull in Moscow in October 1943,

98

to recognize zones of influence—Churchill renewed the attack in May 1944.

2. Just as the initiative for these spheres of influence was taken by Eden in Moscow, in October 1943, so it was Eden who renewed this initiative on 5 May 1944 by proposing the cession of Rumania to Stalin in return for Greece.

3. Although the Russians had asked for exclusive spheres of influence already in 1941, they pressed the British to force the hand of the Americans, not wishing to obtain these spheres without the consent of the United States.

4. Although Churchill knew very well that the official policy of the United States—as expressed by the State Department and by the bi-partisan commission of the American Senate—was against the creation of such spheres of influence, Churchill, with unheard-of stubbornness and by insinuations, untruths, and cheating; working against and behind the back of the Secretary of State of the United States, grasped the consent of Roosevelt for the creation of these zones.

5. This consent was given by Roosevelt *without consultation; without the knowledge of the State Department; of Congress or of the American people.* He faced his own Secretary of State—Cordell Hull—with a *fait accompli*; and so, up to now, the State Department, the Senate, and the American people have absolutely no responsibility in the misfortunes of Eastern European countries—nor for the creation of zones of influence. The American people too, have been victim of the despotic, authoritarian, and anti-democratic acts of their president, Roosevelt, in this matter.

6. In contrast to Roosevelt, Winston Churchill tried to cover his planned baseness by a democratic cloak. He had already asked Anthony Eden for a report on the proposals of division on 4 May 1944, and had informed his War Cabinet—*pro forma*—of the agreement made with Roosevelt on 13 June 1944.

7. Telegraphing to Stalin the agreement with Roosevelt about "the three months' trial," the latter demanded a more forthright expression of consent and postponed the question of spheres of influence. Why? Because, a few weeks later, he was in a position—occupying the entire Balkan zone—to appropriate the zones alone and for always. Why should he tie his hands with some agreement for three months? Especially when the negoti-

ations taking place in Cairo and Stockholm were assuring him the certain unconditional surrender of Rumania.

8. Although the deliberations remained in that phase from 15 July 1944 until October 1944, when—as we shall see—Churchill, obsessed, ill, hesitant in the face of the Russians, went to Moscow to re-open discussion of the zones of influence in the Balkans.

But before examining the events that took place in Moscow on 9 October 1944, let us see—in order to keep them in chronological sequence—what was happening in Rumania. We shall see that both Marshal Antonescu's Government and the Opposition led by Maniu, continued to make desperate efforts to withdraw Rumania from the War.

CHAPTER 15

Armistice Negotiations at Stockholm

In the autumn of 1943, a new minister of Rumania was appointed at Stockholm in view of eventual armistice negotiations, in the person of Mr. Frederick Nano. Mr. Alexander Cretzeanu was appointed ambassador in Ankara with the same aim in view.

Mr. Nano says, in an article in the *Journal of Central European Affairs* of October 1951—after his first meeting with Mr. Johnson, the United States minister in Sweden—that he understood that Europe was to be divided into spheres of influence after the war.

Contacted by the Russians through a Bulgar, Goranoff, Mr. Nano got in touch first with Spichinski, at Christmas 1943 and then with Semenoff. As was natural at the beginning, everyone was feeling his way.

As we shall see, in the next chapter, the Rumanian Prince Barbu Stirbey arrived, in March 1944 in Cairo, to negotiate an armistice for Rumania, with all three Allies.

Thus, the Rumanian Marshall Antonescu was negotiating with the Americans in Madrid, with Russians, alone, in Stockholm, and with all three Allies, in Cairo.

Hoping to get better terms from Madrid, or Cairo, the Rumanian minister in Stockholm, Frederick Nano, was instructed, by Antonescu, to keep in touch with the Russians, so as to gain time.

Things remained like that until 10 April 1944, when the Rumanian minister was contacted again by the Russians, also through the Bulgar, Goranoff. Next day, Mr. Nano was summoned by Semenoff who dictated a text in French, which was to be sent to Bucharest.

> We Russians [said the message] prefer to discuss with the actual Government of Rumania and we are ready to help them to break

with the Germans and to free their country if the Government can organise resistance. At the same time we are ready to have talks with the Rumanian Opposition—Maniu and Bratianu.

One should note at once that the Russians preferred to negotiate with Marshal Antonescu, and also that the latter was in agreement that Maniu and Bratianu should negotiate the armistice if he—the Marshall—should not be preferred by the Allies or if they (Maniu and Bratianu) would obtain better results than he, himself.

Next day, 12 April 1944—the same day on which Novikov handed the armistice terms to Rumanian Stirbey in Cairo—Mr. Nano called on Madame Kollontay—Russian ambassador in Stockholm—at the Grand Hotel where she was convalescing. She told him that the Russians took the talks at Stockholm very seriously and asked him to keep them secret. She added that Stalin had come to the conclusion that it would be better to be on friendly terms with the neighbouring countries and therefore he was disposed to be generous. Mr. Nano's impressions were that the Russians were in a hurry to discuss the matter directly and to sign the armistice quickly.

Next day, 13 April 1944, Semenoff summoned Mr. Nano again and handed him the armistice terms, adding that they had also been sent to Prince Stirbey in Cairo, but that they (the Russians) would prefer the discussions to continue in Stockholm.

We should note that the Russians had been continually urging that the negotiations take place in Stockholm, or at least directly. Novikov, the Russian ambassador in Cairo begged Prince Stirbey, on April 1944 (secret telegram, London, number 848) to realise that the final arrangement would have to be made between Russia and Rumania and he asked him (Stirbey) to come and inform him *regularly, in person* about the progress. Therefore, the least possible tripartite discussion.

Semenoff asked the same of Mr. Nano, reproaching him because Prince Stirbey had passed through Ankara and had gone to Cairo, instead of going *direct* to the Russian ambassador there to negotiate.

What were the armistice conditions communicated to Mr. Nano?

1. The Rumanian troops should surrender to the Russians or else attack the Germans. They (the Russians) would hand over all the Rumanian troops to Marshal Antonescu, and equip them to fight

the Germans in order to establish the sovereignty and independence of Rumania.

2. The frontiers of 1940 to remain; therefore the loss of Bessarabia and northern Bucovina.
3. Compensations.
4. Repatriation of war prisoners.

To this, Semenoff added orally, that the Russians would not occupy Rumania, but only in passing if the military situation should demand it. In addition, the Russians would give Transylvania to Rumania.

Then a memorandum followed from Mr. Nano to ameliorate these conditions. The reply came, promptly, on 31 May 1944. Points 1, 3, and 4 remained intact. The grave situation in Rumania would be kept in mind regarding point 3, i.e., compensations. If the Rumanian government wished to have their seat in a province where there were no Russian troops, Stalin would agree. Lastly, the Rumanians could give a respite of fifteen days to the Germans to evacuate the country, before declaring war on them.

To the clarifications demanded by the Rumanian minister, Molotov replied next day that if the Germans left the country within fifteen days, Rumania could remain neutral. He insisted that he was ready to receive a delegation to Moscow immediately. This reply came on 3 June 1944.

It should be emphasized at once that—in comparison with the terms proposed in Cairo on 12 April to Prince Stirbey—as will we see—the final terms of 3 June 1944 in Stockholm were much more favourable to Rumania.

Speaking of the comparisons between the two negotiations at Cairo and Stockholm, Mr. Nano asks himself, in his article, whether the three Allies in Cairo had been informed of the negotiations in Stockholm, by the Rumanian delegates Stirbey and Visoianu.

The reply is categorically "yes." Thus, on 26 May, as results from a telegram from Lord Moyne to Eden (number 1134), Mr. Visoianu informed them that Marshal Antonescu, through Madame Kollantay, had obtained more favourable terms, in Stockholm.

Also, on 8 July 1944, Mr. Visoianu's body-guard had received (and censored, of course) a letter from Alexandru Cretzeanu to the latter in which Cretzeanu gave Visoianu the armistice terms from Stockholm of the 3 June 1944, i.e., with the three major improvements obtained by Mr. Nano.

Hearing of this, the only reflection of Lord Moyne was that if that were true (*for they did not know about the Stockholm negotiations*), it meant that the Russians preferred to deal with and sign the armistice with Marshal Antonescu.

The Allies were also informed of the Stockholm negotiations in Madrid by the three Rumanian diplomats. They informed the Americans about the Stockholm negotiations of Antonescu's government and underlined the better conditions obtained by it, compared to those which had been proposed in Cairo.

Probably that preference to negotiate with the Marshal rather than with the Opposition, caused Molotov to refuse at first (as seen in document R.4634, telegram to Ambassador Kerr, on 23 March 1944) to negotiate with Stirbey. Molotov agreed to discuss the matter in Cairo only after Eden had insisted, but, as he says, without any hope. Besides, at the Conference of Foreign Ministers in October 1943, in Moscow, when Anthony Eden spoke of the Rumanian emissaries and of an eventual revolt on the part of the Opposition, against Marshal Antonescu, the latter replied that what Eden said was "a pipe dream" and he could never believe in it.

It is clear that Molotov wished to discuss directly with Marshal Antonescu—without the other Allies—and to sign an armistice with him and not with the Opposition.

But the Marshal beat about the bush. He did not want to sign any armistice whose terms would not be guaranteed by the Anglo-Americans, because he put no trust in the word of the Russians.

He was extremely prudent, especially as the newspapers had written about the arrival of Prince Stirbey in Cairo, and he was afraid of Hitler and the eventual reproaches of the Russians that he was negotiating in two or three different places. It seems that the Marshal believed in a separate Stalin-Hitler peace, and he was afraid not to be shown up to the Germans. However, he still hoped for an Allied landing in the Balkans or for Turkey's entry into the war.

It is surprising and inexplicable how Marshal Antonescu—an intelligent man and of exceptional valour—could deceive himself so seriously in the question of the armistice.

Why did he not get out of the war in 1943 as he wished?

Why did he not accept the armistice terms obtained in Stockholm on 3 June 1944, at the time? Especially when those terms were better than those in Cairo communicated on 12 April 1944, to Stirbey?

That question must remain unanswered in the meantime.

The absolute preference of the Russians to sign an armistice with Marshal Antonescu is confirmed also by the talks of Mr. George Duca with Madame Kollontay. As emissary of Iuliu Maniu and of Dinu Bratianu, he presented himself before the Russian ambassadress and told her that the Opposition could not accept the terms of 12 April 1944, in Cairo, which were less favourable than those obtained on 3 June by Marshal Antonescu and that the situation demanded that the three favourable clauses obtained by Antonescu be included in those of Cairo.

To this demand, Mr. Duca received no reply.

Madame Kollontay's silence is inexplicable. The Russians insisted in dealing with Marshal Antonescu, without the other Allies, if possible.

I would like to stress that a very serious question arose, in these negotiations over Transylvania.

In Stockholm, the Russians granted Transylvania to Rumania, upon the signing of am armistice, without any reservation of the approval of the Peace Conference, and the signing of the peace treaty.

The second Rumanian delegate in Cairo, Mr. Constantin Visoianu, as we shall see later, had contested (and under oath, in a Paris tribunal, in 1952) that in Stockholm Transylvania was granted, by the Russians, to Rumania. Visoianu even contested, on the same occasion, that in Stockholm were conducted "negotiations" for an armistice, or that he went to Cairo, with the knowledge and the consent of Marshal Antonescu.

But all these allegations of Constantin Visoianu are bare lies.

These were made—in bad faith—but for the obvious purpose of emphasizing his "merits" of bringing—at Cairo—Transylvania, back to Rumania.

Not only did this clause of granting Transylvania to Rumania figure in the Stockholm conditions of armistice granted to Marshal Antonescu, but even Constantin Visoianu, personally, in the name of Iuliu Maniu, asked in Cairo, that the three Allies grant Rumania at least the same conditions granted to Antonescu, at Stockholm, by the Russians.

In regard to this, I quote the ultra-secret telegram of 5 July 1944 of the British Colonel Talbot Rice:

I believe, however, that when Madame Kollontay presented

the terms to Mr. Nano, she omitted the words "subject to confirmation at the Peace Conference" regarding Transylvania—words that we included in ours.

And on the same date, "the volte-face" plan of Iuliu Maniu was commented on in London (DTR/RO/2757) in the following way:

> Not one of the factions favourable to the Allies can accept the grave responsibility of agreeing to conditions less favourable than those *accorded to Marshal Antonescu.*
> Moreover, definite information exists that as far as the Marshal is concerned, certain modifications in the Armistice conditions of Stockholm were agreed to.

What does the hero of the unconditional surrender in Cairo—Constantin Visoianu—say when he reads this? Does he pretend any longer that he brought Transylvania to Cairo? Or that the Marshal did not negotiate at Cairo?

But, if he also reads the resolution put by Anthony Eden on 5 May 1944 (PM@@/308) about the request of Grigore Gafencu to come to London:

> "We are in direct touch with both Maniu and Antonescu through Cairo and Ankara, and if we now start trying to work through Gafencu too, we shall only become confused."

I also have to remind this Constantin Visoianu what he, himself, told the three Allies, on May 25, when he arrived in Cairo:

"When the Rumanian opposition saw the preference of the three Allies for the "volte face of Rumania" to be made by Marshal Antonescu, the opposition granted the Antonescu government more time, in order to permit him to take the necessary steps with regard to the concluding of an armistice."

Even more, because the Marshal had undertaken—not only with Maniu, but also on the insistence of the latter, with the King himself—to demand and carry out the Armistice alone.

These declarations of Visoianu in Cairo should be complemented by the ultra-secret telegram of Lord Moyne, to London, of 2 June 1944 (number 1385) in which he says:

Nothing could illustrate better than the above, the impossibility of obtaining any practical results through Maniu. Such chances as there were of obtaining some concrete action on the Rumanian side lay *only in winning over Antonescu.*

That is why Mr. G. Duca, Iuliu Maniu's emissary in Stockholm, never got any reply from Madame Kollontay.

Because the Russians had granted more favourable terms to Marshal Antonescu than those of Cairo, appreciating that the withdrawal of Rumania from the Axis was a military matter that only the Marshal could solve.

CHAPTER 16

Rumanian Armistice Negotiations in Cairo

This long chapter, which seems at first sight to be of special interest only for Rumania, is, on the contrary, of great capital interest to all readers. It is closely connected with the policy decided upon, with the duplicity that went into its making, with the whole series of errors committed by the Allies on that occasion, by giving away in an unwarranted way the entire Eastern Europe to Stalin.

We must therefore follow, step by step, these negotiations, which are given in detail, and which sometimes appear as a real imbroglio. But the details are of the utmost importance, essential in this particular case.

The same applies to the next chapter concerning the switching of alliances by Rumania on August 23, 1944. A "volte face" was eagerly sought after by the Russians and the great Allies, and for which they were ready (with proper skill and loyalty on the part of the Rumanians) to pay the right price, but which they received gratuitously, owing to the tragic Rumanian errors.

On 24 December 1943, Iuliu Maniu, the leader of the Rumanian Opposition, wrote to Marshal Antonescu asking him to withdraw from the war and sign an armistice. The Marshal replied that he was ready to step aside for the good of the country and to transfer his power to him, if he, (Maniu) could get assurances of Rumania's sovereignty and independence. The dialogue continued in that way. Maniu replied that if the Allies were to ask for unconditional surrender, the Marshal would have to do it, as that was a military matter. If it were to be a question of a negotiated armistice, he (Maniu) was ready to assume the responsibility and to make contact with the Allies to see what should be done. With that in view, he asked Marshal Antonescu to authorise the sending of an emissary at once. The Marshal accepted.

In agreement with the King and Dinu Bratianu, leader of the Liberal Party, Maniu proposed to send Prince Stirbey, who immediately obtained a passport from Antonescu.

The journey was planned via Ankara to London. Before leaving, Stirbey, as well as the King, the Opposition, and the Rumanian government were all aware of the "negotiating" conditions established by the foreign ministers in Moscow, which had been communicated to Bucharest on 9 November 1943 by the British government.

They knew that:

> The British Government cannot consider any demand for a discussion on the part of the Rumanian Government or from any individual Rumanian unless it is addressed at the same time to the United States and the Soviet Union.
>
> Such a demand must be accompanied by a special power of attorney presented in legal terms, in order to sign the unconditional surrender before the Three Allies. Any other discussion, or procedure is of no interest whatever to the Allies.

Now let us examine—in the light of the British and American secret documents—how the discussion went at Cairo. As the documents are so numerous, I will take them in chronological order so that the reader may more easily follow what went on there.

On 4 March 1944, London asked its ambassador, Clark Kerr, in Moscow, to get in touch with Molotov and convince him to authorise Novikov—Russiam ambassador in Cairo—to take part in the interview with Prince Stirbey.

Telegram number 606 insists on the fact that this interview—between Novikov and Stirbey—would

> make the Rumanians see the reality and especially, put them in direct contact with the Russians.

Ambassador Kerr asked Molotov also whether the Russians were preparing terms for an armistice, with Rumania.

This telegram was necessary, because—although, on 10 January 1944, Decanosov had agreed that Novikov should take part in the inter-

109

view with a Rumanian emissary—Molotov himself said, on 16 February 1944, to Churchill in person that the armistice discussions proposed by Rumanian Victor Cadere, Minister, in Lisbon, were *premature*—a fact that surprised the British Prime Minister who asked for an explanation.

Also on that day—4 March 1944—Lord Killearn asked for instructions from London, in view of the discussions, and emphasised that in order to avoid Soviet suspicion, he ought to explain to them that the Three would only listen to whatever Prince Stirbey would have to say, especially as he (Killearn) saw that Marshal Antonescu was involved in the affair.

On 6 March 1944, Anthony Eden (secret telegram number 628) told the British ambassador in Moscow to ask Molotov:

(1) whether the discussions with Stirbey would take place in London where the European Advisory Committee had its seat and which normally discussed the armistice problems;
(2) whether they have made a project for an armistice, with Rumania. *Eden emphasised that the emissary, Stirbey, was coming in the name of Marshal Antonescu; of Maniu; of the King and of the Communist Party.*

As the Russians were opposed to having the talks in London, it was decided to hold them in Cairo. Prince Stirbey arrived with a passport in the name of Bond, which did not prevent a Reuters' agent from identifying him and from writing of his mission already on 14 March 1944 in all newspapers, all over the world.

This fact weighed heavily on what followed and had serious repercussions on Antonescu's effort to conclude the armistice. The Germans were warned. By whom? Why?

The first meeting in Cairo was held on 17 March with Lord Moyne presiding (he was a minister in the British government) in the presence of the American and Russian (Novikov) ambassadors.

When asked whom he represented, Stirbey replied that the spoke on the part of Maniu and that he had a letter from him for Benes. He said he did not represent Marshal Antonescu, but that he had seen him before leaving and knew that he was ready to sign the armistice.

As can be seen in telegram number 614 sent to London by Lord Moyne, as well as a later report, Stirbey had emphasised that the only one in a position to make an armistice was Marshal Antonescu, who was convinced that he had to make a *"volte face."*

Stirbey added that if the Allies insisted that *Maniu had to make the change, he was ready to do so and that it would be done with the co-operation of the government and of Generals Nicolescu and Potopeanu.*

Maniu had asked for assurances on three points: the independence of Rumania; her territorial rights (Transylvania), and status of co-belligerent.

Stirbey insisted on joint action with Hungary, Bulgaria, and Turkey.

In a summing-up, which Lord Moyne described as dignified and impressive, Prince Stirbey, recognising that Rumania was a defeated country, appealed to their noble sentiments and evoked the principles of the Atlantic Charter.

Comments on the meeting were sent next day to London (document number R4272): that impressions of this first contact were favourable. The British asked what the procedure should be—to encourage Maniu to overthrow Antonescu or to accept his surrender? But—heavens!—Sir O. Sargent said categorically that the last word lay only with the Russians; that the Russians would not cooperate, firstly because they wished to be on the Rumanian frontier and then that they did not wish the British to meddle in the problem of Rumania, which was their affair.

Could anything be clearer? As we have already seen from 18 March 1944—before the Churchill-Roosevelt agreement on spheres of influence in the Balkans—the British had respected the Russian sphere in Rumania.

On 20 March, Lord Killearn (telegram number 555) proposed to Anthony Eden that he contact Marshal Antonescu direct by special radio, as in the case of Maniu. According to him (Killearn), only Marshal Antonescu was capable of making this *volte face*, especially as he had declared that he would oppose with armed force any attempt by the Germans to occupy Rumania.

This is evident, especially now, after the occupation of Hungary by the Germans [adds Lord Killearn].

The three ambassadors who saw Stirbey had the same impressions and opinions. Telegram number 633 of 20 March 1944 from Lord Moyne to London, tells of the impressions of Novikov and MacVeagh (American ambassador). They believed that only Marshal Antonescu was capable

111

of making this *volte face* and that he must surrender to the Russians.

In the meantime, Prince Stirbey had realised that the only thing to do was to speak directly with the Russians who had the first and last word. He said this in a private discussion with the British officer who was in attendance.

As things are here, I would have done better to go to Moscow [he said].

On hearing this, Lord Moyne asks for instructions from London as to what he should reply if the Rumanian emissary should ask to go to Moscow, or to go—alone—to see Novikov.

An important reply intervened on 26 March 1944, when Molotov communicated to the British Ambassador Kerr in Moscow, that:

on the insistence of the British Government, they were ready to negotiate with Marshal Antonescu and to contact him.

Molotov asked—along with the conditions of General Wilson, already sent to Marshal Antonescu—to put forward two others:

(1) That the Rumanian armies still fighting in the Crimea and on the Dniester should surrender to the Russians who would take them across the River Pruth and hand them over to Marshal Antonescu to command them in the fight against the Germans.
(2) That the Marshal should send an emissary or one of the Rumanian generals taken prisoner—to act as a liaison to make the necessary arrangements.

(As can be seen: on 26 March 1944, the Russians had said nothing to the British about their negotiations in Stockholm, which had begun in December 1943, direct with Marshal Antonescu.)

I emphasize that General Wilson had *direct* contact with Marshal Antonescu, through the British and Rumanian military attachés at Ankara. By this, the British general asked them, on 23 March, not to go to see Hitler. On 29 March 1944, in conformity with Molotov's demand, General Wilson sent the following message, by the same way:

112

1. The Soviet Government are ready to establish direct contact with him.
2. The Marshal must order the Rumanian troops in the Crimea and on the Dniester to surrender, as Molotov proposed, and to delegate a liaison officer.

In connection with this important message, and in order to establish the full historical truth, I must emphasize at once the false affirmation made by the former ambassador of Rumania in Ankara: Alexander Cretzeanu, in his book, *The Lost Opportunity*, on page 132, that "Marshall Antonescu did not even reply to General Wilson's message."

The truth is that Marshall Antonescu did answer General Wilson, and in a superb manner.

However, the fact that Alexander Cretzeanu could make, in writing, such untrue statements, is highly distressing, for many reasons. Alexander Cretzeanu, a nephew of Prince Barbu Stirbey, was Rumanian ambassador in Ankara, and he played a very important part in the Cairo negotiations. Most of the messages exchanged between Iuliu Maniu and Cairo passed through his hands, before being retransmitted to Cairo.

In the last weeks before the unconditional surrender of Rumania, on the 23rd of August 1944, all further communications between Iuliu Maniu and Cairo having been cut off, the only communications left were exclusively in the hands of Alexander Cretzeanu in Ankara, and Niculescu Buzesti—the son-in-law of Prince Stirbey—in Bucharest.

It is alarming to see that the whole fate and destiny of the entire Rumanian people rested—during those tragic days—on the discretion and the judgment, good or bad, of those two persons.

How can we trust Alexander Cretzeanu's statements and allegations concerning the whole of the Cairo negotiations, when we find that such an important document as the message of Marshall Antonescu to General Wilson, is totally unknown to him, or worse, that the existence of such a message was categorically denied by him?

Are we not entitled to look at the whole activity of Alexander Cretzeanu with reserve and suspicion?

How could he ignore the existence of such a document? Ignorance? Or the utmost bad faith?

In Lord Moyne's secret telegram (number 930), we have Marshal Antonescu's reply to General Wilson, Commander of the Allied Forces in the Middle East, in its entirety, concerning the unconditional surrender. (It is a pity I cannot give it in his own words, instead of paraphrasing it, owing to the British copyright laws. But surely it could be found, for history, in the State Archives in Bucharest.)

Reading it, I had the impression that I was hearing the greatest Rumanian poet, Mihail Eminescu, in his *Letter III*, when Mircea the Old, says: "I? I defend my poverty, my needs and my nation."

MARSHAL ANTONESCU REPLIES TO GENERAL WILSON

Your message received. Please do not ask a small but heroic people who for 2,000 years have fought for its life, liberty, and faith, to dishonour and destroy itself. Do not ask an old man and honest soldier to end his days in humiliation. I am fighting for my country first as you are for Britain. But you cannot realise the sufferings, struggles, and the menace under which we live. We attacked no-one, but were attacked. They took what was ours and has been ours for centuries. European events in 1940 forced our Allies and friends to abandon us entirely, allowing all our cowardly neighbours to rob us. In reply to our cry of alarm, no-one of our then great Allies could guarantee our reduced frontiers. We were forced alongside Germany to oppose Russia who menaced and humiliated us daily. Germany was the only country in the world who, at our own request, agreed in difficult circumstances to guarantee the continued existence of the nation. . . . As a great and glorious soldier who, I am sure, will understand and help me to save a people—do not force me to throw it into the bottomless pit of shame and destruction. We are your friends, not enemies. I am sure that no people with its forces almost intact as are ours, could capitulate and withdraw from action in which her very existence and liberty are at stake, without some serious guarantee for her future. I rely on you as a soldier to ensure no indiscretion regarding this message.

Two things must be remembered from this message, in spite of all the political and military mistakes attributed to Marshal Antonescu.

First of all, he mentions the importance of Rumania's "almost intact" forces, in order to show that he can still put up opposition to the Russians and therefore prolong the war, but that—in honourable conditions—Rumania could make an important contribution to the Allied victory.

114

Secondly, Marshal Antonescu asks for "certain guarantees for the future of Rumania," from the part of the Anglo-American Allies.

These guarantees—direct consequence of this message sent immediately to Moscow and Washington—came from the Russians, in the Declaration made on 2 April 1944, when, in a specially convened press conference, Molotov declared, "that the Soviet Government does not intend to annex any part of Rumanian territory or to change the existing social system in Rumania."

This declaration was made with the consent of Cordell Hull and Anthony Eden.

On 3 April 1944, frightful bombardments took place on Bucharest and Ploesti. It was said—even by distinguished and serious Rumanians abroad, that the bombardments had been requested by Iuliu Maniu. This is absolutely a calumny and an unwarranted accusation. Not only Maniu did not request such bombardments, but—as we shall see later—he protested and begged the Allies to stop them.

Iuliu Maniu had the same attitude concerning the demands of the Allies to effect sabotage and acts of rebellion in Rumania.

This is his reply given on February 3, 1944, to such a demand:

> You ask me to commit acts of sabotage or violence. How could I do this when my country is threatened by the Russians and Hungarians? If we destroy our means of communication and our defence system, we could no longer defend our country against the Russians and Hungarians. And even more because it is in your interest to find it intact when you arrive here.

The same applied to acts of rebellion. He said he could not overthrow Marshal Antonescu unless they—the Allies—were in his country or on her frontiers; otherwise, it would invite a Russo-Hungarian attack and their occupation of the country.

Obviously Iuliu Maniu, on 3 February 1944 still believed sincerely in an Anglo-American landing in Rumania. He refused to sabotage the Rumanian Army to provoke acts of rebellion.

His aim was clear: the withdrawal of Rumania from the war as soon as the Anglo-Americans had landed in the Balkans or in Rumania. He was ready, together with the King, to overthrow Antonescu—*but only if the latter did not make a volte-face himself and sign an armistice at an opportune moment.*

This is clearly stated in Maniu's message. He says he has no ambition. If the Marshal would make a change, all the better; if not, he would do it himself when the time was ripe. This was because he could not get rid of the Germans: "by one door, so as to invite the Russians in by another."

And so, in view of "the opportune moment," he asked urgently for some plan of cooperation with the Allies.

Next day—4 February 1944—in another telegram from Istanbul (FO 371/43992), it was declared precisely by the British Major Masterson, after his interview with the Rumanian minister in Ankara:

1. Neither the Marshal nor Maniu seek any action against the Germans so long as the Anglo-Americans will not be close enough to come to their aid.
2. That in case Hitler should attempt a military occupation of Rumania, Marshal Antonescu would fight them.

The military importance of the withdrawal of Rumania from the war and the turning of her armies against Germany cannot be doubted. She shortened the war considerably; saved hundreds of thousands of lives of Russian and Allied troops and—perhaps—caused the war to be won by the Allies. Because if Rumania had continued to fight with the Germans during those six to eight months of the Rumanian withdrawal, it would have enabled Hitler to perfect and utilize his secret, new weapons, which were being experimented with.

This fact did not escape the High Command who, on 29 March 1944, sent the telegram number 1583, through Lord Halifax, to London, from which I quote the most important passage:

As was noted in earlier letters about this subject, the High Command of the Combined Allied Armies believe that the withdrawal of Rumania and the other Satellites in the Balkans from the Axis *is of capital importance from a military point of view* and it is especially hoped that by detaching themselves, they will participate with the maximum of effort in the interests of the Allies. Given the actual deployment of the military situation, a prompt, immediate result would be of the greatest importance and urgency.

For these considerations, "The Heads of the High Command are of the opinion that no sort of political conditions should be formulated which would hinder the capitulation of the Rumanian Forces.

The heads of the High Command recommended, in consequence, that Mr. MacVeagh (American ambassador in Cairo) should be present at the communication that the three governments would make to Prince Stirbey.

For the record, I will state that Maniu and Bratianu had delivered a letter to the Swiss Legation in Bucharest, on 3 March 1944, giving the assurance to the Allies that when they would make their "about-turn," they would seek for an armistice, with the Allies.

In the meantime—before the bombardments on Rumania—Marshal Antonescu, replying to the British General Wilson—by the same channel of the Rumanian and British military attachés in Cairo—asked the latter what military help he could count on from the Allies in the event of an about-turn.

On 4 April 1944, by telegram number 826, Lord Moyne informed London that Mihai Antonescu had asked that Marshal Antonescu be immediately informed in a general way as to what the minimal Soviet demands were for an armistice. He asked that Russia should not insist on a military occupation of the country and be satisfied with a corridor for their armies in northern Rumania; and the return of Transylvania, to Rumania.

In the same telegram Mihail Antonescu said that "Col. de Chastellaine is well."

I will return to the latter immediately. But first I want to make a note of the telegram (number 827) of 4 April 1944 from Lord Moyne, replying to the Marshal that the Three could not discuss terms of an armistice in the then-present situation, nor the question of the military occupation of Rumania: that the Marshal had to be content with the declaration made by Molotov on 2 April 1944.

On April 5, 1944, the British ambassador in Moscow—Kerr—in telegram number 999, informed the British government that *Molotov had written to him saying that Marshal Antonescu had accepted their proposals but that they had no knowledge that he had named a liaison office with valid powers to discuss the question*; and that therefore, the communication of that acceptance could not be considered valid.

Also, on 5 April, in Cairo, Novikov, the Soviet ambassador sent after Prince Stirbey and reproached him that Marshal Antonescu had not

117

sent a liaison officer to them. The latter sent on the Russian demands formulated by Molotov to Bucharest immediately.

NOVIKOV WANTS THE NEGOTIATIONS
TO BE MADE EN TÊTE-À-TÊTE

On April 10 a second urgent meeting was convened between Prince Stirbey and the Soviet ambassador alone. The first one had taken place on 31 March, when Novikov, summoning him, told him that if Maniu wanted to overthrow Antonescu, the Soviet government would be ready to give military assistance. When Prince Stirbey asked whether Transylvania would be restored, the Russian ambassador replied that he had not been authorised to make that promise, but he showed the prince a map on which northern Bucovina and Bessarabia were incorporated into Russia and Transylvania into Rumania. He asked the Prince to draw his own conclusions.

At length, called for the third time on 12 April 1944, and also in the presence only of the Russian ambassador—Novikov gave the prince the armistice conditions. These were addressed both to the Antonescu government and to Maniu and were drawn up with the consent of the British and Americans.

From a long telegram sent by Lord Moyne (number 946), on 14 April 1944, we learn the content of Novikov's communication:

1. The Rumanian troops, consisting of approximately thirteen divisions that were fighting in Russia and in the district of Chisinau, were to turn round and, under the command of Antonescu, to fight against the Germans. The Russians undertook to equip them and give all military assistance, the two commands coordinating their military action.
2. The minimal terms of armistice:
   a) A common fight alongside the Russians to restore the independence and sovereignty of the country.
   b) Re-establishment of the 1940 frontiers between Rumania and the Soviet Union.
   c) Reparations for war damage.
   d) Repatriation of all war prisoners and internees. If these con-

ditions—Novikov added—were not accepted soon, they might be changed for the worse in future.

He added that Russia did not want to occupy Rumania militarily; that they would have the right to move about wherever and how they wish, and asked that the Rumanian government should ensure means of communication on the ground, in the sea, and in the air.

Novikov added that the Soviet government considered null the decision made in Vienna regarding the division of Transylvania and looked favourably on the retrocession of that province—or almost all of it—"*with the reservation of its confirmation at the Peace Conference.*"

(This reservation was demanded by the British government.)

To this message, Iuliu Maniu replied to General Wilson on 14 April 1944, demanding:

—Notification to be given to the Germans of an armistice and that war would be declared, if they do not leave Rumania in fifteen days.

—No foreign troops to occupy Rumania, without the express wish of the Rumanians.

—Two airborne divisions to be parachuted into the country.

—The restitution of Transylvania.

—No foreign interference in the country.

From this message, I retain for the moment the clause: "*Previous notification of the armistice to be made to the Germans.*" Because, as we will see, Marshal Antonescu did just this on 22 August 1944. He informed the German Minister Clodins of his demand for an armistice. But the Marshal was arrested on 23 August 1944 on the excuse that once the Germans were informed, they would make reprisals. The same clause of 15 days notice figured also in the Stockholm conditions.

From Maniu's message of 14 April as well as from that of 17 April 1944, which completed it, we see that Iuliu Maniu was working hand in hand with Antonescu and keeping each other informed. Maniu said so "before the tribunal who judged Marshal Antonescu. That General Wilson asked him to keep the Marshal informed; and he personally kept contact with Mihai Antonescu and informed him regularly so as not to obstruct him in his negotiations in Madrid.

On 17 April 1944, the ambassadors in Cairo were becoming im-

119

patient and were ready to give an ultimatum to Antonescu to make a decision within seventy-two hours, sending a message through De Chastellain (supposed to be under arrest, but in reality working with Antonescu). In the meantime they told Maniu, who sought better conditions that it was not he who might discuss and decide on the conditions, but that he would have to accept, or reject, the conditions made by the Three.

On 19 April, Maniu sent a message—through Cretzeanu in Ankara—begging the Allied Military Command to cease the bombardments of the country; that they would only harm the Allied cause and bewilder the Rumanian leaders who were on the Allied side.

On 20 April 1944, Maniu sent another message saying that, on principle, he accepted the conditions offered and wished to "negotiate." (In the meantime, on 17 April, as we have seen, the Three had called on him to reply—yes or no, which was a true ultimatum.)

(A note in passing: Novikov had proposed, in a direct talk with Prince Stirbey on 15 April, that Maniu should eventually form a government in Moldavia, under the Russians.)

On 26 May 1944, Visoianu came to Cairo with a service passport—therefore with Antonescu's consent—as a second emissary from Maniu.

He was received—with Stirbey—by all three ambassadors and he gave them an up-to-date account of events in Rumania. Speaking of the armistice conditions put forward at Stockholm to Nano, he told them that these do *not contain the clause with the reservation about Transylvania (which the British Government had requested).*

The British, on hearing of these negotiations, thought they were "interesting" but that it was of no account, that the Russians were negotiating behind their backs. Probably it was of no interest because of their consent to give the Russians a free hand in Rumania. Nor did the Americans say something. In general they were of the same opinion as the British (telegram number 1334 of 26 May).

At the meeting in which Ted Masterson—a British colonel who had worked in the oil-fields in Rumania—took part, the two Rumanian emissaries pointed out that a volte face, now, was impossible due to the large concentrations of German troops in the southeastern part of the country. Therefore, in agreement with the King, Maniu proposed to make such a volte-face on the Front.

Both the British and the Rumanians emphasised the difficulty of

120

communicating with Maniu, or with Colonel de Chastellain and the fact that they have to communicate with Bucharest through Cretzeanu in Ankara, a very slow procedure.

NOVIKOV'S ULTIMATUM

But the Russians were becoming impatient in spite of the difficulty and dangerous attempts to communicate with Rumania, by her emissaries. On 31 May, Novikov called the two Rumanian emissaries urgently, once more, to the Russian embassy, to convey the Soviet reply to Maniu's suggestions. Maniu's conditions had been rejected until Maniu should declare, categorically, whether he accepted, or not the armistice of April 12, 1944. Novikov added that Maniu must understand that those conditions would be changed for the worse, in the future.

To this ultimatum, Iuliu Maniu communicated on 10 June that he accepted the terms of the armistice (also via Cretzeanu, in Ankara). He announced that he had formed a Democratic Bloc and that they were working out the details and would present their plan of action soon. He added that now that he had accepted, he hoped the armistice conditions would be improved.

In a telegram (number 1385) of 2 June, sent to London, (secret document number R8748), Lord Moyne speculated about the relations between Prince Stirbey and Visoianu. According to the officer in attendance, the relations between them were far from cordial. Stirbey had the impression that the arrival of Visoianu was a reproach on the part of Maniu because he (Stirbey) has not succeeded in improving the conditions of armistice. For instance, the officer claimed that Stirbey was ready to break with Maniu, whose policy he considered to be fatal and useless. He (Stirbey) was of the opinion that the only person capable of making a *volte face* was Antonescu, who must be convinced to do so.

Lord Moyne immediately informed Novikov of this attitude on the part of Stirbey against Maniu. Novikov was enchanted that Maniu "would not be able to play them—one against the other—as he would have liked to do."

On 13 June 1944, Visoianu called, alone, on Novikov to hand over Maniu's agreement of 10 June, which had arrived by courier *via* Ankara. He tried to discuss the "improvements," but Novikov refused.

On the same day, the Rumanian emissary complained that their

121

correspondence was censored, reaching first the Russians and British and them lastly. The Russian replied that, in that way, they gained time . . . they knew sooner what was at stake.

PRELIMINARY CONCLUSIONS

Before examining the discussions in Cairo any further—and to prevent the reader from being swamped by too many details—I will make a synopsis of the essential conclusions, so as to remain faithful to the facts already presented:

1. Travelling on passports given by Antonescu, Stirbey and then Visoianu spoke—of course—also in his name. It was only a question of "diplomacy" for them to pose as emissaries of only the Opposition.
2. All parties were agreed that the Marshal should be convinced to make an about-turn. The Allied Commanders were agreed on this, insisting that no political conditions should be included.
3. The armistice conditions of 12 April 1944 had been refused by Marshal Antonescu who sought guarantees from Britain and the Americans, as well to the Declaration made on 2 April by Molotov. The Marshal had better conditions—obtained at Stockholm, both on 13 April and the improved version of 3 June 1944—than those offered at Cairo.
4. Iuliu Maniu—after endless attempts to get better conditions—accepted them on 12 June and once again sought "improvements."
5. Maniu's conditions included the warning to the Germans and a term of fifteen days for them to evacuate the country—the same conditions, obtained at Stockholm and as those communicated by Antonescu to the King on 23 August 1944.
6. Communication with Bucharest had become very difficult, both with Colonel de Chastellaine and with Maniu by radio. So the only link was through Ankara, between Cretzeanu and Niculescu Buzesti. (So, one cannot prove what was sent from Bucharest, but only what arrived in Cairo).
7. All Maniu's proposals about *volte face* were based on cooperation with Marshal Antonescu, on that of the Opposition and of the

King. He had never dreamt of deciding anything alone, except in case of Antonescu's refusal to comply. The Marshal had told him, in 1943, that he would step aside if the Allies were to offer better conditions to Maniu and more guarantees for the good of the country.

8. In accepting the armistice conditions of 12 June 1944, Iuliu Maniu proposed to send a courier to Cairo with a plan for joint action in view of this *volte face*.

9. Maniu refused to commit any acts of sabotage or rebellion and implored the Allies to cease bombarding Rumania.

IULIU MANIU'S PLAN OF ACTION

This plan arrived by courier via Ankara, certainly by diplomatic bag (sent by Nicolescu Buzesti to Alexandru Cretzeanu). Maniu's message was handed to Visoianu on 27 June (Document R10114 FO).

(Prince Stirbey was ill and was transferred, on 22 June 1944, to Lebanon.)

The essential points of this plan of action were as follows:

1. Drawn up by the King and the Democratic Bloc, the plan provided for a change of government and signing of an armistice.

2. In order to succeed in withdrawing from the Axis, the change of government had to be synchronised with: a great offensive on the Rumanian front, not later than twenty-four hours after the change. Orders would be given to the Rumanian troops to fight against the Germans until Transylvania was completely free. The change of government would be made concomitently with the landing of two air-bourne brigades as well as 2,000 parachutists of the Allied forces at places to be indicated. These troops could be either Anglo-American or Russian. The troops would go into action immediately after the Allies had accepted this plan.

The "Maniu Plan" demanded that the signing of the armistice be done in Cairo, by the two Rumanian emissaries and the three Allies, BEFORE ANY CHANGE OF THE GOVERNMENT IN RUMANIA WAS CARRIED OUT.

123

The "Maniu Plan" for the execution of the *volte face*, reached Cairo by diplomatic bag—but was followed by three cables from Bucharest. In his report to London, Lord Moyne in his telegram number 155 of June 26, resuming the "Maniu Plan" as we have seen, mentioned in paragraph 4, a strange message "from the followers of Iuliu Maniu," "Maniu supporters."

In this message, the Allies were put on guard against "any illusions they may have had that Marshal Antonescu was ready to do something." Of course, Anthony Eden, receiving this message from Lord Moyne, immediately informed Molotov about them.

WHO were the "supporters of Maniu" who were putting the Allies on guard against Marshal Antonescu? Who sent such a message to Cairo?

Whose interest was it to sabotage Marshal Antonescu's armistice negotiations in Stockholm, where he got better conditions than in Cairo?

Who? History must clarify this message. It is of capital importance for the tragedy of the Rumanian people.

It is all the more necessary that we find important documents, revealing that Marshal Antonescu continued to negotiate for better terms, all this time.

On 2 July, Mihai Antonescu asked the Swiss minister in Bucharest to intervene, so that a Russian emissary could come to Bucharest to sign an armistice.

At the beginning of August 1944, Professor Giurescu and Colonel Teodorescu informed the Allies in Ankara that the Marshal wished to send another emissary to Cairo (Filderman?).

MARSHAL ANTONESCU AND THE IULIU MANIU PLAN

There is no more doubt today that Marshal Antonescu knew about the Maniu Plan, and that he, like Maniu, had been waiting since June 26, 1944, to hear from the three Allies of their approval.

To this effect we have the telegram of Marshal Antonescu of August 18, 1944 to Alexandru Cretzeanu, his ambassador to Ankara, asking him why there was no reply by the Allies to this plan.

Cretzeanu answered—see point 6 of its telegram of August 18—that "The delay is due to military problems raised by the Plan."

Under such conditions, when Marshal Antonescu was waiting—like Maniu—for a reply from the Allies, in order for him to carry into effect the same *volte face*, how was it possible for "the supporters of Iuliu Maniu" to put the Allies on guard against Marshal Antonescu?

Who did it? And why?

The reply to the "Maniu Plan" for action never came, in spite of some serious British interventions.

So, on the insistence of Lord Moyne, Sir Archibald Kerr, the British ambassador in Moscow, wrote, on July 19, 1944, a long letter to Molotov in which he asked for the earliest possible reply regarding Maniu's plan for action.

The Americans replied on 24 June that the plan was the Russians' affair and that they (the Americans) knew *nothing about the better conditions obtained by Marshal Antonescu at Stockholm.* (Hence, the State Department was not speaking the truth because they had been informed both by their embassy in Madrid as well as their ambassador in Cairo, who was aware of the text already on 8 July).

Other desperate messages from Maniu in Bucharest brought no response from the Russians. In another telegram (number 2570), Lord Moyne asked the Russians on 28 July to hurry and give a reply to the "Maniu Plan." The ambassador, Kerr, replied on 29 July that there was still no reply from Molotov.

On 5 August 1944, the operator of the clandestine radio station in Bucharest was arrested. The only connection with Cairo now was Niculescu Buzesti and Cretzeanu.

On 7 August, Ambassador Kerr telegraphed to Lord Moyne that, on the evening of 6 August, he had seen Vishinsky and had asked him to hurry up the Russian reply to the plan. The latter replied that he would discuss it with his government.

But no reply came from Cairo. The last document from Cairo that spoke of the plan or of the armistice—before the act of 23 August 1944—was a telegram signed by Sir. O. Sargent on 24 August 1944—(he knew nothing yet of the *coup d'état* in Bucharest) saying that there had been no reply from the Russians and—he believed that was because they had no faith in Maniu's capability to fulfil the "proposed plan."

Before dealing with the event of 23 August 1944, I must say that Maniu's plan provided some clauses of capital importance and that did not coincide at all with what happened on that day.

First, Maniu asked for the armistice to be concluded *before* the change of government. Unfortunately, after the event of 23 August 1944, the armistice was signed only on 12 September, after 130,000 troops had been taken prisoner as well as tens of thousands of deportees between 23 August and 12 September 1944.

Second, this plan also provided that the Rumanian Army would fight only until Transylvania was completely liberated. In fact, after the act of 23 August, 1944, Rumanian troops were fighting—after the liberation of Transylvania, also in Hungary, and in Czechoslovakia. They had losses of 50 percent of their forces, because the Russian Command put them always in the first firing-line.

Third, Maniu's plan had been based on a coordinate action (in the absence of any Allied reply) for 26 August 1944.

As it was made on 23 August 1944, nobody was prepared for it. But the height of irony is that Maniu announced, in a telegram from Bucharest, dated 23 August 1944, but which did not arrive in time—why?—that he would change the government on 26 August. But his telegram—which should have been sent by radio Niculescu-Buzesti to Cairo, *via* Cretzeanu in Ankara—did not arrive at its destination in Cairo until several days later. Why? Who was responsible for the delay?

That is another puzzle for the historians of tomorrow.

With the regret that I must depart from the line of conduct I had decided on—not to arouse any polemic with any Rumanians in exile—I am obliged to make an exception, because it is a question of establishing some extremely important facts.

I refer to the three declarations made by Constantin Visoianu—who, for about twenty-five years had been president of the National Committee in Exile—at the lawsuit of the former Minister Plenipotentiary, Nicolae Dianu, against the Communist Renaud de Jouvenel, under oath, in Paris on 11 March 1952, in connection with the negotiations at Stockholm and Cairo.

Here are the three completely inexact affirmations made by Constantin Visoianu under oath:

First, he went only as an emissary of the "Rumanian Resistance" without the knowledge, or consent of Marshal Antonescu and without a passport given by him. It is true that he was sent by Iuliu Maniu to help Prince Stirbey. But Prince Stirbey arrived in Cairo with a passport from Antonescu, whom he had seen before his departure, and in whose name the prince was negotiating. (Visoianu was not sent to negotiate but to assist Stirbey in editing the Acts, which Maniu believed had still to be edited.)

Visoianu was sent when Maniu made the remark that "the problems raised are more the problems of the Peace Conference, and that he must therefore send another emissary to help Stirbey "edit the documents."

As we have seen, Maniu kept Antonescu informed day after day, and had regular meetings with Mihai Antonescu.

Iuliu Maniu, at the trial of Marshal Antonescu, said that General Wilson had asked him personally for a delegate to be sent, and that Marshal Antonescu should be informed of this. Maniu said he had done this, asking Antonescu to authorise Stirbey's departure for Cairo.

Constantin Visoianu's claim that he left without the consent or knowledge of Marshal Antonescu was denied, under oath, by Iuliu Maniu on 12 May 1946 at Marshal Antonescu's trial.

> I sent the telegram from General Wilson to Marshal Antonescu for his information. At the same time I asked him through a third person to be so kind as to facilitate the departure over the frontier of Prince Stirbey, by giving him an exit visa.
> *But later, being delegated to send another Counsellor to Mr. Stirbey, I proposed Mr. Visoianu, whose departure from the country Marshal Antonescu also helped to achieve.*

I, for one, do not wish to discuss the statements made under oath by Constantin Visoianu and by the great national martyr and hero, Iuliu Maniu. I take as true what Iuliu Maniu said. Maniu did not lie.

The more so because the evidence of Iuliu Maniu was published in the newspaper *Dimineata* of 13 May 1946, of which the founder was Constantin Visoianu himself.

Second, also under oath and at the same trial and on the same day, Constantin Visoianu made a second inexact statement: that in the negotiations at Stockholm, between Mr. Nano and the Soviet ambassador, Transylvania was not discussed.

Was Transylvania not discussed at Stockholm? The documents of the negotiations have now been declassified, and the truth is just the opposite to that maintained by Visoianu.

And, on 26 May 1944, as can be seen in the telegram number 1334 from Lord Moyne to London, *Visoianu in person informed the Three about the armistice conditions obtained by Marshal Antonescu from Madame Kollontay without any reserve*—like that put by the British government—*with regard to Transylvania.*

This document, now declassified, says clearly that the Russians held no "private conversations," but *very* serious armistice discussions direct with Marshal Antonescu through his minister in Stockholm, Mr. Nano.

Now let us see something even more serious regarding the evidence given under oath by Constantin Visoianu. In a top secret telegram (number 1614) from Lord Moyne to London, the British minister informs London that he had received—via Cretzeanu, therefore from Marshal Antonescu—a letter containing *the clauses of the armistice proposed to the Rumanian government by the Russians*—(therefore not from a "private conversation" over a cup of coffee with Mme. Kollontay as Visoianu pretends—and which were more favourable both to Maniu *and to Marshal Antonescu* than those offered in Cairo.

Referring to Transylvania, the top secret document remarks that the restoration clause offers more favourable armistice conditions in Stockholm and gives a firm undertaking to restore the province to Rumania. The Cairo clause—under British pressure—only promised conditional "approbation by the Peace Conference," which, obviously, could have refused it (as we have seen in the previous chapter).

On 8 June 1944, the courier from Ankara had brought Visoianu the armistice conditions—in a letter from Cretzeanu—obtained by the Marshal at Stockholm. Who could have given them, except either the Marshal or Mihai Antonescu? By that divulgence, the Marshal tried to obtain, in Cairo, at least the same conditions so that they could be, in this way, guaranteed not only by the Russians, but also by the British and Americans.

Visoianu communicated these armistice conditions made at Stockholm to his officer attaché "in great secrecy," and asked him not on any account, to mention his name or that of Cretzeanu if the matter came under discussion by the Russians.

The only reaction of the British as we show was a remark full of tact, i.e., if it is true, *this means that the Russians prefer to sign an armistice with Marshal Antonescu and that is why they are postponing the Maniu Plan.*

WHY DID VISOIANU HIDE THE TRUTH?

Why did Visoianu not admit, in 1952, that armistice talks had been held in Stockholm and that they had been embodied in the conditions granted to the Marshal on 3 June 1944? Why did he deny this when he himself presented them to Cairo as "conditions of the armistice"—not as the result of a private conversation—and that he himself had asked in Cairo that they should be given the *same conditions (by the Allies) as those granted to Marshal Antonescu by the Russians*?

The armistice conditions offered at Stockholm—had they been accepted by the Marshal (and he did accept them on 22 August 1944)—would have made the act of 23 August 1944 useless and perhaps the fate of Rumania, at least in the period following the war, might have been more human, more bearable.

Constantin Visoianu was a "hero" of Cairo by this 23 August 1944 act. But let us review the three better clauses obtained on 3 June 1944, in Stockholm, by comparison with Cairo:

1. The Russians agreed that the Rumanian government could be installed in some province of the country where Russian troops could not enter. In this way, the sovereignty and independence of the government would be guaranteed.
2. The Russians undertook not to occupy Rumania—they sought only the right of passage in pursuit of German and Hungarian troops and only if military necessity demanded.
3. The Russians—at Stockholm—agreed for the Rumanians to give the Germans an ultimatum, and a period of fifteen days before declaring war on them. And further, they agreed that in the event of the withdrawal of the Germans without fighting, that Rumania should remain *neutral*, obviously, after the reoccupation of Transylvania, which had been granted, by the Russians.

The difference between the two armistice conditions is obvious and this is why Constantin Visoianu—co-author of the Cairo one—denied those of Stockholm were negotiations.

Visoianu's "armistice" handed the country over to the Russians. The army were taken prisoner; tens of thousands of civilians were de-

129

ported. The Russians occupied the whole country—not only the northern part—to make a passage for their troops.

The king and the government became prisoner of the Russians instead of having their constitutional freedom and independence in a province of the country, not occupied by the Russians.

According to the Stockholm conditions, the Rumanian troops would have had to fight only for the freedom of Transylvania, and not in Hungary and Czechoslovakia with appalling losses.

War damages—promised by Molotov at Stockholm to be reduced—would not have been added to by astronomical sums for the "upkeep" of the Russian occupation armies all over the country. Russian armies would not have been able to loot the whole country, because they would have been obliged to confine themselves in a corridor in the north of Rumania.

Of course—without the presence of the Russians all over the country—the Communist Party would have been able to develop only in their transit corridor.

In this light must be seen the declarations, under oath of the former emissary to Cairo and president of the Rumanian National Council in Exile for twenty-five years—Constantin Visoianu.

CHAPTER 17

Rumanian Jews
and the Armistice Negotiations

I do not want to conclude the discussion of the efforts made by Rumania
to achieve a *volte face* in her alliances, and to end the war, before stressing
the loyal and courageous attitude of the former leader of the Jewish
Community in Rumania: the former lawyer, Mr. Filderman.

In a letter written in French, and addressed to the Rumanian Prince
Stirbey on the eve of his departure to negotiate an armistice for Rumania,
the leader of the Rumanian Jews wished the prince the best of success
in his negotiations. At the same time, Mr. Filderman underlined in his
letter, which was clearly destined to be read by the three Allies, some
historical truth of the greatest importance:

1. The huge sacrifices made by Rumania in World War I, fighting
   alongside the Anglo-Americans, and the Russians, against the
   German armies.
2. The legitimacy of the Rumanian war against the Russians during
   World War II when, owing to the Hitler-Stalin Pact of August
   1939, the Rumanian territory was mutilated on all four cardinal
   points.
3. That, owing to Marshal Antonescu, the Rumanian contribution
   in men, and economic aid to the German war against Russia,
   was less important than if another government than Marshal
   Antonescu's had been installed by Hitler in Rumania.
4. The fair and humane treatment of the Jews in Rumania by Marshal Antonescu, who did not follow Hitler in his mad and criminal
   ways of treating them all over Europe.

The leader of the Jewish community in Rumania had excellent relations with Marshal Antonescu, as well as with the King of Rumania. In June 1944, the King of Rumania received Mr. Filderman in audience, and Marshal Antonescu wanted to send him, in June 1944, as a third emissary to the Cairo negotiations.

(Max Auschnit, an important Rumanian Jew, appeared also in Cairo, and was heard there by the three Allies.)

But let us read Mr. Filderman's letter in full:

To His Highness, Prince Barbu Stirbey
My Prince,

You are leaving us. I do not know whether I will ever see you again. The nearer the end of the war approaches, the more we feel the approach of death.

Indeed, on one hand, there is the threat of air-attacks; on the other, the German threats.

That is why I have decided to write to you, not only to wish you *bon voyage* and success, but also to confide my testament to you. That is the reason why I beg you to consider this letter.

And, in doing so, I can not think in terms of persons before thinking of Rumania and the Rumanian people.

I want my opinion about them to be known: that the Rumanian people were dragged into the war by circumstances beyond their control.

Indeed, in 1914, Rumania broke off the alliance which had united her with Germany and she entered the war on the side of the Allies. Since then, she had no other foreign policy than that of the Allies.

The new war found her faithful to her alliance, but she was subjected to a dynastic crisis and was obliged to allow herself to be dismembered on all sides and to lose territories which the Allies had recognized as Rumanian: northern Bucovina, the southern Dobrudja, Transylvania in the west and Bessarabia in the east.

To declare war on the Axis would have meant allowing herself to be occupied, i.e., to witness the assassination of the whole Rumanian élite who were faithful to the Allies and—I add—of the 320,000 Israelites and—last, but not least—would have increased the war potential of the Axis.

For it is no longer a secret to anyone that the Rumanian Government resisted all demands and bargained to reduce her economic contribution. We, who have known life in the Rumanian territories occupied in 1916—when we were dying of hunger and looking on at the actual wealth of food-stuffs—are able to judge that the war potential of the Axis would have been much greater had it not been for the fact of her alliance with Rumania.

Besides, when she would have been occupied, millions of Rumanian workers had to leave the country to go to work in Germany.

Let us recall again the whole gesture of having refused the territories offered to her—even the Yugoslav Banat which she (Rumania) considered to be Rumanian, having claimed it as such in 1918.

And now that I have said what I think about Rumania, I will explain why I believe I feel the brush of the wings of the angel of Death.

One speaks of air-raids. Almost forty per cent of Rumania's Jewish population live in Bucharest. Many Rumanians have evacuated the Capital. The Government is in the act of moving to the country. But the Jews must remain.

I think that thirty years of public life, in which I have ceaselessly given proof of courage—I say so without false modesty but also without fatuity—give me the right to hope that no one will offend me by calling me a coward. And certainly no one can believe either that I prefer our life to victory, since all my life I have fought for the same ends.

Life is a matter of indifference to me. I raise only a question of principle.

To die, yes! If victory demands it and without our death it was not certain, or whether it would be postponed. If that is the case, not only do we submit, but we will bless our death for we will have the consolation that those who survive will live in freedom at last.

But if that is not absolutely necessary, let us think that our contribution to the war is already the most important and that we leave the few survivors to enjoy life.

And especially, because it was only a week ago that I read that in Washington an American Committee has been formed for the defence of the Israelites of Europe, under the direction of Messrs. Frank Murphy, Henry Wallace, Wendell Wilkie, etc. If this Com-

133

mittee exists, it means that people are thinking a little about the Jews who found God in their cradle and that no one wants to see them exterminated completely.

But millions have already been exterminated. It was only two or three days ago that it was announced from London that 7,000 Greek Jews had been deported to Poland and assassinated in the course of the journey. Here too, their total deportation has been demanded, but it has been refused. But a part of the deportees have found death all the same. Happily, as soon as I returned from my exile in Transristria, I fought for the repatriation for those who had survived and my work was crowned with success because 7,000 deportees have already returned; 5,000 children died *en route* and the *Aide* of the Marshal told me of the latter's decision to repatriate all the other deportees.

So, my Prince, that is what I had to say; what I would say about Rumania if I survive the war; what I ought to say during the war itself, because it is approaching our frontiers.

And now, before closing, I must also speak of our rights. Two problems arise: the situation of the Israelites in the different countries and the problem of Palestine.

These problems appeared already in 1918. The first has been definitively resolved; the second only partially. And it is known that I made my contribution to it as well as to the vital problem of the participation of American Jews in the Jewish Agency. My correspondence with Louis Marshall is proof of this.

The first problem no longer exists. It is simply a question of abolishing the restrictive laws and to replace them by a *restitutio in integrum*. It is again a question of a better guarantee of these rights; in the future. It is an important problem, but it is enough to recall it.

As for the Jewish homeland: the evolution of this problem has made considerable progress owing, at the same time, to the deserving work of the Jews in Palestine, and to anti-Semitism which is being definitively restrained.

My Prince, I have a last request for the owner of my Will. That is, to show it at the moment when it could serve the Rumanian cause and to give a copy to my children as a witness that it was always of them I was thinking in putting my last thoughts on paper.

In renewing my wishes for the success of your journey, I beg you, my Prince, to accept the expression of my most sincere sentiments.

SS. Filderman

I would like to stress that, in my opinion, the figure of 320,000 Jews in Rumania, put forward by Filderman in his letter, does not include the Jews from Bessarabia and Bucovina, where most of them were. Maybe he avoided including them, so as not to offend the Russians who claimed that those provinces were Russian, and not Rumanian.

The famous American newspaperman Reuben H. Markham, in his excellent book: *Rumania under the Soviet Yoke*, gives the figure of 850,000 Jews in Greater Rumania, in 1939.

I do not intend to enter into such a discussion—which is not the aim of this book. Readers may find more about this matter in a very well-documented, and very well-written book: *Aspects des relations russo-roumaines*, by a Rumanian team: G. Gorcanescu, G. Filiti, R. Florescu, D. Germani, A. Gorjiu, M. Korne, and N. Neculce, edited by Minad 1967.

However, it is my duty to establish the historical truth that, in spite of the totally unjustified reputation of anti-Semitism, Rumania was, in the last two centuries, the haven of all the persecuted Jews from Russia and Poland, fleeing terrible pogroms. All found new homes in Rumania.

The figure given by Reuben H. Markham is likely to be the correct one, keeping in mind that nowadays, in the State of Israel, are to be found more than half a million Jews from Rumania. We must add to them all the other hundreds of thousands who left Rumania for other countries than Israel, after 1944.

Keeping in mind the extermination, and the persecution of the Jewish people in all European countries during the war, the Jews in Rumania lived, and survived better than in any other European country. It is a historical fact that the Rumanian people received them and lived with them in a very humanitarian way, and that the government of Marshal Antonescu made it a point not to follow Hitler's orders and way, and to save the Rumanian Jews.

Filderman's extraordinary letter confirms this historical truth.

135

CHAPTER 18

The Act of 23 August 1944 in Bucharest

This was the situation on the morning of 23 August 1944, in Bucharest: everybody—including Marshal Antonescu—was awaiting the reply from Cairo to Maniu's plan, which was two months overdue. . . .

As we have seen, the Marshal had decided to withdraw Rumania from the war and had sought an audience of the King to inform him about the armistice, which he had demanded on 22 August and on the morning of 23 August.

The audience was granted for 4 P.M., and the Marshal presented himself, without any special guard, accompanied by Mihai Antonescu.

In the course of that audience, both Marshal Antonescu and Mihai Antonescu were arrested by the Palace Guard, kept in the King's safe-room and in the evening, handed over to a Rumanian officer of Russian origin—Bodnaras, *alias* Spataru. They did not appear again until the trial in 1946, having been held all that time in Moscovite prisons.

King Michael I appointed General Sanatescu Prime Minister on 24 August. The latter formed a government of National Unity.

On the evening of 23 August, the King spoke to the Rumanian people and to the army on the radio:

> "From this moment, the struggle between our troops and the Forces of the Soviet Union must cease and the state of war between our country and Great Britain and America must end. Receive the soldiers of the Soviet Union with confidence. The United Nations have guaranteed our independence and non-interference in our internal affairs."

As a result of that proclamation, the Rumanian armies coming in contact with those of Russia, ceased to offer any resistance. But they were disarmed, taken prisoner, and sent to Russia.

An agreement was made on 24 August 1944 with General Gerstenberg for the German troops to leave Rumania. Under direct orders from Hitler, General Gerstenberg did not keep his word and attacked and bombarded Bucharest. From that moment, Rumania declared war on Germany.

That is a summary of the events.

Now let us see them in greater depth, in the light of the new documents.

What exactly happened in Bucharest on 23 August 1944?

Alexandru Cretzeanu gives two contradictory versions. In an article published by him in the *Journal of Central European Affairs*, in October 1951, on page 255, he writes:

> On the morning of 23 August, Maniu announced to his representatives in Cairo that the action had been planned for 26th August. But before that message could reach its destination, last-minute events intervened. It was found out that Marshal Antonescu meant to leave Bucharest on 24 August. Therefore, in agreement with the Opposition, the King summoned Antonescu on 23 August and insisted on his concluding the Armistice immediately. When the General refused, the King, supported by a small group of intimates, acted quickly. By the time the telegram had reached Cairo, the Government in Bucharest had been overthrown and replaced by one under General Sanatescu.

So it must be noted, from this first version by Alexander Cretzeanu, that:

—Maniu handed in a telegram to be sent to Cairo saying that everything was ready for 26 August.
—That the King, on hearing that the Marshal would leave for the front on 24 August, summoned him to the palace on the 23rd.
—That this meeting took place with the consent of the Opposition.
—That the King demanded that the Marshal sign the armistice immediately.
—That, on the Marshal's refusal, he was arrested and replaced.

137

Now let us look at the second version of Alexandru Cretzeanu as it appears in his book, *The Lost Opportunity*, p. 148:

Really, everything was prepared for 26 August as the telegram announced. But on the afternoon of the 23rd, Marshal Antonescu came to see the King and told him that he intended—himself—to seek an armistice. He added, in spite of that, that he considered it correct to inform the Germans of his intention.

Until then, the young King had had no occasion to show either his authority or his initiative. Now, he thought quickly. As the Germans might act first, he realised that action must be taken quickly and decisively. The King passed into the next room and ordered the Officers on Guard to arrest the two Antonescus, *etc.*

This version, written and signed by the same Alexandru Cretzeanu, is, as one may see, quite different from the first. The results from these two versions are:

—That everything had been prepared for the *coup d'état* to take place on August 26.
—That Marshal Antonescu went to the palace on his own initiative—not summoned by the King.
—That the King did not consult the Opposition before arresting the Marshal on 23 August 1944, because he had planned to go to the front on the 24th.
—That the Marshal did not intend to go to the front, on the 24th.
—That the Marshal had asked for an audience on his own initiative, in order to tell the King of his intention to seek an armistice.
—That the Marshal had taken the first step in that direction because he had informed the Germans already.

Which of the versions is true?

As I know how controversial is this problem and I do not wish to contribute to a discussion that has done so much harm among Rumanians in exile, I will try only to draw definitive conclusions about this act, especially as I have not the Rumanian dossier, and so my information is incomplete.

Nonetheless, from Alexandru Cretzeanu's second version, we must retain what is logical:

1. That Marshal Antonescu had decided to conclude an armistice and towards this end had even held a Council of Ministers on the morning of 23 August 1944.
2. That he had asked for an audience, in order to inform the King.
3. That certainly—wishing to conclude this armistice—he had, as a soldier, taken all the necessary measures, and even more had informed the German minister, Clodius, so he could have expected reprisals on the part of the Germans.
4. That it is unbelievable that—wishing to conclude an armistice and having informed the Germans of this—he should wish to leave the capital to go to the front.

Among the secret, declassified documents that I have consulted in the State Archives in London, I found a report regarding 23 August 1944.

This is the document number FO 371/43988 of 13 October 1944, containing—in English—an article by General Aldea from the paper *Curierul* of 13 October 1944:

> The day of 23rd August—a day of salvation for our country—found us unprepared from a technical point of view.
>
> The *coup d'état* had been planned for 26th August, but on the morning of 23rd I was informed by the King that he would grant an audience to Marshal Antonescu and Mihai Antonescu that afternoon.
>
> On the morning of 23rd August, a Council of Ministers was held of whose decisions I was not informed.
>
> Lunch at the Palace—at which were present General Sanatescu, Niculescu Buzesti, Mocsony Stircea—was followed by a conference in which we all asked each other what could have decided Marshal Antonescu to ask an audience of the King.
>
> At his audience, Marshal Antonescu had communicated his decision to conclude an Armistice, adding that he had already spoken with the Minister, Clodius, about that.
>
> That would mean the Occupation of the entire country by the Germans, and possibly the arrest and deportation of the King and of those who support him.
>
> During the conversation with Marshal Antonescu, in which General Sanatescu took part, His Majesty interrupted the audience for a few minutes to communicate with us, who had remained in an adjoining room to await the Marshal's decision about an armistice.

After we had discussed it a little, we came to the conclusion that—without waiting until 26th August and thus risk our lives—we should proceed at once to arrest the Marshal and Mihai Antonescu.

After the King had left the room a Major of the Palace Battalion, accompanied by a Sentry informed the Marshal and Mihai Antonescu that they were under arrest. They submitted, without the slightest opposition, and were led to the Palace cellars.

General Vasiliu, General Pantazi and Col. Elefterescu were summoned to the Palace, one by one, by General Sanatescu and arrested immediately. Eugen Cristescu and General Tobescu refused to answer the summons by Sanatescu and went direct to the German Legation where they reported on what was happening at the Palace.

What conclusion can be drawn from this article from the report of an eye-witness who took a direct part in the Act of 23 August 1944?

—Firstly that from a military point of view, we were not prepared for this *volte face* on 23 August, because it had been planned for 26 August.
—That Marshal Antonescu himself had asked for an audience.
—That, in the palace—apart from the King—General Sanatescu, Niculescu Buzesti, Mocsony Stircea, and General Aldea were present. Therefore, not the leaders of the Opposition.
—That General Antonescu had informed the King that he had decided to seek an armistice, and had informed the minister, Clodius, of this.
—That the King had gone to the adjoining room to inform them of the armistice decision. That, quickly discussing it, it was decided to arrest Antonescu. Why? Because, says General Aldea, without that, the Germans would have occupied the whole country, and would probably have arrested the King and those in the plot.

As I have said, I have not the Rumanian dossier of the scene at the palace, but from the above, related by General Aldea, I ask without hesitation, why "the Germans could occupy the whole country" with Marshal Antonescu leading, but could not do so when he was arrested? Was it not just he—Marshal Antonescu—who could have hindered a German occupation? Especially as having decided on the armistice and having informed the Germans of this, he surely awaited reprisals and must have taken all the necessary precautions in consequence. He had even ordered general mobilisation.

140

In compiling the document about 23 August 1944, and the events at the palace on that day, I found an article in *Miroir de l'Histoire*, of September 1970 (number 249) entitled *"L'Armistice—sovieto—roumain,"* signed by the historian, Jacques de Launay, which I will reproduce, almost entirely, although I have grave doubts about the exactitude of the facts related.

The article, accompanied by four photographs (one of which shows the King and Marshal Antonescu, both kneeling in church and praying together) was certainly inspired by someone who was in possession of the secrets of the interview at the palace on 23 August 1944. As this article claims to give a faithful account—from a registration on a recorder—of these talks between the King and the Marshal, I give the account of this dialogue below from the original French version, but with reservations as I have said:

(English Translation)
On 20 August 1944 the IInd and IIIrd Ukrainian Armies, commanded respectively by Marshals Malinovski and Tolboukhine pierced the Germano-Rumanian Front in the Jassy-Kichinev sector. The plans prepared by the King's Cabinet and the Roumanian Civil Resistance were to be executed.

In the Capital, the insurrectional operations were launched on the 23rd. The leader, Antonescu, was summoned by the King.

Before the entry of the Marshal to the Cabinet, His Majesty opened a drawer in his desk and turned on his dictaphone.

Antonescu: Long live your Majesty!

The King: There is no time to waste. In spite of all protestations, you have got the country into such a situation that only the immediate cessation of hostilities and the expulsion of the Germans could still save us.

Antonescu: You are mistaken.

The King: I beg you, when you address me, do it correctly. What does this "you" mean?

Antonescu: You . . . Your Majesty . . . Your Majesty is nervous today . . .

The King: Yes, because when I called for you to come today, you treated me with disdain. Do you imagine that I permit you to usurp my prerogatives and that I can be content, like an imbecile, to see my country collapse?

Antonescu: And who is busy doing it?

The King: All of you, and even so, when I summon you, you have no time to meet the King of this country.

Antonescu: I must tell you that if you believe the country can be saved by an armistice, you are mistaken.

The King: I have not summoned you here in order to ask your advice or to find out your opinion. I have called you here to transmit this telegram concerning the cessation of hostilities to the United Nations.

Antonescu: Who edited it?

The King: What does it matter? If you refuse, I will have it sent myself.

Antonescu: Do you imagine that the Marshal could betray his German allies? And throw himself into the arms of the Russians?

The King: (shouting) Who is the betrayer? You or the Germans? Was it you who guaranteed the frontiers of Germany or Germany who guaranteed those of Rumania?

Antonescu: I am not deaf. Why do you shout?

The King: Yes, you are deaf. Otherwise you would have heard the murmurings of the country. In short, Marshal, will you—yes or no—send this telegram?

Antonescu: No, not in this form.

The King: Then, in what form?

Antonescu: I must make contact with Germany.

The King: How? Is it a question of bargaining, Mr. Antonescu?

Antonescu: Marshal Antonescu.

The King: Mr. Antonescu. For four years you have been usurping my rights; you have had neither my trust nor my sympathy. For months I have been working with the Opposition to save my country. You—I know it—take me for a child. My Rumanians will decide.

But if you consider me to be a traitor, you are wrong. I am the King of my country and your King. I wish to save the country [he shouts and bangs his desk] and nobody can prevent me!

Antonescu: Your Majesty is young and without experience.

The King: You deceive yourself. Suffering is an experience.

Antonescu: You cannot dispose of the country if—

The King: I am head of the Army, and my orders have already been given.

Antonescu: [violently] Given? What orders? Does your Majesty know that you can lose your throne?

The King: Is that a threat? But do you imagine that you have the power to give any order? From this moment, it is I who make decisions. You are under arrest.

Antonescu: How? I? The Marshal? We shall see!

The King: Rubbish! Take him away.

142

It was 5:15 P.M. The King went out and ordered a Major of the Battalion of the Guard to proceed with the arrest of the Marshal. The others members of the government, including Mihai Antonescu—who had also been summoned to the palace—were arrested, one after the other.

This is why the "recording" above seems to me to have been invented by the author:

1. The King could not have said to Marshal Antonescu that he had "summoned him this morning to the Palace," for the truth is that the Marshal had sought an audience for himself and for Mihai Antonescu, the prime minister.
2. At the interview Mihai Antonescu and General Sanatescu also took part. In the "recording" made by Jacques de Launay, they are not mentioned. Even more, the latter affirms that Mihai Antonescu was called to the palace after the arrest of the Marshal, which is also a mistake.
3. The "telegram" seeking an armistice could not have been refused by the Marshal, because he himself had accepted the armistice the evening before—on 22 August, and even on the morning of 23 August.
4. Nobody before Jacques de Launay had claimed that the King himself had said to the Marshal "You are under arrest." The truth, up to now, was that the King had left his study and after consulting those in the adjoining room (General Aldea, Niculescu Buzesti, Mocsony Stircea) returned and said to the Marshal that he was dismissed from his post as leader and then left the room. After his departure, a Major from the Battalion of Guards entered and declared the Marshal and Mihai Antonescu to be "under arrest."
5. The "recording" of de Launay does not say anything about the Marshal's informing the King of the armistice that he had sought. And we do not find the name of the German minister, Clodius, which the Marshal had pronounced when informing the King that he had already told Clodius of his intention to seek an armistice.
6. Lastly, the "historian," de Launay, commits another clumsy error when he affirms, towards the end of the article that the

143

armistice of Moscow, of 12 September 1944, was signed by Stirbey and Visoianu. As Reuben H. Markham shows in *La Roumanie sous le Joug Sovietique*, p. 66, the armistice was signed, for Rumania, by Patrascanu, Damacianu, Stirbey, and Pop.

I must add to this chapter an excerpt from the very serious document of Messrs. Cioranescu, Korne, Filiti, etc., that I mentioned before *(Aspects des relations russo-roumaines)*, which gives a very close version of the 23 August 1944 events in Rumania, and which, it seems to me, is based on first-hand documents and knowledge, from the Rumanian Archives, the book having been published in 1967, before the top-secret documents of the military and political archives in London and Washington became available in 1972. There are, of course, many differences.

This is the excerpt from page 179 of this book:

The big Russian offensive is launched on 20 August, on the Rumanian front. The King, Maniu and the leaders of the opposition take measures in view of putting an end to the alliance with Germany on August 26. Maniu sends a cable to Cairo asking that air borne troops should be sent to Rumania as soon as possible. Back from inspecting the troops, Antonesco sees the leaders of the National-Peasant party to examine the possibilities of an armistice [August 22, 1944]. On the morning of August 23, the Liberal leader Georges Bratianu brings to the Marshal the support of all the parties to sign the armistice. Antonesco seems to agree. An audience with the King is set for the afternoon. Antonesco sees also the German Minister Clodius, to whom he explains the necessity for Rumania to halt the war with Russia. On the morning of the same day, the MAE Micheal Antonesco sends a diplomatic messenger to Stockholm, requesting Nano to go to see Ambassadress Kollontaï, and, to see if Moscow maintained the armistice conditions of 29 May, and 2 June, to choose a place and the date for the negotiations.

Informed that the Marshal was going back to the front next day, King Michael decides to precipitate events.

At the time of the audience Antonesco is of the opinion that the Germans should be given two weeks to withdraw from Rumania (Russian counter-propositions of June 2 1944). The King insists that all military operations should be stopped at once. After deliberation with his counsellors, the King declares Antonesco to be dismissed, and under arrest. The War Minister [General Pantazi] and the Home Secretary [General Vasiliu] are also arrested.

At 22 P.M. the King announces by a radio proclamation the conclusion of an armistice, and orders the Rumanian troops to stop the fighting. The German Minister Von Killingen is summoned to the Palace, and asked to communicate to the German Government to withdraw without delay their troops from Rumania. The next day, the German aviation bombards Bucharest. Rumania declares war to Germany.

The merit or demerit of the act of 23 August cannot be attributed either to Maniu or to Dinu Bratianu. They were not at the palace, nor were they even in Bucharest; nor were they even consulted, according to all available documents up to now. What they wanted was a *volte face*—a change of policies and alliance to be made by the Marshal. Only in case he did not accept, would they have been obliged to conclude an armistice, but also with the concourse of the Marshal. The *coup d'état* had to be made against the Germans, not against the Marshal, who had agreed all along that an armistice must be concluded. The proof is that he sought it on 22 August and had informed the Germans of his decision.

It should be remarked also, that on 22 August, Iuliu Maniu in person, accompanied by Ion Mihalache, not only had no intention of arresting Marshal Antonescu, but asked him for an audience; saw him and begged him—the Marshal—to conclude an armistice and according to Maniu: "as regards the Armistice, Marshal Antonescu was very well disposed."

This Maniu declared at the trial of Marshal Antonescu and added afterwards:

> I entered the Government on 24th August, after the incident at the Palace, so I had no chance to find out what happened there, nor could I have been in any way responsible for what happened there.

That is the historical truth.

Until now I have used the expression, that Marshal Antonescu asked for an audience: "to inform the King that he had decided to sign an armistice," which was used in both versions of Cretzeanu's report, as well as in General Aldea's, because I wished to respect their vocabulary.

But I must emphasise that Marshal Antonescu did not intend to seek an armistice when he went to the palace, *because he had already done so the day before*—on 22 August.

This is shown by a telegram sent by the British ambassador in Ankara to the Foreign Office on 22 August 1944 (telegram number 1386).

In it, the British ambassador informed his government that the prime minister of Turkey had communicated to him the contents of a telegram from the Turkish minister in Bucharest, saying that the latter had seen the Rumanian prime minister—Mihai Antonescu—who told him that he had the consent of the Marshal, of the King, and of the leaders of all parties to ask for an urgent reply, within twenty-four hours, from the British and American governments as to which of the three following proposals they were in agreement:

—That the Marshal send a delegation to Moscow to conclude an armistice?
—That he (the Marshal) should contact the Russians and Anglo-Americans, at the same time, to fix the armistice conditions?
—That his government should discuss the armistice conditions with the Allies, in Cairo?

Mihai Antonescu wished to know on which of the three formulae the Anglo-Americans would like the Marshal to follow.

At the same time, the Turkish prime minister informed the Russian and American ambassadors of Mihai Antonescu's request.

On 23 August 1944, at 12:40 P.M. the Foreign Office in London (top secret telegram number 2646) sent confirmation of their receipt of telegram number 1386 to the ambassador in Moscow—Sir Archibald Kerr—and gave the ambassador instructions that if the Soviet government agreed, he should reply at once to Mihai Antonescu through the Turkish prime minister, that the Rumanians should at once send a delegation to Moscow, either by the front lines or by Turkey.

The telegram concluded by suggesting that the Soviet and American governments should inform their ambassadors in Ankara of this decision.

Marshal Antonescu's intention to conclude an armistice is also confirmed by the British ambassador in Stockholm, in his telegram number 985 of 1 September 1944 (top secret document number R13785/g, declassified), sent to his government.

In it, Sir W. Mallet informs his foreign minister that he received a communication from the Swedish foreign minister in which the latter tells him that the Swedish minister in Bucharest had informed him by telegram—*which had been delayed for eight days*—that a special courier

146

from Marshal Antonescu had left for Stockholm to conclude the armistice.

That delayed telegram had therefore been sent on 22 August—therefore before the arrest of the Marshal on 23 August.

I have also seen the telegram sent by the ambassador, Lord Halifax, in Washington, on 24 August, informing the State Department of the Marshal's request made through Turkey.

What had happened to Marshal Antonescu's diplomatic courier who had set out for Stockholm with his acceptance of the armistice terms handled by Mr. Nano, Rumanian ambassador in Sweden and Madame Kollontay, Soviet ambassador there?

He arrived in Stockholm only on 24 August 1944. Mr. F. Nano tells us, in an article published in the same journal as that of Alexandru Cretzeanu, in October 1951:

> I was therefore surprised when the Courier [Mr. Djuvara] rushed into my office and hardly able to breathe, said to me: Mr. Antonescu agrees with you and so I am bringing instructions for you to see Madame Kollontay immediately to see whether the conditions you have obtained are still valid or will have to be renegotiated; or whether the Russians wish to discuss them with the Opposition or with the present Government. Mihai Antonescu told me that the Marshal is ready to withdraw and that he had given him a free hand to sign the Armistice.

Mr. Nano replied that he was afraid he had come a day too late. It was 24 August 1944.

What happened in Bucharest after 23 August is well known. I will therefore say what happened in Moscow, according to the Anglo-American documents I have consulted.

On 24 August, the American and British ambassadors asked Vishinsky to complete the terms of the armistice treaty with Rumania, which—in its edition of 12 April 1944—was only a synopsis of the essential clauses. The British and Americans wanted to discuss, at their leisure, the sum asked for damages, which seemed to them enormous in view of the weak Rumanian economy, as well as the Control Commission in which they wanted to play an "active and equal part."

Vishinsky replied that since 12 April the conditions had changed and that as a result, the problem would have to be studied from the beginning. (In the meantime, Churchill and Roosevelt had accepted Russian control of Rumania).

On 25 August 1944, Molotov—at 2 A.M.—summoned Harriman and Kerr to the Kremlin and read out to them the declaration that the Soviet government was to publish in the morning:

> The Supreme Command of the Soviet Army believes that if the Rumanian Armies will cease all action against the Red Armies, and if they will ally themselves with the Soviet Armies and, hand in hand, will fight against the Germans to free Rumania or against the Hungarians to free Transylvania, the Red Army will not disarm them, but will leave them armed and will give every help towards this end.

The same day—25 August 1944—Molotov repeated the Declaration of 2 April 1944: that

> the Soviet Government declare that they do not aim to annex any Rumanian territory, apart from Bessarabia or to change the social structure of Rumania which exists today.

But, although Rumania ceased to fight against the Russians on 23 August, Russian troops—between that date and 12 September, the day of the signing of the capitulation—took 130,000 prisoners after the fighting had ceased. In addition, they deported 20,000 Rumanians from Moldavia and Transylvania as well as 72,000 Rumanians of German ethnic origin.

In Moscow, Ambassador Harriman was advised by Roosevelt—in the absence of Cordell Hull who was in hospital—to ask for a share in the Allied Control Commission *but not to insist; to be "discreet."*

In his report to Washington of 14 September 1944, Averell Harriman says clearly: that the Russians will do "whatever they like in Rumania, as they did in Bulgaria and Poland."

Concerning the Allied Control Commission, Molotov was precise and categoric: only the Soviet head of the Commission would have the right to give orders to the Rumanian government; executive power would be exercised only by the Soviet Command. On 20 September, Vishinsky specified to the Anglo-American ambassadors that they must not have more than five members each on the Control Commission, that their role would be subordinate to the Soviet Command, that they were not to

148

communicate with the Rumanian government except through the intermediary of the Soviet head of the Commission, and, lastly, that they were not to travel in Rumania without special permission from the Soviet head of the Commission.

The protests of the Allies were purely formal; "discreet," as Roosevelt had recommended and as Churchill explains in his *Memoirs*: That he could not protest too strongly "because he had come to an agreement with the Russians that, in Rumania they were to have 'the first say.' "

Before ending this chapter, I must mention a sensational document, dated 23 August 1944, from Cairo. It is a telegram to Lord Moyne, British Cabinet minister, sent from Cairo to London. It bears the number 1946.

Discussing the proposal to send a new emissary to Cairo by the Rumanians (Marshal Antonescu was thinking of Filderman), Lord Moyne opposes this, saying that this would only be one more attempt to form intrigues among the Three allies and that any discussion would be useless before the military surrender.

Lord Moyne suggests, however, that in the *event of a* volte face *in Rumania*, he (Antonescu) *must make direct contact with the Russians*.

As seen, on the morning of 23 August, Lord Moyne still believed that Marshal Antonescu could make a *coup d'état* against the Germans. On the same day—23 August, at 4.30 P.M.—the Marshal was arrested.

In another telegram, of the morning of 23 August 1944, with the following number—1947—also to Lord Moyne—speaks of a message received from Cretzeanu from Ankara on the same day. (It should be remembered that the only link with Bucharest was through Cretzeanu.) The two other posts had ceased contact, apart from the radio station Nicolescu-Buzesti-via Cretzeanu).

In this message, presented by Prince Stirbey to the American chargé d'affaires (because Novikov did not wish to accept it until the next day, 24 August) and to the British Major Russell, Stirbey told them that as he had received no news for a long time about Maniu's plans, the Opposition were completely in the dark and did not knew what to do: whether to act before receiving the reply asked for, without any coordinated action by the Allies? Or to wait for a reply, which might come too late? (As is known, the day for the *Coup* had been fixed by Maniu for 26 August in "the Maniu Plan").

The two diplomats replied to the prince that the final decision was, and remained, in the hands of the Russians, and that they (the Anglo-Americans) would agree to any decision made by Novikov.

Notice should also be taken of a telegram—(number 2649, of 24 August 1944), the day following the act of 23 August—sent by Anthony Eden to Ambassador Kerr in Moscow.

In this document, the foreign secretary tells the ambassador that they have had no official confirmation of events in Bucharest, and begs him to find out from the Russians. He also asks him to find out whether the Russians are ready to conclude an armistice on the conditions laid out on 12 April 1944, on which the Three had agreed, or were they to be revised? Anthony Eden asks to participate in the discussion and at the signing of that armistice wherever it would be concluded.

We shall see how Molotov, alone, dictated to the British and Americans who were only present *pro forma*; how the armistice was signed by Malinovsky, and in the name of His Majesty and of the United States.

THE CASE OF FINLAND

As is known, Finland had been under Swedish domination until the reign of Peter the Great. Since then her fate wavered as a result of frequent wars between Sweden and Tsarist Russia. But from 1909, Finland was integrated into Russia with a semi-independent statute of a Duchy.

After attempts at forced Russification under Tsar Nicholas II, Finland became an independent republic by the peace of Brest-Litovsk (capitulation—more exactly—of Lenin). On 17 June 1919, Finland proclaimed herself a republic and later was recognized as a sovereign, independent state, in the League of Nations.

By the Hitler-Stalin non-aggression pact of 23 August 1939, the Soviet Union obtained spheres of influence, not only in the Balkans, but also in the Baltic countries and Finland.

The three Baltic countries immediately granted military bases to Russia and were later completely swallowed up by the latter. Finland refused Stalin's demand to provide him with military bases and to sign a non-aggression pact with the Soviet Union.

In November 1939, after the incorporation of half of Poland, Stalin attacked Finland. Britain and France helped Finland, while on 10 December 1939, the Soviet Union was expelled as an aggressor from the League of Nations.

After a heroic struggle—which roused the admiration of the entire free world—a peace treaty was signed in Moscow on 13 March 1940.

150

The Soviet Union obtained 10 percent of Finnish territory—Karelia and a water line in Lake Ladoga—as well as a contract for the Hangoe Peninsula to last thirty years and the right of transit across Petsamo.

When Hitler attacked Russia on 22 June 1941, Finland joined the Axis, with whom she fought until the conclusion of an armistice on 4 September 1944. The terms of this armistice, known on 19 September 1944, were not those of an unconditional surrender. Far from it. However, the 1940 frontiers were recognized. Petsamo was ceded to Russia. For Porkalla, a contract was signed to rent it for fifty years and reparations amounting to 300 million dollars had to be paid.

But the independence of the country was scrupulously respected by Russia. Although existed in Moscow a "Democratic Finnish Government" (Communist), which was recognized by the Russians, no one bothered about it; in negotiations no one interfered as in Poland or in Rumania—subjugated countries.

Why this favoured treatment?

Certainly international public opinion played a role, but a minor one; world-wide admiration for the country and her heroic army had surely influenced Stalin, especially as he had been the aggressor. It was good propaganda for him.

But I believe that because the British had recognized Russia's rights in Finland in 1941, and Roosevelt in 1943, Stalin had a free hand in bargaining for the spheres of influence handed over on 9 October 1944 by Churchill in Moscow. Finland did not enter into the bargaining between them. Stalin was given a free hand in the Balkans, and he knew how to make full use of it.

Moreover, in the case of Rumania, the resistance put up by the army and Marshal Antonescu's tenacity to obtain the best conditions, were shattered by the Act of 23 August 1944 when the whole of Rumania was handed out on a tray, together with the rest of the Balkans and the shortening of the war. Who would not have profited by such an occasion?

But the case of Finland explains several things clearly:

—Wherever the Anglo-Americans wanted, they could have influenced the behaviour of the Russians. They did not want to in the Balkans.
—Marshal Mannerheim, Finland's great military hero, in resisting, saved his country. He was honoured by his country—not shot by a firing-squad, like Marshal Antonescu.

151

Did Marshal Antonescu make mistakes?

Of course he did, as I have pointed out. But I do not think that the fate of Rumania was too much influenced by them. Declaration of war on the United States? A diplomatic formality, which no one took seriously. The American Air Force, which bombarded the Rumanian country and people pitilessly, were welcomed as heroes, when they fell prisoners.

Ought he to have halted on the Dniester? Possibly. But would Stalin have been content—once the war was over—without "a friendly government" and military bases in Rumania? Certainly not. If necessary, he would not have hesitated to install it. But I think that Marshal Antonescu made, nonetheless, a great mistake: he allowed and encouraged armistice negotiations with too many parties.

He had to remain firm on Rumania's withdrawal from the war, together with Iuliu Maniu and Dinu Bratianu and Titel Petrescu, as he had wished in January 1943.

But the armistice negotiations should have been conducted by him—by the government. The parallel negotiations (disguised) showed weakness and undermined the national unity. The entire nation wished to be alongside the Allies and to withdraw from the Axis. But this should have been negotiated by Marshal Antonescu and his army because they counted with the Russians. The Army was commanded by Marshal Antonescu and they respected him.

The diversification of the negotiations and their parallelism, showed up the weak points of the Rumanian moral and political front and Stalin profited by it. He expected Rumania to fall alone by an act like that of 23 August 1944 and waited.

The negotiations in Cairo should have been held openly with the Rumanian government—not disguised. Prince Stirbey had been identified before his arrival in Cairo. The secret was now pointless.

In the "negotiations" in Cairo, no secret was divulged: the Allies knew that Stirbey was speaking also in Marshal Antonescu's name. (Molotov said so sharply in the case of de Chastellaine.)

The Germans? Hitler may have been mad, but he certainly was not stupid. He could not imagine that Stirbey was negotiating in Cairo without the consent of the Marshal, while "the plotters"—Iuliu Maniu and Dinu Bratianu—were walking openly through the streets of Bucharest and meeting each other in Snagov, with the Gestapo all over Rumania.

By taking charge of the negotiations in Cairo, misunderstandings arising from the communications system would have been surely avoided.

But the way they were transmitted no one could find out what messages were sent by Maniu and what was sent by the Three in Cairo. And *vice versa*. All messages passed through the censorship of Niculescu-Buzesti-Cretzeanu. Marshal Antonescu ought not to have left the fate of the country to these lines of communication. He ought to have controlled them himself.

By doing that, the Marshal would have realized in time the advantage of the armistice proposed to him by the Russians at Stockholm, had he accepted it.

The Cairo conditions were unconditional surrender. The conditions in Stockholm meant an armistice—as we have seen—which might have changed—at least for a while—the fate of Rumania.

In any case, the act of 23 August handed the whole of Rumania to Stalin on a silver tray. Who, in his place, would not have taken advantage? Rumania's fall meant the collapse of the entire Balkan region: Bulgaria, Yugoslavia, Greece, and Hungary, followed by Czechoslovakia and Germany.

By her political and military importance, Rumania was the cornerstone of the entire front in Eastern Europe. The act of 23 August 1944, meant the collapse of this whole front, without any benefit to Rumania, which she deserved for such a gesture. The Russians were ready to pay the price for it. They offered it in Stockholm, and they wished to deal with Marshal Antonescu personally, because they knew that the Rumanian Army could still resist for a long time. The Russians knew that the fate of the war depended on Hitler's secret weapons and were anxious to shorten it. The Russians were disposed to pay a great price for the collapse of the entire front in the Balkans! But they obtained it gratis!

CHAPTER 19

The Signing of the
Unconditional Surrender of Rumania

This was done on 12 September 1944, in Moscow. From the act of 23 August 1944, when the Sanatescu government accepted the "armistice conditions"—twenty days had passed. Why this delay? Obviously, so that the Russians could occupy the whole country before discussing or signing anything.

What was there to discuss? The "armistice conditions" had been formulated by the Allies on 12 April 1944. They had been formally accepted by Maniu, as we have seen. On 12 June, General Sanatescu had accepted the same conditions. No one had suggested any change. But the Russians were not in a hurry to sign. According to the documents I have seen, the Allies discussed among themselves whether or not the initial conditions fixed would be the same. Evidently, the Anglo-Americans considered that the Russians had "the first say" in Rumania, and would therefore have to prepare the armistice project.

But Molotov prevaricated. It was only on 31 August that he handed the project to the British and American ambassadors in Moscow.

The British and American replied on 3 September 1944, making certain suggestions to Molotov's proposals. In this way, the question was delayed even longer, because these suggestions had to be discussed anew among the Three.

The Rumanian delegation arrived in Moscow on 30 August. It was composed of Lucretiu Patrascanu, Ionel Pop, Christu, General Damaceanu, and Colonel Focseneanu. To these were added Prince Stirbey and Visoianu, who had come from Cairo, via Teheran.

154

Until 10 September 1944, nothing happened. We must suppose that discussions were being held among the Three, but we do not find anything of importance in the documents we have consulted. The British suggestions were minor and already known (reserves about the recognition of the Rumanian frontiers with Transylvania before the Peace Conference), and smaller reparations. They had already made these suggestions before 12 April 1944.

The general meeting (in agreement with the reports that I have been able to consult) opened on 10 September 1944. The ambassadors, Kerr and Harriman, took part. Molotov handed the project for the armistice to Patrascanu and asked him whether the Rumanians wished to discuss it immediately, or whether they wanted time to study it. The Rumanians asked for time, and the meeting was postponed until the next day.

At the meeting on 11 September, the discussions were courteous. Molotov did not raise his voice, as was reported. Each of the Rumanian delegates took part, making suggestions or proposals, or asking for explanations. Ionel Pop said that Rumania wanted a long frontier with Czechoslovakia. Visoianu even succeeded in his request that Molotov's remark regarding the withdrawal of Russian troops from Rumania should be inserted in the minutes. Christu spoke of the economic situation, Patrascanu, of political prisoners, Damaceanu and Focseneanu of military matters.

Each delegate had been able to speak. But next day, at the third meeting, on 12 September, the armistice was signed—without any change—as it had been presented in the project on the first day. The farce had ended.

On the part of the Allies, only Malinovsky signed, both in the name of Russia and of the United States and Britain, although their ambassadors—Harriman and Kerr—were present and had taken part in the discussions. The Three were named "The Soviet High Command (Allied)." As can be seen the "Allies" were in parenthesis, so that there should be no mistake about the role—minor and non-existent—the British and Americans would have to play.

The armistice conditions were much more severe than those offered in Cairo on 12 April and much, much more difficult than those offered to Marshal Antonescu in Stockholm on 3 June 1944.

"Free transport" over the entire country must be ensured by the

Rumanian Army Command. The whole Occupation Army had to be maintained by Rumania. The National Bank of Rumania would have to put any sum of money asked by the Russian Command at their disposal. They could take as war booty, or damages, any factory or other installation in Rumania.

Neither the independence of the country, nor her sovereignty were respected, because the Soviet troops were present everywhere, nor did the war damages mentioned in The Convention reach the 300 million dollars. Transport and maintenance of the military troops for two years cost the Rumanian economy—together with the liquid "fund" taken from the National Bank, together with war damages—not the 300 million, but almost 2 billion dollars, at the 1944–5 rate of exchange.

From every point of view, it was not an armistice, but a dictatorship, an unconditional surrender.

The wording of the Armistice Convention was the most diabolical document ever read by a lawyer. It was couched in vague, general terms with double meanings, which could always have been interpreted in favour of the Soviets. The lawyers had no say in its interpretation. Its legal meaning was arranged by the Russian Military Command or by the head of the Russian Mission.

That is why—as the late Princess Alice Sturza recalled, Iuliu Maniu confessed, after 23 August, his deception and the tragedy, when he said:

Is that an Armistice? It would have been better not to sign it. It is a military Occupation, and in no sense an Armistice.

CHAPTER 20

Churchill Has Not the Slightest Sympathy for Rumania

To what may we attribute Churchill's hostile attitude to Rumania in September 1944? To his physical degradation, exhaustion and loss of memory, or cynicism and total lack of feeling—if not awareness at least—of humanity?

> I have never felt [he writes on p. 181 of Volume Six of his war memories] that our past relations with Rumania and Bulgaria would justify a gesture or some special sacrifice on our part, but the fate of Poland is close to my heart.

How could this eminent historian, this genius with such a vast culture, and extraordinary memory, how could he forget so easily the reasons for having sympathy, a great sympathy, admiration, and gratitude for Rumania?

How could Churchill forget?

The French armies were fighting at Verdun. His British armies were fighting on the Somme. He was personally involved in the unfortunate Gallipoli Expedition. He was fighting for his physical and political survival.

The time was August 1916, and the German victory seemed close at hand. Maréchal Joffre—Commander-in-Chief of French-English armies, asked for Rumania's help, that she should enter the war.

On 14 August 1916, Rumania entered the war, alongside Churchill's country and army. Poorly equipped, without ammunition, without any air force, or heavy artillery, Rumania entered with Europe the war at the side of Churchill's country.

She was solemnly promised, with Churchill's government's signature, the return of the robbed Rumanian territories.

To enable Rumania to enter the war at that time, and under such circumstances, Great Britain promised Rumania to throw a great offensive on the French front (battlefront), one on Churchill's Salonika battlefront, with the armies of General Sarrail, as well as on the Russian battlefront through the Hungarian plain. Rumania was also promised arms and equipment.

None of the promised offensives materialized, and no equipment and ammunition ever reached Rumania.

Could Churchill have forgotten all that?

Could Churchill forget that Rumania was crushed under the mighty armies of the Kaiser and Franz-Joseph, that she was left to fight alone a suicidal battle?

Could the distinguished historian be oblivious of all those facts? Feeling no sympathy for Rumania?

When she fought to her last man, and last ammunition, in the "death triangle" in Moldavia, for her own national aspirations and survival, but alongside the British armies too, for their victory, and their glory? For the glory of Churchill's noble and great country? And for the glory and victory of Great Britain's armies?

What a short memory he has, the political man.

How quickly he had forgotten what he wrote to Stalin on 4 November 1941, when the latter asked him to declare war on Rumania:

> Rumania and Hungary are full of our friends. They have been overrun, subjugated, by Hitler and used as the cat's paw; but if their fate turns against the brigands, they—the Rumanians and Hungarians—can easily come to our side. [Vol. 3, p. 528]

And how easily and quickly Churchill forgot to honour the *solemn guarantees* given by his country and by France to Rumania on 13 April 1939, by which she was promised *"Independence and territorial integrity."*

On March 21, 1939, the British and the French requested Colonel Beck to adhere to a guarantee by the four of the integrity of Rumania. Beck refused to join in such a guarantee with the Soviet Union, and, after having obtained the British guarantee for the integrity of Poland, he refused the same guarantee for Rumania.

"The guarantee granted to Poland was against the General Staff's objections. The General Staff declared that in view of our resources, it was unable to fulfil the obligations we had undertaken. Chamberlain forbade his War Minister, Hoare-Belisha to communicate these objections to the Cabinet Council" (Liddell Hart).

What was going on in the tired brain of Winston Churchill on the way to Moscow in October 1944 to make him sell the territorial integrity and independence of Rumania, so solemnly guaranteed by the British people?

What was obsessing, what was worrying that man who bore the destiny of his own country and of the whole world on his shoulders? In the head of him of whom his doctor, Lord Moran, said that he was not the same man who went to Carthage in December 1943? How could he have forgotten that there is a relationship between the British Royal Family and that of Rumania and, at least out of politeness, refrain from writing as he did on p. 181 of Vol. VI of his *memoirs*?

How could this great statesman, this titan of history, have forgotten the enormous sacrifices made by the Rumanian people when they fought alongside Britain—his own country—in World War I?

Rumania, declaring war on 14 August 1916, when the Franco-British Allies were in front of Verdun and the Douaumont Fort, they obliged the Germans to concentrate their military and economic efforts on the Rumanian front.

Entering the war when Germany was preparing to launch a powerful offensive, in order to deal the finishing stroke on the Allies, Rumania, with her frail, badly equipped army; without ammunition, mobilized almost a million men who threw themselves heroically against the Germans, thus easing the pressure on the Allied armies.

In his serious study, *La Roumanie dans la Grande Guerre*, Pamfil Seicaru writes, with reason, that by her entry into the war, Rumania *prolonged it*, thus permitting the Allies to win.

Fighting on the longest front of 1350 kilometres, as compared to the Franco-English front of 800 kilometres and along 1100 kilometres of Russian front, Rumania immobilized great numbers of German troops, which would otherwise have been hurled against his—Churchill's—country, Britain.

Let me give you the text of the telegram from Lloyd-George, the former colleague of Winston Churchill in the British Cabinet, addressed

159

to Ionel Bratianu, in 1916, when Lloyd-George became Prime Minister.

Now when I am asked by the King to form a new Cabinet, I
want to assure Your Excellency of the great admiration I feel for
the courage and tenacity in the fighting, shown by your country,
in these difficult times for her, and the unshattered decision of His
Majesty's Government to give Rumania every possible help and
cooperation with others of our common Allies, up to the final victory, which will be ours.

Of course, Winston Churchill, in October 1944, on his way to Moscow, forgot about this telegram also, as he forgot Rumanian sacrifices
during World War I, the British guarantees he gave Rumania, which was
facing the two brigands: Hitler and Stalin. He forgot all that should have
made him feel sympathy for Rumania.

But was it the same Churchill in 1944 who was going to Moscow
to hand over to Stalin the whole of Eastern Europe? Or was it an old
gentleman weary of all the great battles and responsibilities he had to
assume for four years, and who started to doze off in his old age, as every
one of us does.

How could he have forgotten this fact; as a statesman; as British,
as a military strategist? Was it not a gratuitous insult on the eve of his
visit to Moscow, to be preparing to hand over a civilized, Christian, Latin
people to the Soviet hordes and who had already lost almost a million
men in World War I fighting on the side of his country?

Could it have been wickedness; tiredness; senility? On the physical
side—after his serious illness at Carthage in December 1943—after Teheran—Churchill was a failing man, exhausted. Lord Moran wrote in his
diary on 10 December 1943, p. 143:

He knows, without my telling him, that he is finished; it seems
that Teheran destroyed him. He is clearly in decline. It is plain he
is riding for a fall.

In order to understand Churchill's state of mind and spirit on the
eve of his visit to Moscow in October 1944, we must refer, in the first
place, to the diary of his personal physician who had attended him, night
and day since 1940, but not to his own *Memoirs*. These were written
five years later with the help of a whole staff of collaborators—military,
political, and historians. As usually happens, these *Memoirs* may have

160

been slightly "doctored," four or five years after the events took place.

But the diary of his physician, Lord Moran, is more faithful and was written daily. It contains his observations as a doctor, as a man, and as an Englishman. He noted everything and published everything—favourable and unfavourable, as General Smuts requested.

Let us see now what Lord Moran reveals to us about the state of nerves; of obsession and of depression of Churchill:

> "Good God! Don't you see that the Russians are advancing across Europe like a giant wave? They have invaded Poland and there is nothing to stop them overflowing also Greece and Turkey," said Churchill.

It should be noted that he did not mention Rumania, nor Bulgaria, Yugoslavia, nor Hungary. And for a good reason: regarding these countries, he had already come to an agreement with the Russians, and had obtained—as we have seen—the personal approval of Roosevelt, without the knowledge of Cordell Hull, his Secretary of State. He (Churchill) was obsessed by the invasion of Europe by Stalin's hordes (i.e., of the disaster that he, personally, had brought about to this Europe by his own mistakes) and obsessed to the point of neurosis as to how to save Turkey and Greece. He wished to keep the way open to the Mediterranean; the road to the British Empire—a road and an empire now threatened by the Red armies.

On 21 August 1944, six weeks before the Moscow meeting, Lord Moran notes on p. 173:

> Winston never mentions Hitler now. He talks constantly of the Communist peril. At night, he dreams that the Red Army is spreading like a cancer, from one country to another. *This has become an obsession to him*, and he can think of nothing else.

> If only those ten Divisions, [said Churchill repeatedly] had been able to land at Trieste, but the Americans did not consult me. They said that everything had already been arranged.

I must say at once, before continuing the story of Churchill's policy in the Balkans, that for him, Rumania did not form part of the Balkans, that her fate had already been sealed. By the Balkans he meant a way to assure the road out to the British Empire by the northeast coast of the Mediterranean.

161

Considering Turkey and Greece to be threatened (and wishing to neutralize Yugoslavia and Albania), Churchill made his own decisions because the Americans did not help him to come to a direct understanding with Stalin. That was now the source of his obsession to cultivate the friendship of the Kremlin dictator at any price.

Churchill, continues Lord Moran on p. 190, says:

> Stalin will get all he wants. The Americans have taken care of that. Our Army in Italy was too weak to keep them in check.'' *That is why he has to safeguard his interests regarding Stalin by other means; anything could be arranged if only he could win Stalin's friendship.*

This was an obsession, neurosis, his doctor said in August 1944, of Churchill. As he could no longer keep the Red armies in check, he wished at any cost to win Stalin's friendship. With what aim? To save the road to the Mediterranean. That was the reason for his visit to Moscow and the cause of the infamous agreement of the night of 9 October 1944.

That obsession was certainly justified. A patriot and a strategist, Churchill, thus obsessed day and night, by the Communist danger, tried to save what was now left.

As a man, it is possible to understand his desperate attempt—and a much too late one—to purchase Stalin's friendship by selling Rumania and creating zones of influence in the Balkans.

Certainly it was a desperate attempt to repair, even partially, the grave mistakes made by himself and Roosevelt from 1940 onwards. For his country. One can understand his patriotism and his last stand.

This was patriotism, but poor political judgment. It was not the political judgment of a genious, as we are accustomed to look at Churchill, but a desperate attempt to save what was lost, and to correct—in a last stand—against Stalin—his terrible and tragic mistakes.

It was a bad policy toward his own country, Britain, and a cruel and terrible mistake against all the enslaved peoples, by Churchill dealing with Stalin.

CHAPTER 21

Churchill in Moscow in October 1944: Sell-Out of Eastern Europe

Let us return now to Britain and Churchill's obsession with the Communist peril. Readers will have remembered the indiscretions of Dr. Moran regarding this obsession "by Communism which is spreading like a cancer" all over Europe. They will also have remembered the initiative, the insistence, the perseverance of Churchill in May and June 1944, when he succeeded in obtaining Roosevelt's agreement for zones of influence in the Balkans against the official policy of America and how, in order to deceive the State Department, Congress, and the American people, they agreed mutually to pretend that this agreement was only for three months and only out of necessity.

(*Note.*) In *The Reckoning*, Eden recognized without embarrassment, that Maisky, the Russian ambassador, had categorically reopened the question of zones of influence after the war—*therefore definitively*—in August 1943.

> After the War [Maisky told me], each of us will have a sphere of influence in Europe: the USSR in the east; the British and Americans in the west. [Eden replied that he agreed, (p. 408)]

In view of these proofs, who can have the effrontery to speak of "temporary spheres of influence for three motnths"? Especially when the same Maisky had harped on the question since October 1939, at the beginning of the war? And when Stalin was the faithful ally of Hitler? Who, but Churchill?

Let us now see what Churchill was coming to Moscow for in October 1944, after Rumania had already been occupied by Russian troops for

163

six weeks and the armistice—the capitulation of Rumania—had been signed on 12 September. He will tell us himself in his *War Memoirs*, Vol. VI p. 196:

I arrived in Moscow on the afternoon of 9th October [1944]. At 10 P.M. I had my first important interview in the Kremlin. Only Stalin, Molotov, Eden and Major Birse and Pavlov were present as interpreters.

After we had discussed and agreed to invite the Poles, as the moment was favourable for "business," I said: "Let us arrange our affairs in the Balkans. Regarding Britain and Russia, what would you say to 90% of Russian dominance in Rumania, while we would have 90% of the say in Greece and let us go 50–50 in Yugoslavia?"

While the proposition was being translated into Russian, I took a half-sheet of paper and wrote:

Roumania:
> Russia, 90%
> The rest, 10%

Greece:
> G. Britain, 90%
> (in agreement with USA)
> Russia, 10%

Yugoslavia, 50–50%
Hungary, 50–50%

Bulgaria:
> Russia, 75%
> The others, 25%

I pushed this paper across to Stalin, who, in the meantime, had heard the translation. A short pause followed. Then Stalin took his blue pencil and made a large tick—and gave me back the paper.

Everything was translated in less time than it would take one to sit down.

After that, a long pause followed. The paper lay in the centre of the table. At last I broke the silence and said: "Will it not seem cynical if it becomes known that we have settled the fate of millions of people in such an unusual manner. Come! Let us burn this paper." "No, you keep it," said Stalin.

Would the "scrap of paper" below be the historical document to which Winston Churchill referred?

I personally, looked for this document in the State Archives in London, and did not find it annexed to the "minutes" of the report of the conversations in Moscow in October 1944 among the prime minister's papers, nor among those of the foreign secretary (Anthony Eden).

It is very probable that the document was preserved as a historical relic among the personal papers of the prime minister. In any case the writing—as compared with other documents written, or annotated personally by Churchill—resembles it very closely. This document is shown also by Cyrus Sulzberger, in his book *Such a Peace.*

(Note.) This document—published by *Der Spiegel* and reproduced in the Rumanian newspaper *Stindardul,* confirmed also by Churchill's *Memoirs,* Vol. VI, p. 197, in which he speaks of the "tick"—the sign made by Stalin on the "scrap of paper" with a blue pencil. This "tick" would seem to have been the kind of OK, which can be seen on most of the papers referring to Rumania, and which look like a pipe. Did Stalin give his consent only with regard to Rumania, because the sign appears only on the figure referring to Rumania? This seems to be true, the more so because next day we find Eden and Molotov squabbling about the percentages fixed for the other countries.

That is Churchill's version, written *eight years later* and with the help of no less than seven historiographers, written six years after the end of the war when the Moscow agreement—regarding the Russian attitude—had to be presented in another light, i.e., when the mistakes had to be toned down, explained, denied.

Hence the discrepancy between Churchill's version of the Moscow talks and the minutes of the meetings—which I have seen and read and copied in their essential parts.

I consulted these minutes in the Liddell Hart Center for Military Archives in London. They are to be found in the dossier of General Lord Ismay, former chief of the General Staff, who accompanied Churchill to Moscow. They are numbered COS (44) 915 (0), and I have read copy number 2, entitled: *Anglo-Soviet Political Conversations at Moscow, October 9th–17th, 1944.* Let us see them:

On October 9 at 7 P.M., a preliminary discussion took place between Molotov and Eden about the general form of the discussion that was to follow between Churchill and Stalin—a matter of courtesy and current diplomatic procedure—so as to find out what subjects would be discussed. That is how the minutes begin.

The same evening, 9 October, at 10 P.M., the great discussion with Stalin began and where—according to the report that I have consulted—*was*

166

also present Sir Archibald Clark Kerr, British ambassador in Moscow and whom Churchill omitted to mention.

This fact is important, first of all because after eight years, his (Churchill's) memory could have deceived him, and secondly because Sir Clark Kerr knew already on 9 October about this agreement regarding Rumania and the zones of influence. and thirdly, the omission of the ambassador's name in the minutes was *intentional*, so as not to show him up in an unfavourable light in the face of his mission to Rumania in 1946, of which I will speak later. One thing is certain: all those historians—Churchill's collaborators—as well as later historians who were engaged on the problem, made no mention of certain errors of memory, either from uncertainty about dates, or from the deliberate omission of important phrases in the discussions, or because of their distortion in the following days when they were transmitted to Washington.

In other words, I suspect seriously that the *Memoirs* were "doctored" and underwent a cosmetic operation regarding that crucial interview between Stalin and Churchill. They were "touched up" to look historically better.*

THE TOP-SECRET MINUTES OF THE CHURCHILL AND STALIN MEETINGS IN THE KREMLIN

How did that meeting proceed? Churchill offered Stalin an autographed photo of himself. They then went on briefly to the problem of Poland. But now an essential juridical question was raised regarding Rumania. Churchill suggested that the frontiers in general and in Poland, in particular, should be specified in the *Armistice Convention and not in the Peace Treaty*. Why this subtlety? Because, explained Churchill, the armistice is a matter for the president of the United States alone, whereas the Peace Treaty has to be ratified by the Senate. It would therefore be easier for the Americans to solve the questions of frontiers and territories by the Armistice Convention than by treaties.

That was the procedure with Rumania, Bulgaria, Hungary, and Poland too. That explains why we speak of the "agreements" of Yalta or

---

*This cosmetic falsification of history was so flagrant in Churchill's Memoirs that even his faithful shadow, his friend and doctor, Lord Moran, wrote in his own memoirs: "I was astonished to see to what an extent the historian altered the facts. Had he really come to believe what he wanted to believe?"

167

of Helsinki and not of treaties. Agreements—Churchill was right—must not be subjected to debate in the American Senate, and so *they could not be*—eventually—rejected. They were not to be presented to the representatives of the American people who—in this way—had their mouths closed; they were confronted with a *fait accompli*.

The report of the meeting says that Churchill accepted the division of Poland (for whom Great Britain entered the war) as well as the Curzon Line and that he would uphold these at the Armistice Conference and hoped that the Americans would do the same.

The prime minister emphasized later in his conversation that there were two countries that preoccupied him. One was Greece. He was not too worried about Rumania. That was, in the first place, the *business of Russia*. He believed the Russian armistice terms to be reasonable. But Greece was another matter. Great Britain must be the chief power in the Mediterranean, and he hoped that Stalin would allow him to have the last word on Greece as he (Stalin) had in Rumania.

Stalin, admitting that the way to the Mediterranean was essential to Britain, said he agreed that Britain should have the first say in Greece.

Winston Churchill, knowing that his understanding with Stalin was contrary to the policy of the State Department and of the Congress of the United States and that this "agreement" would rouse the indignation of the American people and world public opinion, asked that *spheres of influence should not be spoken of*, but that *other diplomatic terms* should be "used" and gave the assurance that so long as he and Stalin agreed, he (Churchill) would be able to explain everything to the president.

After a general discussion about the Dumbarton Oaks Conference, the British prime minister returned to the question of the Balkans and the interest that their two governments had in each of those countries. It was agreed that they (Britain and the USA) had equal interest in Hungary and Yugoslavia while Russia had a predominant interest in Rumania and Great Britain in Greece.

Churchill emphasized that British interest in Bulgaria was greater than that in Rumania where "she (Britain) was a spectator," while in Bulgaria she wished to be active.

As was obvious, there was no talk of an agreement "of three months" but, openly, of *permanent spheres of influence*, which had to be presented in diplomatic terms—as we shall see.

At the same sitting of 9 October 1944, Churchill and Stalin spoke of Turkey, of the Dardanelles, of freedom for the Russians to go anywhere with their civil boats or warships.

168

Churchill begged Stalin to restrain the Italian and Greek Communists. Stalin replied that he had no influence over them. In that case, Churchill asked him not "to instigate them and not to provoke mobs."

Then they discussed the problem of Germany and of Japan and the meeting rose.

In the paraphrasing rendering of that meeting—for the British laws do not allow publication of the full text without special authorization—I am trying to be as faithfull as possible.

But I do believe that the "scrap of paper" of Churchill's *Memoirs* wasn't written on October 9 but October 11.

Why do I believe this? First, the minutes of the meetings do not mention the "scrap of paper." Churchill speaks of it only eight years later.

This makes me believe, definitively, that the ultimate fixing of spheres of influence took place, not on the night of 9 October in the Kremlin, but on 11 October at the British Embassy in Moscow after 1 A.M. after Churchill had had an interview with Stalin following the banquet given in his honour.

Why have I this doubt, this certainty? Very simply, because next day, on 10 October, Eden and Molotov—at their meeting at 7 P.M. as is clear in the minutes—haggled, like merchants of old carpets, about the percentages of influence in the other countries *outside Rumania and Greece*.

Readers will remember that on 9 October, Churchill asked for 50 percent in Hungary and 25 percent in Bulgaria. But next day, Molotov asked Eden for 75 percent in Hungary and 90 percent in Bulgaria. When Eden refused, Molotov proposed another formula: that Russia should have 75 percent in Hungary, Bulgaria, and Yugoslavia. When Eden refused that too, Molotov proposed 90 percent in Bulgaria and 50–50 in Yugoslavia. In turn, Eden proposed 25–75 in Hungary, 80–20 in Bulgaria, and 50–50 in Yugoslavia. It was a dreadful and disgusting barter.

The discussions of the Armenian carpet merchants ended without agreement, after Eden had declared that he understood Russia's interests in Bulgaria, but he would prefer to have a greater influence in Bulgaria than in Rumania.

As the bargaining of 10 October did not lead to any agreement between Eden and Molotov, it was continued next day, 11 October at 3 P.M. when Molotov asked Eden whether he would accept 80–20 for Hungary and Bulgaria and 50–50 in Yugoslavia. As Eden did not reply, or rather did not agree, they passed on to a discussion of the armistice treaties with Bulgaria and Hungary.

Therefore, if the *entire Balkan problem* had been settled between Stalin and Churchill on a scrap of paper on Oct. 9 as the prime minister affirmed—why did Eden and Molotov spend two consecutive days haggling about it?

They did this just because, apart from the spheres of influence in Rumania and Greece, the discussion remained vague and would have to be resumed by Eden and Molotov.

My point of view is—and it is strange that no historian has up to the present remarked it—that the agreement "on a scrap of paper" was made on 11 October in the interview at the British Embassy after midnight.

On these questions, we have also the *Memoirs* of Lord Moran in addition to the official reports of the Molotov-Eden talks. Lord Moran, on page 194, gives us an account of a discussion between Churchill and Eden—whom he calls Anthony and Winston—in which Eden says, on 10 October, that is, after his first interview with Stalin that Molotov does not want to give them even "a finger" in Bulgaria. But Lord Moran speaks on page 196, of the dinner given at the British Embassy, where the explanation is.

"Members of the British colony in Moscow were not invited to the banquet, but came after the meal, invited for 11 P.M., in order to greet their legendary hero, Churchill. As the banquet did not end until 12:45 midnight," writes Lord Moran, "Churchill—after having cast a glance at them—asked for a glass of champagne and, cigar in mouth, passed into an adjoining room to discuss with Stalin. This discussion lasted until 3 A.M., the members of the colony still waiting to greet 'their great leader.' "

It is certain that, on the orders of Churchill and Stalin, it was at that meeting, *which was not officially registered*, that the misunderstandings between Eden and Molotov about the percentages in the rest of the Balkans arose were settled. This is a little scrap of history, because the fact in itself—the exact day of the unfortunate agreement, one of Churchill's capital misdeeds, has no fundamental importance.

That this little slip was not retained by the historians who studied the Moscow Conference is—certainly—due to the fact that they took as gospel what Churchill wrote (and who could doubt anything he wrote?) as well as the fact that these documents were to have been kept secret for *fifty years*. But, accidentally or voluntarily, General Lord Ismay made them public before that time.

(*Note*.) The fate of Czechoslovakia was not discussed. (It does not

170

appear on the "scrap of paper" of Churchill. On which one of the most shameful pieces of history was written.) Why? Because Benes was in Moscow. He had signed a treaty of alliance with Stalin for twenty years. So Czechoslovakia had a "friendly" government, as well as a solidly Communist one.

Moreover and surely, Roosevelt had given his consent to leave Czechoslovakia in the Russian sphere of influence. Otherwise how could it be explained that the victorious armies of General Patton had been given orders to withdraw 130 kilometres from Prague and Czechoslovakia? In order to leave the glory of its "..iberation" to the Soviet troops and to respect their zone of influence.

CHURCHILL TOAST TO STALIN: "GOD BLESS YOU"

The conference in Moscow continued with the mutilation of Poland, the heroic country that was "close to Churchill's heart" and for which Britain went to war.

At the State dinner, Churchill finished his toast addressing himself to Stalin: "God bless you"! What a blunder: to end the banquet in the house of an atheist who had murdered priests, closed and burned churches, and forbidden religious practices by saying "God bless you"!

His personal physician, in his book *Winston Churchill*, believed as we too have every reason to believe, that on 9 October 1944, Churchill's senility and arteriosclerosis were well advanced.

God to bless Stalin the assassin, as Churchill himself called him in his speeches and articles, years before; Stalin, the murderer confessed that he had killed ten million *Kulaks* (peasants) in the thirties—his own countrymen! What had happened to Churchill's mind?

Dr. Moran tells us that Churchill was ill on 15 October in Moscow with a temperature of 101° F. The situation was so alarming that he sent an urgent message to Cairo to warn the two specialists Drs. Scadding and Puvertaft and to send an aeroplane with two nurses. Probably it was a question of high blood pressure and some heart trouble.

> So far as I can see [Lord Moran wrote in his diary] the affairs of the Prime Minister are prospering. Perhaps our affairs are improving or else Stalin has given him all he wants. In any case, Stalin is more friendly than ever. Only yesterday he assured Churchill that Russia does not wish to Communize the world as he is accused.

171

And, at the risk of repeating myself, I reproduce the reflections of Lord Moran in continuation:

> But do these assurances count with the Prime Minister? The trouble is that when an idea comes to him, he lets his imagination run away with him and does not bother to check his facts. In any case, Churchill makes his plans in the conviction that Stalin is a man of his word and honour. Of course there are moments when the Prime Minister discovers that he has received nothing from Stalin. In a way, he is going up a one-way street. They have got what they want by deceit; by flattery and by force [Churchill told him].
>
> With all that, Churchill wants only Stalin's friendship. I told him this morning that Russia will have a free hand after the war in the whole of Europe. He replied, as if he had not understood: "Oh! I don't think so."
>
> [And Lord Moran, to conclude]
>
> *It seems incredible, but for the moment "the Red Light"* (i.e., his obsession with Communism which is spreading like a cancer and will not let him sleep) *has gone out.*

But his personal physican is more categorical about Churchill's power of discernment in Moscow, when he writes on page 206:

> On his return from Moscow, the Prime Minister seems to realize that *he has received nothing from Stalin and that Poland has been left in the claws of Russia. He did not lose much time in returning to more realistic politics.*
>
> I have come to associate these sudden changes of judgment with his physical condition [concludes his personal physician].

So I repeat the question: was Churchill not already seriously ill when he went to Moscow in October 1944?

The doctor returned to the Moscow Conference in his diary once more in 1953 when Churchill was again prime minister and ill. In spite of his advanced arteriosclerosis, Churchill insisted on carrying on as prime minister and he explains why:

> I can do something which no one else can do with the Russians. That is my sole reason for sticking to this post of Prime Minister. But my head is no longer well. When I wake up in the morning I wish to do a thousand things. I can't any more. Perhaps I need a

tonic. But I can still correct the proofs of my *Memoirs*, for that needs no mental effort.

And, taking a typed page from his bedside table, Churchill handed it to me and said: "Read this."

We made an arrangement with Stalin during the war about spheres of influence, expressed in percentages—Rumania, Bulgaria, Greece and Turkey, etc. Here they are typed. Read the last paragraph. It seems too cynical, I said to Stalin, how we have disposed of the lives of millions of people in this way. Perhaps we should burn this paper? Oh no! said Stalin, you keep it.

We did so, Charlie, on the spot, and in a few minutes. *You see! Men in a leading position can do such things,* which others can not!

In 1953, Churchill no longer spoke of spheres of influence lasting *for three months only, but indefinitely*.

With this in view, Churchill had immediately set to work in Moscow and on 10 October—the day after he had given Rumania and Eastern Europe to the Russians—he sent, together with Stalin, a telegram to Roosevelt saying:

> We must consider the best way, the best solution for a common policy with regard to the Balkan countries, including Hungary and Turkey.

So far, not a word about the arrangement already made regarding these countries. Also next day, 11 October, Churchill sent another personal telegram to Roosevelt, in which he said:

> It is absolutely necessary, urgent, to try to reach a common solution to the Balkan problem, so as to avoid civil war in several of these countries in which probably you and I would sympathize with one part of them and Stalin with another.

Neither in this telegram did Churchill tell Roosevelt that he had *already come to an understanding with Stalin about these countries* on 9 October. Why? Because he knew that Roosevelt was ill, that his telegram would pass through several hands and that somehow, Roosevelt would understand him without too many words. The main thing was to hide the truth from the State Department, from Congress, and from the American people.

173

A day later—on 12 October 1944—Churchill telegraphed to Harry Hopkins, the *alter ego* of the president and did not mention, even to him, that the *Balkan situation had already been arranged by him and Stalin.* The telegram sounded as if nothing had been definitely settled; that they had had only a general discussion:

> The Russians claim complete responsibility in Rumania, but are disposed to lose interest in Greece. They show great interest in Hungary and claim, mistakenly, that she is their neighbour.
> We have so many bones to collect in the Balkans at this moment that I think it would be much better "to carry the matter further *a deux,*" i.e., to discuss and resolve the question of Balkan problems with Stalin, without the participation of Harriman.

When did Churchill tell the truth? In his *Memoirs*, in volume VI, on page 197, when he says that he settled all within a minute with Stalin, or now on October 12th when he does not mention any agreement to Harry Hopkins, but informs him about *what the Russians want?*

On 12 October, also from Moscow, Churchill sent a telegram to his colleagues in the government in which, with great ability, he says that he had come to an understanding with the Russians about spheres of influence, but that the question must be treated in the meantime "with gloves on."

> "The percentages indicated are not meant to show the number of members composing the different Commissions of the Balkan countries. They are rather to show the *interest and feeling* with which the British and Soviet Governments discuss the problems of those countries.
> "As is natural, Soviet Russia has vital interests round the Black Sea, one of which, Rumania, attacked her furiously with 26 divisions. The second, Bulgaria with which Russia has ancestral connections. Great Britain believes that it is right that special respect should be shown to those two countries, and to Russia's desire to control them, practically, *by leading and advising these countries in the common cause.*"

After having mentioned Greece and Yugoslavia, in point five, Churchill says to his Cabinet colleagues:

As it is the Soviety Army which will control Hungary, it is normal that a large share of the influence be given to them, with the reserve that Great Britain and *probably* the United States would regard Hungary as a Central European country and not one of the Balkan States.

Why this reserve with regard to Hungary? For the simple reason that Roosevelt considered that Hungary—he "loved the Hungarians"—should return to the West. That is why Churchill telegraphed to Hopkins that "the Russians show a great interest in Hungary" so as to prepare Roosevelt.

IN MOSCOW CHURCHILL DETHRONED FOUR KINGS: THE RUMANIAN, THE YUGOSLAV, THE GREEK, ALL RELATED TO HIS ROYAL FAMILY, AND THE ITALIAN

On 16 October—also in Moscow—Churchill "with humble duty" sent to the King of England a very devoted telegram, *but did not mention in it anything about the agreement on spheres of influence.*

This fact seems curious; unbelievable, when we consider the close relationship between the British Royal House and His Majesty King Michael I, of Rumania whom Churchill dethroned on 9 October 1944, in Moscow, after the former king had risked his life and shortened the war by six or eight months and perhaps even brought them (the British) victory. The same should be said of the kings of Greece and Yugoslavia, for whom Churchill had accepted a plebiscite. Certainly Churchill feared the reaction of the British Court on hearing the truth; for that reason he said nothing to his king about that so important agreement.

With the same preoccupation to hide the truth, to "wrap it in chocolate," "to arrange it cosmetically" for history, Churchill claims to have written a letter to Stalin on 11 October *with his true thoughts and feelings,* which he reproduced on page 198 of the same volume, but which he never sent.

But even in that letter—which I believe may have been written by the historians who helped him with his *Memoirs* in 1952/53, rather than on 11 October 1944—we find the wish to hide the truth from the world.

175

As I have said, it will be considered barbarian and even dishonest if they—the Agreements—were to be exposed to the eyes of the experts of the Foreign Ministries of the whole world. Therefore, *they cannot form the basis of a public document, still less at this moment.*

Why should they not become public "at this moment"—11 October 1944? Because Roosevelt was to hold elections on 4 November 1944, and the latter asked, as we shall see, that the spheres of influence—to which Congress and the American people were opposed—should on no account be spoken of.

Now let us see Roosevelt's reaction to the Moscow Conference and to the telegrams he received.

An extraordinary, unbelievable fact should be noted. President Roosevelt wished, before Churchill's departure for Moscow, to authorize him to stand proxy for him (Roosevelt) and to speak with Stalin in his name. As the historian, Arthur Schlessinger writes in *The Origin of the Cold War*, that Roosevelt, prepared a proxy telegram for Churchill and only at the last moment; this was stopped by Harry Hopkins who realized what the consequences would be.

How could the president of the greatest and most powerful country in the world, who had an ambassador—Averell Harriman—in Moscow; and a foreign minister, a vice-president, dream of delegating his exclusive duty to the American people who elected him to a foreign head of state?

Does not this fact alone show evidence of the Roosevelt's deteriorated state of health, just six months before his death?

Constitutionally, such a suggestion of proxy was an aberration and, on a political level, a mistake, a shame, and a humiliation. Harry Hopkins realized that. Instead, he asked Stalin to allow Harriman to be present as an "observer" at the meetings. The percentages had not been arranged at these meetings, but *en tête-à-tête*, Harriman being informed only next day.

Replying to their common telegram of 10 October, Roosevelt telegraphed that he was "most pleased" that Churchill and Stalin had come to an understanding. This was sent on 12 October 1944, i.e., three days after Harriman, his ambassador, had informed him—on 10 October—about the agreement on spheres of influence, as Eden had already informed him, using the expression "spheres of influence."

In this telegram, Roosevelt replied to Harriman—on 12 October—

> At the moment my interest in the Balkans is that practical measures should be taken to assure us that those countries will never again take part in an international war.

No comment!

Also, for home consumption, Roosevelt added in his message to Stalin on 8 October—one day before the arrival of Churchill—the following sentence:

> There is hardly any problem, either military or political in this World War, in which the United States is not interested.

Lord Halifax comments on this clause in the following way:

> Roosevelt must be extremely careful, especially in the weeks leading up to the Presidential Election, to forestall any indiscretion about the secret treaties connected with the explosive question of Eastern Europe.

The President himself says it, quite unashamedly, in a telegram to Churchill on 22 October 1944, about Poland:

> I am enchanted to hear of the progress made by you in Moscow on the question of Poland. When you have come to a solution, I wish to be consulted about the necessity to *postpone its publication for about two weeks*. You will understand.

The telegram was sent on 22 October. The elections were to take place on 4 November, in exactly two weeks. Also, Roosevelt did not wish to share in the search for a Polish solution—already found by Churchill and Stalin—but was only interested in its *publication* later.

The complete and unquestionable consent of Roosevelt to the division of Europe is without any doubt.

In January 1945, before leaving for Yalta, he said categorically for those who had ears to hear, addressing several senators who were worried about the fate of Europe:

> The Occupation Forces have the power in the zones they oc-

cupy, and each of them knows that no one will question this in any way. The Russians are dominant in Eastern Europe. It cannot even be conceived that we might quarrel about that. The only path we have to follow is to find out how best to ameliorate the situation.

Clear, precise, definitive! Without Congress; without the State Department; without the consent or knowledge of the American people who had entrusted him with their honour and destiny!

Roosevelt personally, as well as his supporters, took the view that as the Russians were in the Balkans, there was nothing to be done; they were "in possession" and could not be displaced.

I pointed out that Eisenhower had ordered General Patton to withdraw from Prague and not to occupy Czechoslovakia, because that country came under the Russians according to the agreement. Eisenhower did the same regarding Berlin. They withdrew, leaving the glory of occupying it to the Red Army. Therefore formulae to restrain Stalin existed and could be discussed if Roosevelt wanted that. Stalin withdrew from Iran, following an ultimatum from Truman later on.

I will stress that several of Roosevelt's counsellors proposed to him from the beginning of the war that on the conditions of delivery of material to Russia according to the Lend-Lease arrangement, political clauses should be attached in order to prevent unilateral occupation and Communization of the Balkans by the Russians. What an efficacious tool that would have been, had Roosevelt taken heed!

But in his advocation of Stalin, Roosevelt told Cardinal Spellman that Russia had absolutely everything. She "had achieved extraordinary things and she needed only a few trucks from the U.S.A." So Roosevelt didn't think he could use a lend-lease clause. However, in the toast raised on 11 October 1944, at the dinner given at the British Embassy in Moscow, Stalin spoke otherwise:

> If someone were to ask me whether we Allies could win without the help of the United States, I would reply *no*. Even if France had not capitulated, the Allies could never have won the War *without the help* of the United States.

Without the heavy American armaments, Russia would have been at the discretion of Hitler. How right were Roosevelt's advisers, his deputies, and senators who asked for political guarantees with regard to the Lend-Lease programme! But those were voices lost in the desert. They remained only for history in the State Archives. As well as those voicing the intervention of the senators, Styles Bridges and Harlan Bushfield—who recalled that for a thousand years Russia had been aiming at an outlet to "the warm sea" and that now was their moment—remained unheeded. Or the voice of Senator Burton Wheeler, who, on 14 January 1944, speaking of the danger of Russian territorial expansion, shouted prophetically:

> Sympathy for the Soviet Union has increased enormously in the last years, but if she will lay a hand on Poland, Finland, the Baltic and Balkan countries, the feelings of the public will change just as quickly.

Means were not lacking to exert pressure on the Russians to oblige them to retire behind their own frontiers. What was lacking was *the will to use these means*—among them the Lend-Lease, which would have been one of the most effective.

At the Moscow Conference, Peter the Great's Testament had become fact. Zones of influence so dear also to Tsar Alexander, had been reestablished in the Balkans. The Dardanelles were opened, and Soviet ships were reaching the "warm seas."

But by doing this, i.e., *by handing the Balkans to the Russians*, the British and Americans *lost the moral right to protest and to complain of Russian expansion. They legitimized it by secret agreements, which invited expansion and aggression later on.*

The Western forces, i.e., Britain and America, promoted Communism in the whole world, for they legitimized it and made it respectable.

That is why any revision of Western policies must begin by denouncing these agreements; by denouncing, courageously and firmly, the errors of Churchill and Roosevelt, which have brought us to the threshold of a third world war. Their physical incapabilities must come under the serious discussion and scrutiny of competent men, without embarrassment. However genial, politicians are men like all of us. The misfortune is that from that point of view, they cannot be put under observation, like any ordinary man. But their mistakes are more wide-reaching than ours and are paid for by the blood and tears of the innocent.

President Roosevelt was canonized in Moscow and with reason. But even he—as well as Churchill—should be reviewed. Both of them must be reappraised and their mistakes judged objectively, in order to be corrected.

Why should the two greatest democratic countries in the world—Britain and America—not have the civil courage to mount such a historical trial? The merits of both Churchill and Roosevelt remain intact, but their mistakes must be pointed out in discussion and debate by public opinion. That should be the procedure of a true democracy.

The Russians, in spite of their dictatorial, inquisitorial system and their theory of the infallibility of the Communist doctrine and party, had the courage to denounce Stalin for his mistakes and to exhume him and bury him more deeply.

OTHER GRAVE-DIGGERS OF THE EASTERN EUROPEAN COUNTRIES

Right through this book, I have affirmed that American official policy was opposed to spheres of influence and even Roosevelt, personally, was against them in public. But I wish to emphasize the baleful role played by three persons in the formulation of that policy. The first was the former War Secretary, Henry Stimson, who thought that the Russian demands were admissible for security reasons. Russia wanted a *cordon sanitaire*, in the inverse sense.

The second was Henry Wallace, also a cabinet member, who asked openly for spheres of influence for the Russians. This pro-Russian and pro-Communist, went so far in September 1946, when President Truman was struggling to correct the mistakes made by Roosevelt as to state publicly in Madison Square Garden in New York:

> For our part, we must recognize that we have no right to poke our noses into the political affairs of Eastern Europe, just as the Russians have no right to interfere in Latin America (the Monroe Doctrine), Western Europe or the United States. Whether we like it or not, the Russians will try to Communize their spheres of influence, just as we wish to democratize ours.

For his pro-Russian attitude and policy, Wallace was dismissed by Truman, in 1946.

The third person was George Kennan—at that time counsellor at the American Embassy in Moscow—who asked Roosevelt in 1944 for:

a clear and immediate recognition of the division of Europe into spheres of influence and a clear policy based on that division.

This baleful personage Kennan shapes American policy towards Russia for forty years. From the policy of "containment," he went on to the *unilateral* nuclear disarmament of his own country—the United States. Now a pensioner, he preaches it to-day in all the churches in Harlem, New York, or in parishes where the population is poor. He is preparing a Fifth Column for the final assault against this great and generous American people—a noble people who honoured him by appointing him ambassador in Moscow and other great capitals of Europe for forty years.

THE MORAL PRINCIPLES BETRAYED

We see, therefore, that the State Department and the bi-partisan committee of the Senate were against spheres of influence. Let us enumerate their arguments briefly:

Cordell Hull believed, rightly, that such spheres contained within the seeds of a third world war. That the security sought by the Russians could be better assured by a powerful international organization.

Any creation of spheres of influence weaken and reduce to zero all authority and possibility of action on the part of the United Nations who wished to create them. In the United Nations, the friendship of neighbours desired by the Russians was self-assured.

The creation of spheres of influence was immoral; contrary to the generous, sound, and humane ideals of the American people. They were in flagrant contradiction of the Atlantic Charter, of the Declaration of Human Rights of the Declaration of the Four Freedoms. In a word, the creation of zones of influence trampled on the whole ideal for which the American people forged a country, a democracy. It trampled on the ideal for which the American people fought in two world wars.

Even more! Cordell Hull was certain that the zones of influence would be used later by the Russians as a new platform from which to launch themselves into Western Europe.

How right he was.

* * *

181

The Russians denied that Churchill and Stalin made any deal in Moscow. . . . (*Soviet History 1960–63*, IVOVSS V.P. 134, Istorya Velikoi otechestvaunoi Voiny Sovetskogo Soyuza.)

In connection with Churchill's visit to Moscow, I wish to point out also a tragicomic situation. Among the top secret documents that I consulted in the State Archives, I found a telegram from Mr. Le Rougetel, political counsellor of the British mission, who suggests to the British government that Winston Churchill visit Rumania in Bucharest, i.e., to stop for a few hours in Bucharest after his visit to Moscow. He assured them that Churchill would be received as a true liberator, as a messiah.

The reply came that Churchill "had not time." And a good thing it was, for the Rumanian people would never have forgiven the tears of joy he would have shed, had the visit taken place. A grotesque situation was avoided.

ROOSEVELT'S EMISSARY AT WORK
TO FOOL THE AMERICAN PEOPLE

Roosevelt-Churchill's decision to hand over Eastern Europe to the Russians—already made by them in 1943—was confirmed—as if there were any need—also by the great American journalist, Walter Lippman.

This was one of the journalists closest to Roosevelt, the eye and ear of American public opinion. He helped the president to manoeuvre that opinion—and how skilfully! and to fashion his enthusiasm and decisions.

Walter Lippman—in 1943; in time of war and full censorship—advocated zones of influence in his articles and lectures. He could have done this only with the permission and knowledge of Roosevelt. I might even say: *placed by Roosevelt to prepare the Americans*.

Even more, Walter Lippman published a book, *U.S. War Aims* (Hamish Hamilton) in London, in 1944, in which—on page 48—we find the following:

> There are, of course, also small, but important States which are not included in the system of Atlantic security, which I named earlier. For example, Czechoslovakia, Poland, Finland, Rumania, Bulgaria, Yugoslavia, Hungary and Austria. The vital, strategic connection of these States is not bound to the maritime power of the Atlantic but to *the dry-land power of Russia*.
> Their independence can only be continued by a policy of good-

neighbourliness with Russia; for them to keep their independence and Russia to keep her own security.

And on page 52 of the same book, speaking of "regional State constellations," he says that "this is the shape of things to come," i.e., the way things will develop. He foresaw and advocated Yalta, in 1944, when he wrote:

Other regional combinations which are taking shape in the world the most important is that of which the Soviet Union is the nucleus. The frontiers of this nucleus—which I call the *Russian orbit*—are not clearly defined. But certainly they extend from Prague to Vladivostock; from Eastern Europe to Eastern Asia.

And in order to prepare the American people and world public opinion—Walter Lippman ends (a year before Yalta) with the following sentence:

Therefore it is natural that the Russians consider the whole region east of Germany as a separate system (from that of the Atlantic) of their own, for security.

I ask, with a sinking heart, whether the Eastern European diplomats abroad at that time, ever read Walter Lippman? Whether they understood and whether they informed their governments and the leaders of their countries? And if not, why?

Churchill thought it unnecessary to officially inform the French government about his arrangement with Stalin.

Nonetheless, twenty days later, on the occasion of his visit to Paris, he told General de Gaulle about the "scrap" of paper arrangement of the zones of influence in the Balkans.

"In Rumania," writes General de Gaulle, "Churchill told us that the Russians will have 90%, and we and others 10%. In Bulgaria the Russians will have 75%, and we 25%. In Greece, however, we will have 90%, and the Russians 10%. In Hungary, and Tchecoslovakia we shall split 50/50."

Thus, General de Gaulle knew about the Churchill-Stalin infamous arrangement and failed to protest, and failed to inform the Rumanians.

On the other hand, I will stress again that, from what General de

Gaulle wrote (page 62; Vol. III of his *Memoirs*) it is crystal clear that the percentage arrangement was final, and not temporary, for three months, as Churchill wrote later.

Two weeks later, on Nov. 24, 1944, General de Gaulle went to Moscow. During his conversations, he asked Stalin what fate he had in store for the Balkan states.

Stalin told him that Bulgaria could remain independent, but that she would get the deserved punishment, and that she (like Poland) had to become "democratic" (Communist). The same applied to Rumania. In Hungary, "if they will revert to a 'democratic' government, we shall help them fight the Germans."

No problem with Yugoslavia, which was "democratic." As far as Greece was concerned, the Russian troops did not enter the country, and it was left to the British. Thus, de Gaulle had to ask the British about the fate of Greece.

In that manner, Stalin confirmed to de Gaulle the October 9, 1944 Churchill-Stalin deal, in the Balkans. He knew therefore the fate of those countries, and he wrote on page 81, of the same volume:

"From this conversation it was clear that the Soviets were determined to treat after their own pleasure, will and interest, the occupied territories by their troops.

"Therefore we could expect from them a terrific political oppression in Central Europe and in the Balkans."

General de Gaulle, listening to Stalin, got this terrible impression, but failed to say one word of sympathy to Stalin, on behalf of those countries. No wonder Stalin took it for granted that General de Gaulle was in full agreement with him, Churchill, and Roosevelt.

NO. General de Gaulle did not protest to Stalin, nor did he inform the Rumanian king, the government, or the Rumanian political leaders. The little "sister," the Latin sister, was forgotten. This is all the more true when we know that General de Gaulle defended vigorously Poland and her government in London.

It is also true that General de Gaulle, not having been invited to Yalta, stated for the record the position of France, on his speech on the radio of February 5, 1945: "The independence of Poland, Tchecoslovakia, Austria and the Balkan states, is the condition that France judges to be essential for the peace."

But the fate of these countries was already sealed. General de Gaulle knew it, and he spoke only for the record of History.

What had General de Gaulle thought himself of Winston Churchill:

"Fools and cretins. Look at this rabble, *cette canaille*, cheering the old bandit."

This story is told by J.R. Tournoux, the de Gaulle biographer, in his book *Pétain and de Gaulle* (page 329) and referred to the visit paid by Churchill in October 1944, in Paris, when he was cheered by a million French people, on the Champs Elysées.

CHAPTER 22

Iuliu Maniu Begs Churchill
to Tell the Truth

Even if the Rumanian Opposition—Iuliu Maniu, Dinu Bratianu, and Titel Petrescu—were deceived during the war in their belief in an Anglo-American landing in the Balkans, they had no doubt at all about the real situation once the Russians were in their country. The Opposition knew the truth.

This was easy to understand. Because—though they formed part of the government, as members of the Democratic Bloc—the Communists, with the help of the Red Army, had set fire to the country, disorganized it, installed their own people, by force, in the town halls, police prefectures, and in all other key posts. All this at the height of the war against Hitler, while heroic, but unfortunate Rumanian armies fought for the Allied cause when the country was struggling to fulfil the difficult armistice conditions, or to be more exact, the unconditional surrender.

To Iuliu Maniu especially, everything was now clear. He had understood, though late, that Rumania had been given to Russia. That the latter wished to liquidate "bourgeois" Rumania and hand her to the Communists, under the rigorous control of Moscow, of course.

From a series of top secret documents, declassified after thirty years, we realize now that the Rumanian Iuliu Maniu supported by Dinu Bratianu and Titel Petrescu, struggled to force the British to tell him the truth, however, painful it might be: *"Has Rumania been given to the Russians? Have the Allies put her in the Russian sphere of influence?"*

As I write, I have before my eyes, and with a sinking heart, a top secret report, number 265486 of 2 November 1944 of Air Vice-Marshal Stevenson (head of the British Military Mission in Rumania) sent by him from Bucharest to London.

186

On four pages in ten paragraphs, the vice-marshall reports: That on 25 October 1944, Iuliu Maniu asked him urgently for an interview, but that he refused, so as not to compromise himself with the Russians, and advised him (Maniu) to approach the political counsellor, Mr. Le Rougetel. That, on 1 November, the vice-marshal received an urgently written message, through an emissary, a personal friend of Iuliu Maniu and who was also a member of the government, with the following content—in synopsis:

1. That Iuliu Maniu prefers to make contact directly with Vice-Marshal Stevenson, owing to the gravity and urgency of the subjects to be discussed.
2. That Iuliu Maniu has information that his assassination was being plotted at the meeting of his Party on 28 October 1944, but that he does not believe the Russians to be capable of such a political mistake, because his assassination would strengthen the National-Peasant Party even more. But in any case, that Maniu would reinforce the guard.
3. Iuliu Maniu—the report continues—is afraid of the annexation of Rumania by the Russians either by force or by the Rumanian Communist Party. He points out how, in Hungary, the Russians behave much better than in Rumania, purposely to convert the Hungarians to Communism. But—adds Iuliu Maniu—if Hungary should become Red, then there would be no possibility of avoiding the political—or perhaps even physical—annexation of Rumania to the Soviet Union.
4. In consequence—continues Iuliu Maniu—if Great Britain's intention is for Rumania to pass—lock, stock and barrel—under Soviet control, *he Iuliu Maniu, is ready to sacrifice himself and to prepare the Rumanian people for this tragic eventuality.*
   "By doing so we may avoid a massacre and a civil war, if this land is allowed to be prepared by the Communists."
5. But Iuliu Maniu adds—in that ultra-secret letter—that if Rumania was not given as a Russian sphere of influence by the British Government, then he—Iuliu Maniu —is ready to fight with all his strength against the Communization of his country.

At the same time, in that memorandum, Iuliu Maniu suggests that he, personally, should fly to London, while Mihalache and Niculescu

Buzesti should fly to Moscow in order to clarify the situation.

Vice-Marshal Stevenson reported to London that he had assured the emissary of Maniu that it was not a question of Russian control in Rumania and that he was not of the opinion that the suggested visits would serve any purpose.

When Vice-Marshal Stevenson's report reached London, together with the letter of Iuliu Maniu, it was first of all examined by the Ministry of War.

In the top-secret document number R17822 of 3 November 1944, we find the following stupefying comments:

—that Stevenson did well not to receive Maniu, but he should not even have received the emissary;

Let me quote, textually, from the astounding ultra-secret document, number R 17822 from the London Public Record Office. "Maniu seems to be nothing now but a drivelling old fool and I can quite sympathize with the Russians if they are trying to get rid of him by fair means or foul."

—that if Iuliu Maniu wishes to have another interview with the vice-marshall, the latter should refuse any demand for an interview.
—that, if Iuliu Maniu should see Mr. Le Rougetel, political counsellor, the latter should try to rid him of the idea that Rumania has been given to the Russians and that he—Maniu—should prepare the country to suffer under the Russian yoke.

After repeated refusals on the part of Vice-Marshal Stevenson to receive Maniu, the latter went to see the British political counsellor—Mr. Le Rougetel. The counsellor tells us of this interview in his ultra-secret telegram, number 230, dossier R19567.

The telegram begins by saying that he—Le Rougetel, had had a long interview with Iuliu Maniu in Bucharest on 27 November, and had found him depressed and "perplexed." He (Maniu) told him that the present situation could not continue because the Communists were now working openly against the government, of which they were a part. Iuliu Maniu could overthrow the government immediately, but he did not wish to do so because they were just waiting for some such provocation in order to liquidate him.

Iuliu Maniu—continues Le Rougetel's telegram—said that his situation is absolutely intolerable from a personal point of view. He had been a reliable partizan of Anglo-American cooperation. But that when he began to negotiate the armistice in Cairo, he did it on condition that the independence and sovereignty of Rumania would not be endangered.

Mr. Le Rougetel adds that Iuliu Maniu told him in the course of their conversation *that it is now* clear that in negotiating this armistice, he had been deceived and in turn, he had deceived millions of Rumanians who had looked on him as their leader.

In his telegram, the British counsellor adds that Iuliu Maniu spoke with impressive sincerity. That the actual situation in Rumania was extremely worrying and that the country's chances of remaining a sovereign state were very reduced.

In a second telegram, from Mr. Le Rougetel, and also ultra-secret, in number 247, of 1 December 1944, we see that, again, Iuliu Maniu comes to see him about what he had said, that, if the military and political circumstances demand it and if the British government wishes Rumania to enter the Soviet sphere of influence, he, Iuliu Maniu, could understand this only too well.

But he begs the British government—and would be extremely grateful to them—for a precise answer to this question.

CHURCHILL, PERSONALLY, REFUSES TO TELL RUMANIA THE TRUTH

Because of the extreme importance of Iuliu Maniu's demand and his insistence on having an urgent and precise reply to his question as to *whether Rumania had been given to the Russians as a sphere of influence, or not,* the telegram of Le Rougetel was transmitted at once to the prime minister of Great Britain—Winston Churchill.

Churchill, as we can see in the top-secret document number R1978–230/37, rejected Iuliu Maniu's request. Writing and signing it (W.S.C.)—saying, "SURELY WE ARE NOT CALLED UPON TO MAKE SUCH ADMISSIONS."

Churchill signed this reply on 2 December 1944, i.e., less than two months after the hand-over of Rumania by himself, personally, to Stalin in Moscow, on the evening of 9 October 1944, as we have seen.

I add, in this connection, that also in Moscow, on 16 October 1944,

189

Anthony Eden asked Molotov whether he was satisfied with the situation in Rumania, because he had heard that the Rumanian Communists were on the point of leaving the Democratic Bloc. Molotov replied that he was not satisfied by the way things were going in Rumania, because a leader of that Bloc, Iuliu Maniu *had not yet expressed himself in favour of the armistice.*

Also on 16 October 1944, as can be seen in the ultra-secret report of the Moscow discussions (p. 36), Anthony Eden asked Molotov what he thought of the former King Carol II of Rumania. Molotov replied that he had been of interest to the Russians only so long as the war lasted. Now he was of no further interest.

Above, I have presented a series of documents that will certainly weigh heavily in the history of the Eastern European countries. They show the Machiavelliansm, the insincerity, the perfidy, the cruelty and cynicism by which the Rumanian people were deceived, sacrificed, and betrayed.

That the fate of the Rumanian people and others was decided as early as in 1941, when the Russians demanded her from the British and if she had to be sacrificed for Britain's private interests, we could eventually have understood. It was a case of political myopia with the tragic and incalculable consequences that we now know.

What surprises me, however, is that the leader of the great, worthy, noble English race, who had always given precedence to honour and fairplay, did not—when he was asked a precise question such as life and death—tell the truth. On the contrary, he concealed the truth thus exposing both the leaders and the entire peoples to grievous suffering, misery and despair.

Part of all this could have been diminished or avoided by a different internal policy, *if the truth had been known.*

To hide such truth is a mortal sin, which can not easily be forgotten, or forgiven.

If Churchill had told the truth to Iuliu Maniu even as late as 2 December 1944, Rumanians might have been saved from savage and murderous repression and terror, as he—Iuliu Maniu—would have prepared the people by trying to save the intellectual substance of the country. He would have tried to put a more humane Communist—inevitable—regime in power, one with a more Rumanian conscience and soul.

CHAPTER 23

Tragic Illusions: Landing in the Balkans

Churchill's supporters pretended and still do, that he had wished to cut short the inroad of the Russians into the Balkans and, towards that end, had fought, unsuccessfully, for an Allied landing by the Turks in that region. That, because Churchill was a prisoner of Roosevelt who opposed this idea, he was therefore not guilty of the tragedy that followed.

It is true that an invasion of the Balkans was an elementary affair to be considered on the military level—not by a general, but even by a corporal. Knowing that the Balkan countries were ready to receive the Anglo-American and Turkish armies with open arms, it was obvious that they would welcome an Allied front in the Balkans. It was to have been a military move in which, unfortunately, Marshall Antonescu also believed as well as the Rumanian opposition, with Maniu at their head. So did all others in Eastern European countries. They clung to the belief in the good judgment and military logic involved, as well as to the policy that would have dictated such a movement. But they were all under a delusion and many of them paid with their lives, as Antonescu and Maniu of Rumania did.

But the historical truth is that if such an invasion had been discussed—even hypothetically—and was an idea very dear to Churchill, so as to rehabilitate him after disastrous Gallipoli, it was rejected from the outset, before the Teheran Conference in 1943. Moreover, as we shall see, this hypothesis was in no way concerned with the entry of troops into Rumania, at all.

What Churchill really wanted (however much the historians may have touched up the problem of a landing in the Balkans) was to replace the landing in the South of France (first called Anvil and then Dragoon) by a landing in the northern Adriatic, so as to enter then in Istria and Trieste and to advance by the valley of Liubliana—Zagreb to Vienna.

191

He had never advocated an advance into all of the Balkans, but only into Yugoslavia so that the English enter Vienna first. Thus, the German armies would have had their lines of communication cut off behind them while in view of the pressure from Eisenhower's troops in France, they could have forced the Germans in the Balkans to surrender or else be annihilated by them, by the Partisans, and by the Russians.

It therefore can be seen that even then, when he wished to "touch up" history and present it more favorably for his own good, Churchill did not go farther than Central Europe (Hungary and Austria), for his landing—and there was no mention of Rumania or of "cutting off the Russian advance into Europe."

Proof of my statements is furnished by Churchill himself on page 127 in Volume VI of his *War Memoirs*. These were written in 1952, with the aid of a group of historians and experts, i.e., six years after the talks at Fulton, four years after the Berlin Blockade, and two years after the beginning of the Korean War, therefore in full time of war—both hot and cold.

At that time, Churchill had every interest to show himself up as a visionary, a political prophet, who had wished to land in the Balkans and bar the way to the conquest of Europe by the Soviet hordes. He had every interest in pointing out that he was a victim of Roosevelt's refusal and that Roosevelt was guilty, and not he, himself.

But Churchill—in spite of every desire to stick to this argument, did not dare to do so. Why? He could not go so far. Therefore, he wrote the truth, which is otherwise:

> Another serious problem is pre-occupying me. I was very anxious that we should reach *certain parts of Central Europe before the Russians*. [Neither Rumania nor Bulgaria form part of Central Europe. Author's Note.]
>
> The Hungarians, for instance, expressed their intention to fight against the Russian advance, but that they would surrender to the British troops if they were to arrive in time. Therefore Alexander must take Trieste and occupy Istria and try to reach Vienna before the Russians [Vol. VI, p. 127].

But the military means did not exist for that operation either, which, in any case, did not refer to Rumania, which in 1943 had made desperate efforts to convince the Anglo-Americans to land, symbolically, two divisions in Rumania, so that they (the Rumanians) could withdraw from the German side and turn their arms against them. But Rumania was not on the road of the British Empire—like Yugoslavia, Greece, and Turkey—nor like Hungary and Austria in Central Europe. The fate of Rumania had been sealed on 8 March 1941, in so far as the British were concerned, when Maisky, the Russian ambassador in London, told Eden categorically that they wished to have military bases in this country.

On discussing his plan for a landing in Trieste and Istria with Roosevelt, he opposed it because he wanted all military efforts to be concentrated on Operation Overlord, i.e., the landing in Normandy, France. There were not enough troops, while the American military leaders did not wish to renounce the landing in the south of France, which had already been prepared.

Commenting on this refusal, Churchill wrote on page 56 in Volume VI of his *Memoirs*: "No one involved in those discussions had ever thought of moving armies into the Balkans; but Istria and Trieste were strategic and political positions."

Discussing, in a telegram, this matter, with Roosevelt, (the landing at Trieste and Istria), Churchill wrote:

> On military grounds—Stalin—might have been greatly interested in the eastward movements of Alexandre's army, WHICH WITHOUT ENTERING THE BALKANS, would profoundly affect all the forces there, and which, in conjunction with any attacks Stalin might make upon Rumania or with Rumania against Transylavia (Hungary) might produce the most far reaching results. On a long term political view he—Stalin—might prefer that the British and Americans should do their share in France in the very hard fighting that was to come, AND THAT EAST, MIDDLE AND SOUTHERN EUROPE SHOULD FALL NATURALLY INTO HIS CONTROL.

STALIN AT TEHERAN: "LEAVE TURKEY IN PEACE"

To make sure that "no one" wanted to move British, American, or Turkish armies into the Balkans, and as Churchill heard that Stalin suspected him of such thoughts, at the Teheran Conference, the prime minister went to see him *en tête à tête*, to appease him:

A mistaken idea had formed itself in Stalin's mind, that I wish to invade the Balkans intead of France. So it was my duty to disabuse his mind of the idea, and I went to see Stalin personally with this aim.

And to make sure that there should not be the least doubt about the invasion of the Balkans, Churchill returns again to this question, in the volume V, page 346, of his *War Memoirs*.

NO SUCH IDEA HAD EVER CROSSED MY MIND

"No such idea had ever crossed my mind."

In the opinion of many people, the idea of a landing in the Balkans was connected with the entry of the Turks into the war, along with the Allies. But this had never been seriously considered by Churchill. Eden told the Turkish prime minister that he was not interested in whomever entered the Balkans first but only in shortening the war. Stalin had negotiated the entry of Turkey into the war in November and December 1943, directly with the Turks, but no understanding had been reached.

When Churchill discussed the problem again in a telegram to Stalin on 11 July 1944, he only proposed the breaking off of relations between Turkey and Germany, but not Turkey's entry into the war, adding that Turkey could not do so *because no one would be able to equip her*.

Stalin replied on 15 July 1944, that it was better to leave Turkey in peace.

In these conditions, who could still speak of an intention on Churchill's part, to land in the Balkans? It was an illusion, a tragic illusion, which did much harm to Rumania, and all the peoples of Eastern European countries.

CHAPTER 24

The Yalta Conference

Yalta was more than a *crime*, it was a *mistake*, as Fouché would have said.

Contrary to an opinion, which has been rooted for almost three decades, the fate of Eastern Europe was little discussed at Yalta (except for Poland and—vaguely—Yugoslavia) and especially it was not decided there. The decisions were made before, as I have shown and tacitly accepted by the Big Three. The Rumanian problem was not discussed at all, still less decided.

Dozens of books have been written about Yalta. I do not intend to repeat already familiar questions. I will only recall that the president of the most powerful state in the world was forced to travel—ill and dying as he was—from 23 January until 4 February 1945, covering 16,000 kilometers, in order to reach the home of Stalin in the Crimea. Why? Because, out of different pretexts, neither Scotland, nor Rome, nor Egypt, nor Constantinople could become the venue—only the Soviet Union. It was a deliberate humiliation for America. The moment for the conference, which Stalin chose at his discretion, was decided to coincide with the victorious advance of the offensive that he had launched on 12 January 1945, on the Eastern Front. This coincided—curiously and unhappily—with the reverse suffered by Eisenhower's Army on the Western Front in the extraordinary battles of the Ardennes. So Stalin chose not only the place, but, also the favourable moment to hold talks.

So that the humiliation should be more complete, Stalin was not present, either at the arrival of Roosevelt or of Churchill. He came by train several hours after they had landed.

The guests were so lodged as to separate the American delegations from those from Britain, having the Russian delegation in the middle of them in order to separate, to isolate, them. The sixteen tons of caviar and fifty tons of Crimean champagne were distributed generously and equally between the two delegations. The Americans had 400 participants and the British, about the same.

Now let us make a short review of the events of 4 to 11 February 1945.

1. Sunday, the first day, a *tête-à-tête*—Stalin, Roosevelt. The general meeting from 5 P.M. was confined to a review of the military situation on both fronts. In the evening a great dinner was given by Roosevelt. He raised a toast to "the small nations," while Churchill toasted "the proletarians of the world."
2. Beginning on Monday, 5 February, three meetings were held daily, one military, one political (the three foreign ministers to lunch), and a general meeting of the Big Three in the afternoon. At this, Alger Hiss, member of the American Communist party, was always present in the American delegation.
3. Tuesday, 6 February, at the general meeting, the Russians accepted the Security Council, asked for three supplementary votes, and Poland was again discussed.
5. Thursday, 8 February: At 3:30 P.M. *tête-à-tête* took place between Stalin and Roosevelt in which—in half-an-hour, and in Churchill's absence—the entry of Russia into the war against Japan was decided and the price it would cost. Thirty minutes were sufficient to decide the fate of Asia and the future of mankind, as we shall see. An ultra-secret treaty—of which we shall speak—was to be prepared and signed. The seeds were sown for the war in Korea and in Vietnam and the fate of China—to be Communized—was assured.

   At lunch, the foreign ministers spoke of the withdrawal of troops from Iran, without reaching any agreement. The frontiers of Yugoslavia, the Control commission in Hungary and Bulgaria were also discussed. *Nothing was mentioned about Rumania. The State Department prepared special dossiers regarding the behaviour of the Russians on the Control Commission in Rumania, but no discussion took place.*

   None of the compiled dossiers (which had been entrusted to Alger Hiss) were opened or consulted by Roosevelt. He decided everything by sight or smell or by the notes that Harry

196

Hopkins or Alger Hiss sent to him He was already . . . moribund.

In the full session on Thursday, the discussion was resumed about the United Nations, with Poland, Greece, and Yugoslavia. Nothing about Rumania.

6. Friday, 9 February, Saturday, 10 February, and Sunday, 11 February, Rumania was never mentioned in any of he discussions, nor were spheres of influence.

The word 'Rumania' appeared only in the final communication, where it was said that the British raised the question of compensation for their oil installations. Nothing was debated. Only a note was made for the dossier.

Some claim that the fate of Rumania was connected with the Yalta Declaration concerning Europe. We shall return to this later. The declaration was nothing more than a screen, a mystification.

We shall return to this, but until then let us summarize the decisions taken, both in the public communication and in the protocols and secret treaties published by the Americans in 1955.

From this point of view, the present volume has no new declassified material regarding the Yalta Conference as such. Everything had been declassified long ago.

The Protocol, refers, as I have emphasized, to the *heads of governments*, not to their countries and the "agreements," not the treaties.

TO AVOID THE CONSTITUTIONAL CONTROL
BY THE AMERICAN CONGRESS

The juridical term "agreement" was used, instead of "treaties" as we have seen, in order to avoid the ratification by the American Senate of the arrangement made. Agreements made by governments are not required to be ratified, being "administrative" (governments). Treaties must be ratified by the Senate, according to the Constitution, then, made public, discussed, approved or disapproved.

In order to avoid such ratification (or even debate), the same procedure was used by the Helsinki Conference, later, under Kissinger's reign.

The same misleading procedure was used to avoid the control and censure by the American people of their foreign policy and other matters:

1. The United Nations Organization.
2. Declaration concerning liberated Europe.
3. The dismemberment of Germany.
4. Occupation zones and control commissions in Germany.
5. The question of reparations.
6. The fate of the great war criminals.
7. The Polish situation.

Numbers 7–14, respectively, concern Yugoslavia and her frontiers, Bulgaria-Yugoslav relations (friendship pact). About the claims of the Greeks against Bulgaria. About the question of withdrawal of Russian troops from Iran (postponed) and about the Straits Convention. Thus, the formation of a council of the three foreign ministers and lastly, we have an ultra-secret agreement made on 11 February between Roosevelt and Stalin, regarding the entry into the war against Japan, discovered only after the death of Roosevelt in his personal safe.

ROOSEVELT'S DELUSIONS OF 2 SEPTEMBER 1943 COME THROUGH AT YALTA IN FEBRUARY 1945

I will point out, in a separate chapter, the tragic mistakes made at Yalta by Roosevelt. Naturally, I will deal only with part of these—the more important ones—and I will examine in its entirety, the behaviour of Roosevelt before Yalta as well as during the tragic conference.

But before that, I think it will be interesting to see again how Roosevelt visualized in his morbid fantasies, and his political hallucinations, the post-war world.

For that, we must go back to the minutes and the written notes of Cardinal Spellman, as he took them, after spending the evening with President Roosevelt, on September 2, 1943, and allow the reader to see what Stalin and Russia got out of Roosevelt's generosity and poor judgment.

These are excerpts from those minutes, just as they appeared on pages 222, 223, and 224, from *Cardinal Spellman's Story*.

Collaboration of the "Big Four":

It is planned to make an agreement among the Big Four. Accordingly the world will be divided into spheres of influence: China gets the Far East; the U.S. the Pacific; *Britain and Russia, Europe and Africa. But as Britain has predominantly colonial interests it might be assumed that Russia will predominate in Europe.* Although Chiang Kai-shek will be called in on the great decisions concerning Europe, it is understood that he will have no influence on them. *The same thing might become true—although to a lesser degree—for the U.S.* He hoped, "*although it might be wishful* thinking," that the Russian intervention in Europe would not be too harsh. [Author's italics]

League of Nations:

The last one was no success, because the small states were allowed to intervene. The future League will consist only of the four big powers (U.S., Britain, Russia, China). The small states will have a consultative assembly, without right to decide or to vote. For example, at the armistice with Italy, the Greeks, Jugoslavs and French asked to be co-signers. "We simply turned them down." They have no right to sit in where the big ones are. Only the Russians were admitted, because they are big, strong and simply impose themselves.

Russia:

An interview with Stalin will be forced as soon as possible. He believes that he will be better fitted to come to an understanding with Stalin than Churchill. Churchill is too idealistic, he is a realist. So is Stalin. Therefore an understanding between them on a realistic basis is probable. The wish is, although it seems improbable, to get from Stalin a pledge not to extend Russian territory beyond a certain line. *He would certainly receive: Finland, the Baltic States, the Eastern half of Poland, Bessarabia.* There is no point to oppose these desires of Stalin, because he has the power to get them anyhow. So better give them gracefully.

Furthermore the population of Eastern Poland wants to become Russian. Still it is absolutely not sure whether Stalin will be satisfied with these boundaries. On the remark that Russia has appointed governments *of communistic character for Germany, Austria and other countries which can make a communist regime* there, so *that the Russians might not even need to come, he agreed that this is*

199

to be expected. Asked further, whether the Allies would not do something from their side which might offset this move in giving encouragement to the better elements, just as Russia encourages the *Communists, he declared that no such move was contemplated. It is therefore probable that Communist Regimes would expand, but what can we do about it. France might eventually* escape, if it has a government à la Leon Blum. The Front Populaire would be so advanced, that eventually the Communists might accept it. *On the direct question whether Austria, Hungary, and Croatia* would fall under some sort of Russian protectorate, *the answer was clearly yes.* But he added, we should not overlook the *magnificent economic achievements of Russia. Their finances are sound. It is natural that the European countries will have to undergo tremendous changes in order to adapt to Russia, but he hopes that in ten or twenty years the European influences would bring the Russians to become less barbarian.*

Be it as it may, he added, the U.S. and Britain cannot fight the Russians. The Russian production is so big that the American help, except for trucks, is negligible. He hopes that out of a forced friendship may soon come a real and lasting friendship. *The European people will simply have to endure the Russian domination, in the hope that in ten or twenty years they will be able to live well with the Russians.* Finally he hopes, the Russians will get 40% of the Capitalist regime, the capitalists will retain only 60% of their system, and so an understanding will be possible. This is the opinion of Litvinoff.

Hungary:

He likes the Hungarians. He wants them to come over. He would be ready to accept them on the Allied side as they are, if they come over.

Austria:

No plan for the Austrian Government in Exile is made or tolerated. *There will be no opposition to a Russian dominated Communist Austrian Regime.* The one thing that would save Austria from the Communists would be if Otto of Austria succeeded to gain that throne with the help of Hungary. But even then *he* would have to deal with the Russians.

Croatia:

He opposes the resurrection of Jugoslavia and favors an independent Croat and Slovene State. *Churchill is for the status quo ante.*

Germany:

Agreement has been reached between R[oosevelt] and Churchill, that Germany will be divided into several states. It will have no more central government, but will be under the domination of the Big Four, *mostly Russia.* There will be no peace treaty, but simply a decree of the Big Four. Before that hearings would be held, but these would have no influence. Germany would be divided into the following states: Bavaria, Rhineland, Saxony, Hesse, Prussia. Wurttemberg would become part of Bavaria, Saxony would take parts of Prussia. Hannover would become an independent state; *Germany would be disarmed for forty years.* No air force, no civilian aviation, no German would be authorized to learn flying.

Poland:

Poland, if re-established, would get Eastern Prussia.

Other Countries:

Plebiscites would be held in the following countries: France, Italy, Netherlands, Belgium, Norway, Greece. *No plebiscite is to be expected in Czecho-Slovakia.* [Author's italics]

I do not know what kind of fate Eastern Europe would have had, had Roosevelt survived the Yalta Conference. But I do know that the fate of Belgium, France, and the whole of Western Europe would have been different: Finlandization under the Russian protectorate as Roosevelt wanted it.

This impression is also confirmed by Anthony Eden: Here are some excerpts from his book: *The Eden Memoirs: The Reckoning*.

"It seemed to me that Roosevelt wanted to retain all the strings attached to the future of France, so that he could pull them as he pleased, and determine as he wished the fate of that country [Pages 374, 375].

"Roosevelt then told me how anxious he felt about the future of Belgium, expounding a project he had already mentioned to Oliver Lyttleton; his plan was the creation of a new state: 'Wallonie,' made up of the Wallone zones of Belgium; of Luxemburg; ALSACE-LORRAINE, AND PART OF NORTHERN FRANCE. [And Anthony Eden, himself one of the contrivers of the Iron Curtain, concludes on page 376] Although I greatly enjoyed those conversations, and the President's charm and wit, *I FELT PERPLEXED*.

"His opinions, academical and at the same time revolutionary, that he expounded thereon, were very alarming in their cheerful, utter lack of common sense.

"He brought up to my mind a conjurer who would nimbly play with dynamite balls, unaware of the danger [juggling with friendly and enemy countries alike]."

As we can see, the Roosevelt-Eden interviews took place in March 1943. Roosevelt was firmly entrenched in his opinions (see letter, Zabrousky and Weiss), at least since that time.

CHAPTER 25

"Yalta? I am Yalta," Replies Vishinsky

The Yalta Conference ended on 11 February 1945. In the meantime, the situation had worsened in Rumania: Communist assaults on the town halls, on the ministries. Backed up openly by the Russians, by the army, and by the NKVD, the Rumanian Communists hanged and shot, while at the same time, twenty Rumanian divisions were fighting for the Anglo-American-Russian cause in Hungary and Czechslovakia.

General Radescu, prime minister, sought intervention by the Americans and British to restrain the Rumanian Communist agitators, so that the country could remain quiet behind the front, and that she could support the army both materially and morally so that they could loyally fulfil their commitments to the Armistice Convention.

On 24 February 1945, General Radescu gave a courageous speech on the radio in which he accused "a handful of people without country and without God" of setting fire to the country. Those "without country and without God" replied by attacking their own Minister of Home Affairs with a shower of bullets, as they were doing all over the country and especially in Bucharest.

The prime minister was severely reprimanded by the chief of the Russian armistice commission, Vinogradov, for his radio speech. Next day, a Communist demonstration, backed up by tanks and lorries full of Russian soldiers, raged through the capital, demanding General Radescu's head.

Burton Berry, chief of the American Military Mission in Bucharest, together with the British chief, Le Rougetel, asked in vain for an interview with the head of the Soviet Mission. Truman, not knowing the agreement about spheres of influence, sent instructions to the American ambassador in Moscow—Averell Harriman—to inform Molotov that the United States expected the situation in Rumania to evolve in an orderly and legal manner. Truman demanded application of the Declaration of Liberated Europe of Yalta, and added that the situation in Rumania demanded urgent discussion by the Big Three. This note was presented to Molotov on 26 February 1945.

Churchill did not protest. In keeping with his usual cynicism, he explains why:

> We were embarrassed to protest, [he writes (on page 420 in *Triumph & Tragedy*)] because Eden and I—when we visited Moscow in October 1944—recognized that Russia must have "a largely predominant voice"—the last word—in Rumania and Bulgaria, while we should have the same right in Greece. *Stalin respected this Agreement most scrupulously.*

Molotov's reply to Harriman's note was immediate. On 27 February, Vishinsky landed at the airport in Bucharest and was received with all honours. From the airport—without even calling in at his own embassy, or making contact with the heads of the British or American missions—he went straight to the Royal Palace in the Calea Victoriei. Neither London nor Washington had been informed of this visit. In fact, there was no need because those capitals had given the Russians a free hand, through Churchill and Roosevelt.

The scene at the palace has been told and is well known. Calm, cold, brutal, and direct, Vishinsky demanded from King Michael an immediate change of government, which would be loyal to the Soviet Union, and handed him a list of people who ought to form that government.

King Michael replied calmly, in the presence of his foreign minister, that as Rumania was a constitutional monarchy, he must respect the country's constitution. He would consult his party leaders according to the country's laws, and of course the Soviet demands would be considered.

His Majesty wished to gain time in which he hoped to be able to consult London and Washington. Because not even His Highness knew of the Moscow agreements and even if he had known, he could not have acted otherwise.

Vishinsky left, asking the king to hurry.

The discussions began. At that time, both the Soviet and the Rumanian Communist press published venomous articles. Demonstrations with tanks and Russian lorries full of soldiers appeared in front of the palace to intimidate the king.

The chief of the American mission—Burton Berry—tried to see Vishinsky, but the latter refused to receive him.

Vishinsky returned to the palace, and was much more brutal this time. He told the king that he did not intend to wait much longer. When the foreign minister, who was also present at that second interview, spoke of the Declaration of Liberated Europe, according to historians Feis and Gaddis, Vishinsky replied: "Yalta? I am Yalta."

Then, looking at his watch, he gave the king an ultimatum of two hours and five minutes (according to James Byrne's version, p. 111) until 8 P.M. to change the government and presented once more the list of those people whom he wished to be elected. He slammed the door—both in reality and figuratively—cracking the paint on the palace door and breaking, in the same time, the column of democratic Rumania.

That was how the formation of the Groza government came about in Rumania and the resignation of General Radescu who took refuge at the British Mission, in Bucharest.

It was claimed that if Roosevelt had lived, things would have turned out differently; that the "Yalta agreements" would have been "respected" and that Roosevelt himself, on his death-bed realized the duplicity of Stalin. It is possible that in his last few hours, the president may have had a moment's lucidity and came to realize the immense tragedy of the errors committed. It is a human phenomenon to take stock—if one's brain permits—when death is approaching. It may be possible that he did this.

But I have found *nothing regarding Rumania* in that sense. The Groza government was installed by Vishinsky on 6 March 1945. Roosevelt died on 12 April. He knew what had happened in Rumania. *But he did not protest.*

The claims of Stettinius in his mediocre book—that Roosevelt had complained to Stalin—is completely contradicted by the facts. The telegram from Churchill to Roosevelt of 27 March 1945, in which he suggests that they make a joint complaint to Stalin refers, in reality, only to Poland. Churchill—although the Groza government had been installed on 6 March—does not mention the fact in his telegram of 27 March. He speaks of Poland because he found himself in a painful situation in Britain. In the House of Commons and in the government, everyone was accusing him of having dishonoured Britain and having sold Poland.

To that telegram Roosevelt replied that he had accepted a common intervention to Stalin. Churchill had advised him that the only remaining solution—that they should not both be accused of complicity in the Communization of Poland and of the Balkan countries—*is that they should have their own interpretation about the Yalta Declaration;* and to stick to it.

As the reader can see, everyone has his own version of the Declaration of Liberated Europe, a Stalin one, and a new one of Churchill.

The version of Churchill, proposed to Roosevelt, had to defend him from being accused of betrayal and surrender.

President Roosevelt had telegraphed to Stalin, but spoke only in vague, general terms, and he too, put the accent on Poland. The reply of Stalin arrived on 7 April 1945, just before Roosevelt's death and—as was natural—this also referred only to Poland. No mention of Rumania.

The American historian, Gaddis, in a chapter of *Security versus Self-determination*, p. 164, draws the following conclusion about President Roosevelt:

> The fact that Roosevelt did not wish to demand application of the Declaration for Liberated Europe, when only two weeks after Yalta, the Russians had installed their own Government in Rumania, was—undoubtedly—a precise indication to Moscow that he did not expect the respecting of the Yalta Declaration literally.

That declaration was (as another historian, William McNeill says in *America, England and Russia*, p. 559) in Stalin's eyes like an "inoffensive piece of rhetoric *destined for American home consumption.*" McNeill's conclusion is correct and agrees with Churchill's demands on the night of 11 October 1944, in Moscow, in which he suggested to the diplomats that they "enter the game" so as to "hide the truth," especially from the American people, and make them "swallow the pill more easily."

As I have said, after the death of Roosevelt, the new president, Truman, also asked for agreement with the Yalta Conference, as regarded Rumania and Bulgaria (before he knew the truth).

For him, the declaration was what it appeared to be:

The three Heads of Government (*not the three Heads of State*) must undertake to consult each other during periods of instability in liberated Europe, to assist the former Axis Satellites to solve their problems by democratic means.

To form temporary Governments until the free elections on a widely democratic base, so that eventually, in free elections, these people will be in a position to choose—alone and freely—democratic institutions according to their own wish.

For President Truman, the meaning of freedoms and of elections and the word 'democratic' were one and the same. For Stalin the declaration had another meaning, because being concerned with *Liberated Europe*, a terrible weapon had been placed in his hand, of which perhaps, the Anglo-Americans were unaware and did not realize that when it was drawn up; the seeds had already been sown in the Armistice Convention.

It is a question of Paragraph II (which comes before "largely-representative Governments" and "free elections") where it is stated:

The establishing of order in Europe and national economic reconstruction must be done in such a way as to allow the liberated peoples to destroy Nazism or Fascism to the last trace, etc.

In the absence of any precise definition, anyone in the new Russian Occupation Zone might be labelled as Nazi or Fascist, because this dangerous weapon had been put in their hands by both the British and Americans. After the handing over of Rumania to the Russians, the next step must be the liquidation of the Rumanian elite, towards the denationalization of the country in order to Communize and Russify her.

President Truman was not long in learning the truth. At the Potsdam Conference in July 1945, when he complained to Stalin of the failure to apply the Declaration of Yalta in Rumania, the latter replied:

"Any Government chosen in any one of those countries will be an anti-Soviet one, which is inadmissible" [Stettinius, *Roosevelt and the Russians*, p. 130; and Philip Mosely, *Face to Face with Russia*, p. 23.].

That is why Stalin demanded immediate recognition of the Groza government in Rumania by the Americans before holding any elections.

Also at Potsdam, on the evening of 16 July 1945, when Churchill was *en tête-à-tête* with Stalin, the latter reproached the British prime

207

minister for the American protests and for not having recognized the Groza government.

Stalin also said that he was pained by the American demand to change the Governments in Rumania and Bulgaria, *because he (Stalin) had not meddled in the affairs of Greece.*

When I asked him [continued Churchill, (p. 543, Vol. VII of the *Memoirs*] why the Soviet Government had decorated King Michael, he replied that the King had been decorated because he had behaved courageously and intelligently on the occasion of the *coup d'état.*

The result of the Potsdam Conference was nothing more than a policy of mystification, as we shall see later. A formula had to be found for face-saving, especially that of President Truman who undertook, personally, to recognize the Groza government.

The diplomats returned to their work.

CHAPTER 26

Roosevelt's Last Speech

Let us now see how Roosevelt presented the Yalta Conference to Congress and to the American people, before commenting on the decisions taken.

The president spoke before Congress only on 16 March 1945. Why so late? The conference had ended on 11 February 1945. Because he was seriously ill, though he had tried to assure the American people that he had not been ill in Yalta:

> I have come back from that long journey, [he said—after having excused himself that he could not stand on his feet] reinvigorated and inspired. I felt well all the time. I was not unwell for a single moment before returning to Washington. Here I heard that all kinds of gossip and criticism had been circulating in my absence. But the Roosevelts are not opposed to travels as you might suspect; they prosper and enjoy them.

Why did the president deem it necessary to make these remarks before his speech? The explanation is simple. He had been bitterly criticized because he had agreed to go to Yalta—Russian territory—instead of having chosen neutral territory.

He had been described in his absence as a tired, sick man *who ought not to have gone to meet Stalin*.

I have emphasized the state of Roosevelt's health in another chapter and do not intend to repeat this, but I must say that those who saw him at Yalta—Byrnes, Stettinius, Churchill, Admiral King, his doctor, Lord Moran, etc.,—considered him to be not only ill, but dying. What daring and what self-confidence in his health he must have had to deny the state of his health at Yalta!

As the spheres of influence given to Stalin in Eastern Europe had been already criticized in the U.S.A. the president continued his speech:

> There were moments of political confusion and agitation in those liberated countries, as in Greece, Poland or Yugoslavia and there may be even more. But worse than that: real conceptions of *spheres of influence* had begun to spring up in some of these countries, which were incompatible with the principles at the basis of international cooperation. If these had been allowed to evolve unheeded, they could have led to tragic consequences in the future.
>
> I believe that the Conference in the Crimea was a serious effort on the part of the three leading Nations to find a common basis for peace. *It must mean the end of unilateral actions exclusively on the part of the Allies and of spheres of influence and balance of power* and all the other expedients which have been tried for centuries and proved bankrupt.

The perfidy of this sick man in his efforts to deceive the American people at such a solemn moment, before Congress, is unbelievable.

Not only did he not admit to the American people that he had been involved in, and had agreed to these spheres of influence, he now condemned them as disastrous. Why did he do this? Because he knew that the American people were *opposed* to such spheres of influence. The State Department had been opposing them for *four years*, while Cordell Hull was in office, and Congress too was against them. With what ability he harped on the troubles in Poland, Greece, and Yugoslavia so as to justify the infamous agreement made in his name, as well in those of Churchill and Stalin, on 9 October 1944.

But Roosevelt did not mention anything about Rumania, Bulgaria, or Hungary. This speech was made on 16 March 1945, ten days after the Russian *coup d'état* made by Vishinsky in Bucharest, when they enthroned the Groza government by the power of Russian tanks. That did not prevent Roosevelt from congratulating the hypocritical "Declaration about Liberated Europe," nor from speaking about "democratic governments" and "free elections":

> The Three Great Powers had agreed that all political and economic problems in any country freed from the Nazis or in any of the Axis Satellites must be the common responsibility and competence of those Three Powers. They will work together during the period of instability and when hostilities have ended, to help the

peoples of any of the liberated countries or any of the *former Axis Satellite countries to resolve their own problems by truly democratic means*.

And President Roosevelt made this statement on 16 March 1945, ten days after Vishinsky's visit to Bucharest and *six months* after the so-called Allied Control Commission had been—on paper—constituted, knowing very well that the American representatives on it were being treated like servants by the Russian authorities, as truly subordinate to them.

Common control and responsibility? When the American representative in Rumania *was unable to make any direct contact with the Rumanian government, with the King, or with the leaders of the Opposition*? When for six months, the Americans had had to ask permission of the Russian officers to travel from Bucharest to Snagov, twenty kilometres away?

Roosevelt had been aware for six months of the humiliating situation of the American representatives in Bucharest. Why did he not protest? Because he agreed to it by his acceptance of the zones exclusively for Americans in Italy and Japan. Why did he not tell the truth to the American people?

But another fact of a much more grave nature was hidden from the American people: *the direct threat to the security and existence of the United States. A sin of omission.*

He said nothing of the secret agreement he had made with Stalin (and signed also by Churchill) in the question of the entry of Russia into the war against Japan, at a price. And this price *endangered the national defence of the United States*, as Cardinal Spellman said later in his *Memoirs*:

> Several months after the death of the President [writes the Cardinal, on page 248, as the details of the Yalta Agreements began to seep through], my old fears and doubts about the President were transformed into a true disillusionment.
>
> The height of this disillusionment about my formerly ideal President was when I heard that they had given away not only the south part of the Sakhalin Islands, *but also the Kurile Islands*.

This had reminded Spellman of an evening at the White House, after his return from Alaska, and it was a very painful memory:

Roosevelt had given me an account of the theatre of military operations in the Pacific and, showing me a map of the Pacific with the Kurile Islands, said, dramatically:

"Those Islands are like a fist directed at the heart of America. They must never fall into the hand of an enemy of ours."

And I realized with deep sorrow [said Spellman] that after Yalta, that *fist now belongs to our most dangerous enemy; and that our President is ill and incapable of realizing that it was he alone who handed it over.*

Cardinal Spellman realized long before Yalta, that his venerated president was ailing and incapacitated; mentally exhausted. He realized that at Yalta he had given their deadly enemy the means to murder his country.

But why did Spellman keep silent from 1945 until 1962, when he published his *Memoirs*?

In September 1943, when the mentally ill president had confessed his plan to yield up Europe to Stalin and to create zones of influence, the Cardinal kept silent. At least it was not a question of his country though of Christian, civilized Europe, which was to come under the heel of the pagans and barbarians.

But how could the prelate have kept silent when the sick president had given the Kurile Islands to Stalin? Should he not have denounced him from the pulpit of St. Patrick's Cathedral in New York? To ask the honest American people, guiltless of their president's deeds, to repair them? Why did he wait for seventeen years?

Certainly because he feared a coalition against him and the Catholic Church in the United States, all partisans and admirers of Roosevelt. I can understand, but I cannot approve. I realize that the powerful Democratic Party, together with the powerful Masonic organization—of whom Roosevelt and Harry Hopkins were leaders—would have opposed any revelation on the part of the Cardinal. But how could he—the servant of God, and of truth—keep quiet?

That is why I wrote in Nov. 1978 the following article in connection with the election of the new Polish Pope.

THE NEW POPE, JOHN PAUL II

The elections of a workman's son from the village of Wadowice near Cracow—Cardinal Karol Wojtyla—as the new Pope surprised and stupefied the whole world, from two motives: it was the first time for 455 years that the new Pope was not an Italian and the fact that he comes from behind the Iron Curtain, from Poland.

It is curious that neither the man in the street, nor political leaders, priests nor journalists protested against the qualification of "surprise" of this election, instead of affirming and justifying it as *natural; logical; imperative* and long awaited.

Why a "stupefying surprise"?

That the new Pope is not Italian?

But by the Church's *universal* vocation, by the Faith she propagates—without and beyond frontiers—she may and must elect any other national as Pope, if he has the necessary qualities; if he is "qualified."

The Italian papal monopoly was broken not by "manoeuvres" behind the scenes and electoral meanness, but *deliberately* and *courageously*.

Italian papal monopoly was justified in the past by tradition; by the enormous spiritual and religious authority of the Pope and of the *Vatican* and its influence throughout the whole world.

But things have changed. Papal authority has diminished gradually, gradually by its faults or weakness. The Catholic Church—as all other Churches—is passing through a crisis of Faith; of credibility and authority; which impose daring and urgent *new solutions*.

When 40 percent of the population of Italy (the country of Catholicism) vote for Karl Marx before the Altar of St. Peter; when a Pope can no longer go out into the streets of Rome without a division of tanks and an armoured car, for fear of the "Red Brigades," it was *natural, imperative* and *urgent* that the 111 Cardinals, representing the 750 million Catholics, to ask themselves, in the Sistine Chapel: "How long?" and "What is to be done?"

Searching among the fathers of the Church, they found among them a man qualified to be leader; to be Pope—Cardinal Wojtyla. Young and healthy; fifty-eight years old, which ensured a *long* and *certain* reign, especially after the tragic death of Pope John Paul I, about which all kinds of rumours had circulated, affirming he had been assassinated.

Wojtyla, a modest but worthy man, with a profound and pious faith; intellectually of broad culture, but also a pastor; a chief; an organizer.

Was his Polish origin an obstacle? An obstacle because he came from behind the Iron Curtain?

How could those 111 Cardinals presume to think in those terms? Poland is today a Catholic country where 95 percent of the inhabitants belong to that Church, in spite of all the persecutions (or perhaps just because of them). The Catholic Church is the most pious; most devoted; most united. She has—after thirty-two years of Russo-Marxist terror—26,000 priests, 30,000 monks and nuns, i.e., double the figures for 1939. In spite of all the prohibition to teach religion in schools, the Polish Catholic Church has today more than 20,000 "Parish Schools." The Churches are overflowing with *young people*. The Church plays a leading role in the everyday life of every Pole, in spite of the existence for thirty-two years of a Marxist regime.

What other country can boast of such a situation, either behind the Iron Curtain or especially in this decadent and unmindful Western World?

The Cold War of the Church, of Faith

With regrettable delay, the 111 Cardinals in the Sistine Chapel of Michelangelo realized that the Church was at war—a cold war, hard and continued—with the Marxist-Leninist ideology, which is attacking the foundations of Faith and of the Church with tanks, with money, with propaganda, riding on the horse of pan-Slav imperialism.

And they chose a new Pope from Poland, from millennary Catholic Poland, from the Poland of Jan Sobieski, the defender of Christianity, saviour of Europe by his defeat of the Turks at the gates of Vienna in 1683.

The Conclave chose as Pope a *Pole* who knows that his country was mutilated and bled in 1944, for the fourth time by insatiable Russia.

The Conclave chose as Pope the son of *a worker*, to show that not only the Communist régimes have the privilege of "social promotion" for workers and that, before God, we are equal and have equal chances free of hatred or class struggle.

The 111 Cardinals chose as Pope a *Polish* Cardinal who had witnessed the whole tragedy of the Catholic Church in Poland; who worked under the Primate—Cardinal Wyszynski—in his everyday struggle with the Communist Dictatorship and Russian pressure, helping him, not only to defend the Church, but to make her the *first* and *incontestable* power in the State—something which both the Communist régime and Moscow were obliged to take into account.

214

Indeed, while in Yugoslavia Cardinal Stepinac was condemned; while in Hungary Cardinal Mindtszenty (so ignobly received in Rome after his liberation) was expelled; Cardinal Wyszynski stood up with courage and dignity to the eleven Soviet divisions in Poland as well as to the entire Communist régime. Neither Moscow nor the Polish Communist Governors dared to touch him or the Church. There were infamous, unjust and cowardly persecutions, but the Church ended by being strengthened and the Polish people—like a wall of faith and national determination—stood, as one believer and one patriot behind *the true* leader of Poland—the Primate, Cardinal Wyszynski.

His right hand; his spiritual son; his successor, Karol Wojtyla was by his side, in the front line, in the first trench.

The choice of Cardinal Wojtyla was the indirect choice, as Pope, of the Cardinal Primate Wyszynski—who, at the age of seventy-eight, was no longer able to become a "Candidate."

The choice of Cardinal Wojtyla was a homage to his chief, a homage to the firm, worthy, Catholic Polish people as well as an indirect, but categorical homage to the "Silent Church" behind the Iron Curtain.

"Homages" are pleasant, but they do not win wars. Something *else* is necessary; a *new man* is necessary—who is imaginative, spectacular and courageous.

THE BETRAYAL OF CHRISTIANITY AT YALTA

As I have written innumerable times, at the betrayal at Yalta in 1945, the sale of half of Europe was arranged promised and prepared by Roosevelt as far back as February 1943.

It was on 2 September 1943 when, in an interview of two hours in the White House, Roosevelt said to Cardinal Spellman (I quote from page 223 of his *Memoirs*):

> He intends to form an agreement between the Four Great Powers. *In consequence*, the planet would be *divided into spheres of influence*: China would have the Far East; U.S.A. the Pacific; England and Russia, Europe and Africa. But as Great Britain's primary interests are in the colonies, *it is to be presumed that the Russians will dominate Europe*. But the President "hopes"—that, although all this could only be "wishful thinking"—the behaviour of the Russians in Europe would not be too harsh.

215

What did this eminent Cardinal do in the face of these hallucinatory decisions of his President? What did this Catholic Cardinal do when he heard that the whole of Catholic Europe would be handed over to the Muscovite barbarians? Nothing, or even worse, he sent a letter of thanks to Roosevelt for the dinner. . . .

But should this Cardinal—who was human, faithful and a *convinced anti-Communist*—have remained with folded arms when the entire Catholic Church was threatened with extinction as in the days of Attila or of Genghis Khan?

Ought he not to have *informed the Pope* and the *whole world* of the assassination of Europe and of Christianity, which was being prepared in the White House? Ought he not to have denounced to the American people the crazy project of their president?

> The peoples of the whole of Europe will have, without doubt, to *endure Russian domination*, in the hope that in ten or twenty years, they will become accommodated to the Russians [said Roosevelt to Cardinal Spellman].

The Cardinal said, when there was a question of dividing Poland:

> "But your decision cannot transform Poland into Russian territory without deporting the Polish people. It is immoral to uproot the population like that, depriving them of home, church and cemetery" [page 246].

This was well-spoken on the part of the Cardinal.

But what did he do to defend his Church? Did he take the whip—like Jesus—to drive Roosevelt from the White House, or call the American people—that generous and honest nation—who were in no way responsible for the tragedy that was being prepared—to fight for the defence of Christianity (to mention only that side of the affair)? No.

Neither he, nor the Pope in Rome, nor the Cardinals did anything. The Catholic Church kept silence. The Russians invaded Europe, profaned the churches, imprisoned her servants, pillaged and are still pillaging. The spheres of influence permit them to do so, while the Catholic Church, with all her immense power, did not try to defend herself; the war of the Russian hordes against the Church of Christ is on the point of being won by them. Someone—a new Pope—must cry: *Enough!*

A CHALLENGE FROM THE KREMLIN?

In writing the above, I do not wish to underestimate in any way, the suffering and dignity of so many Catholic and Orthodox priests. In the ten Communist prisons through which I passed, I got to know them; their courage and sacrifice—especially of the Catholic priests who were more closely united than the Orthodox. I wish, however, to emphasize that the *Vatican, and the Head of the Catholic Church—the Pope*—did not do their duty. Diplomatically, they denounced Marxism and Communist totalitarianism, *but did not denounce the Yalta Agreement from the pulpit, from the Altar*, from the balcony of St. Peter's in Rome or through the intermediary of all the Catholic priests in the world. This betrayal ought, first of all, to have been denounced to the American people; this betrayal of Christendom at Yalta. The American people who were unaware of it, would *not have tolerated it*, and would have *forced* the government to *denounce* this agreement. Instead of a policy of offensive against the *causes of the betrayal* of Christendom at Yalta, the Vatican played an active part in the betrayal of Europe at Helsinki, by signing—they too—the consecration of the criminal spheres of influence.

In the face of this weak policy of "détente," by which the Catholic Church lost, without gaining anything, it was natural for the 111 Cardinals to ask the question: how long?

The "liberalization" of the churches behind the Iron Curtain was not the result of a policy of force by the Vatican, but the merit of the faithful of the "Church of Silence," which *forced*—by their unshaking Faith—a policy of liberalization, which suited the Communist government that needed calm. Who intervened—and how—to defend their faith? Their own families, in their own countries, on their own earth?

Who came to the aid of Rumanian Prince Stephen the Great—defender of Christendom against the Turks? Nobody. The pope sent some money, which was stolen by the King of Hungary. Rumanian Mircea the Old? Rumanian Michael the Brave? They struggled alone and died alone, like so many heroes of the Rumanian Nation. Did anyone come to the aid of Rumanian Prince Constantin Brancoveanu?

How actual is one of the books of our great Rumanian writer, Vintila Horia, regarding the tragedy of our rulers, defenders of Christianity, and regarding the indifference of Rome and the West in the face of the religious and material genocide of the Rumanian people! Could it surprise

217

anyone that, on his death-bed, Stephen the Great left, as a political testament to his son, Bogdan, the advice to come to terms with the Turks?

A NEW POPE—A NEW POLICY

Here is the reason why Catholics, Orthodox, the whole Christian world—even the Jews—look with hope towards the new Pope.

Knowing, by the experience of his own body and soul, how Communism works, the new Pope will not let himself be deceived by words; by "slogans" like "*détente*," or any other foolishness. He knows that the only way to talk to the Russians is by holding a whip in one's hands—from a position of strength. When you dine with the devil you need a *long* spoon—says a Rumanian and Polish proverb. The new Pope knows this.

He knows that the Church is in crisis—a mortal crisis; that the only hope is a *new* policy to mobilize the whole of Christendom in the face of the expansionist, anti-Christian imperialism of Moscow. He knows that simply by his election all the peoples behind the Iron Curtain—even the Orthodox believers in Russia—were electrified; overwhelmed, like the saints on icons who received the stigma. The faithful behind the Iron Curtain hope for freedom, for a better life. They hope and believe in the new Pope.

With the new Pope's intention for reform and to fight for more social justice in the West, we await his leadership in a moral crusade to free the countries behind the Iron Curtain. The new Pope must take the initiative for an active, offensive policy, on all fronts, to liberate the believing Catholics, Orthodox, etc., from the Russian tyranny. With patience and perseverance, with courage and ability, a new Crusade for Christendom must be started and ably conducted. The Church is the best ally—the most effective (the existence of the Rumanian nation has proved this)—in winning back the national independence, the liberty of the enslaved peoples of Yalta.

Priests, with the Cross at their head
For the Army are Christians!

218

CHAPTER 27

The British and American Diplomats Lie to the Rumanian People

The foreign ministers of the Three Great Powers had met in Moscow on 16 December 1945 to discuss—among other things—the problem of the "recognition" of the Groza government in Rumania by the Anglo-Americans. Ernest Bevin was present instead of Anthony Eden; and James Byrnes instead of Stettinius for the United States.

What was the need to recognize the Groza government in Rumania? Why had Britain and America not recognized it until then?

Because, as we have seen, it had been imposed by an ultimatum of two hours by Vishinsky. Therefore, it did not represent anything in Rumania from a political point of view, being nothing more than a crypto-Communist improvization, reduced to a small minority. Therefore, it did not implement the conditions demanded at Yalta—concerning liberated Europe—in order to be recognized. As we have seen, on 21 August 1945, the King of Rumania asked Russia, Britain, and America to advise and help him to form a really representative and democratic government, in order to conform to the Declaration of Yalta, so that it could be valid and recognized by all Three.

In the meantime, the king had asked the Groza government to resign. As they did not wish to do so, they remained, without the king's signature and without collaboration between them and the king, until January 1946.

For the Rumanians, a declaration made by President Truman on the Voice of America radio on 18 August 1945, brought new hope:

At Yalta [he said] it was decided that the three Governments would, in common, assume the reestablishment of really democratic

Governments in all the Satellite countries of Europe. The principle was reaffirmed at Potsdam regarding Rumania, Bulgaria and Hungary. *These nations will never fall under spheres of influence of any country.*

On the basis of this declaration (too good to be true), a distinguished and subtle Rumanian diplomat—Savel Radulescu—who had become the King's Counsellor after 23 August 1944—conceived the idea of consultation with the Big Three in the hope of getting rid of the government forced on them by Vishinsky. He advised the King to ask for the Groza government to be dismissed, to refuse to accept the decrees of a government of usurpers, and to ask for the co-operation of the Big Three to get out of the constitutional impasse. (Savel Radulescu—as well as many other great Rumanians—paid with his life for his courage and patriotism.)

The situation in Rumania had been put under discussion in Moscow at the meeting of the Big Three Foreign Ministers in December 1945 where they decided to send Sir Archibald Kerr and Averell Harriman and Vishinsky to "mediate and arrange things."

What had they to "arrange"?

> To broaden the Government by the participation of two Ministers representing the two historical Parties: the National Peasant and Liberal; to guarantee free elections and the elementary constitutional freedom of man. And of course to do this by a common action of the three great powers, [and not by Russia alone].

As I write, I have before my eyes, the report made on 25 January 1946 by Sir Clark Kerr, to his foreign minister, Ernest Bevin, about his mission to Bucharest.

It is marked "Ultra Secret" and is numbered R1880/92/37. It was declassified after thirty years. It consists of seven pages and deserves to be translated in its entirety, but British law obliges me to paraphrase it. So I will sum up the essential parts:

The Allied Commission, which was to advise His Majesty to convince the Rumanian Opposition to enlarge the Government in Bucharest—composed of Sir Archibald Kerr; Averell Harriman, American ambassador in Moscow, and Andrei Vishinsky—set out from Moscow by train and arrived three days later in Bucharest. They did not see Vishinsky until they arrived close to Rumania when they made their plan of action together. Vishinsky was to see Prime Minister Groza and the

220

government first, while the British and American ambassadors were to see the leaders of the Opposition, i.e., Maniu and Bratianu.

The report continues that on 1 January 1946, the three were received in audience by the king to whom they said that they wished unanimously to get out of the impasse and reach a solution quickly to permit Britain and America to recognize that government. Ambassadors Kerr and Harriman emphasized the importance that their governments attached to the holding of really free elections, and that in Rumania fundamental rights and liberties would be respected. In turn, Vishinsky too emphasized the need to hold free elections.

They told the king that the first condition must be the inclusion in the government of two representatives from the Opposition—one from the Peasant Party and the other Liberal. Then, an assurance from the Groza government that they would hold free elections and respect the fundamental freedoms; the recognition of the Groza Government by Great Britain and America would follow.

His Majesty the King promised to listen to the advice given, as he had listened to the decisions taken at Yalta and Potsdam. He added that he would wish that the government, thus formed, should be provisional, only until the elections and that it should include some neutral ministers in some of the departments.

The three ambassadors replied that they had no mandate for anything like that.

After the audience, all three went for an interview with the Groza government where the two ambassadors emphasized, once more, the importance attached by the British and American governments to really free elections. The prime minister—in spite of frequent interruptions by Vishinsky, who did not seem to have much faith in Groza—promised, in the end, to prepare a list of obligations, which they would undertake.

Sir Archibald Kerr, in point eight of his report, emphasizes that he had had plenty of time at that meeting to observe the prime minister and so *he had come to the conclusion that he (Groza) would do absolutely nothing apart from what the Russians would allow.*

Next day, he went to see Maniu and Bratianu, the leaders of the opposition. He found them both deeply worried and suspicious of the actual government and of the Russians, and sceptical, without any faith in the proposed solution.

The British ambassador tells how he used with them every kind of argument—from hot to cold; from flattery to severity—telling them that it was their last chance to receive help.

221

Both Iuliu Maniu and Bratianu insisted that everything possible must be done to save the Throne and that the elections must be absolutely free. If this could not be done, they said that the new Parliament installed by falsified elections, would suggest military annexation to the Soviet Union and would ask for Rumania to be incorporated into Russia as the seventeenth Soviet Republic.

Sir Archibald Kerr replied that they could count on the British and American governments to press the Groza government to respect their promise to hold free elections.

But the British ambassador reports that he realized *that he had not convinced either the government nor the opposition any more than he had been convinced by what they had said to him* (point 10 in the report).

Further, Sir Archibald Kerr describes how he had gone to see Mihalache, who had made an excellent impression on him, and who said he did not want to enter the government. And how the ambassador was obliged to use "cajolement" and "dragooning" alternately, in order to convince him. *Two methods*, added the ambassador, *which were repugnant to him*.

Let us examine further this ultra-secret document, today declassified.

Prime Minister Groza rejected both Mihalache and Bratianu, who had been proposed by their respective parties, without any explanation. As the two ambassadors insisted, however, next day, the 4 January, Groza told them that Mihalache had been a volunteer on the Russian Front while Bratianu was a "reactionary." On that occasion, Vishinsky said that his government was categorically opposed to the entry of those two men into the government.

Again there were interviews with Maniu and Bratianu. The former furnished a list of sixteen names while the latter put forward four, from whom they could choose whom they pleased to enter the new government. They saw Vishinsky again and in the end it was agreed to recommend Hatieganu and Romniceanu. This was done. A lunch followed in Castle Peles in Sinaia, after which Vishinsky left for Sofia while Sir Archibald Kerr and Averell Harriman returned to the capital.

In Bucharest, the two ambassadors saw Groza again and discussed in detail the list of "guarantees" furnished by the latter. This was annexed to the report. They saw Groza again next day.

Sir Archibald Kerr recognizes that he parted from the prime minister knowing that he had been unable to move him or to convince him. But with an extraordinary candour and subtlety of style, he recognized *that*

Groza did not make the slightest effort to leave the impression that he had been convinced, leaving it to be clearly understood that he—Groza—knew only too well that he neither expected them to believe him nor that he would hold to the promises he had given.

The ambassadors expected that Groza would put all the spokes in their wheel, which the Russians demanded and without any embarrassment.

It is a sad matter but he does not see what more he can do. (It is obvious that the ambassador is a realist and very humane.)

Indisputably Groza was a crafty go-between. He was a madman, but likeable. He can be forgiven for the fact that he danced only to the music of Vishinsky, for he was not clever himself. But Tatatescu his foreign minister was "sharper and a liar from head to foot," said Sir Archibald. He was intelligent but not so intelligent as to deceive Sir Archibald when he was lying impudently.

This report, of extraordinary historical sincerity, relieves Sir Archibald Kerr of a part of responsibility, which he personally did not have as he was simply carrying out orders received.

The conclusion of the report is expressed in paragraphs 28 and 29 as:

His personal conviction was that the Groza government had not the slightest intention of respecting either the letter or the spirit of the decisions—to hold free elections—which had been made by the three foreign ministers in Moscow; that the Rumanians had not the slightest doubt—like Sir Archibald—that the elections would be falsified.

Before ending his long report, the British ambassador emphasizes that—with all Vishinsky's efforts to appear sincere—for him it was clear that *Vishinsky was controlling Rumania as if it were a province of the Soviet Union and that the Groza government was only his instrument.*

Therefore, writes this humane man, he left Bucharest with infinite sadness and with deep thankfulness that he had not been born Rumanian.

That is a document of exceptional gravity and sincerity, which does honour to its author.

As can be seen from the Kerr report, the Three went to Bucharest and talked with the King, with members of the government, and with the leaders of the Opposition. Things were "arranged," patched up, but no one was convinced, or hoodwinked.

What is to be retained from this report? The cynicism of the am-

223

bassadors? Their duplicity? The Machiavellianism and egoism? All to-gether and that is not enough.

Sir Archibald was a very distinguished man and very well informed. Ambassador in Moscow, he was present on 9 October 1944 when his chief, Winston Churchill, ceded 90 percent of Rumania to the Russians in his interview with Stalin. He was with the British prime minister both at Yalta and Potsdam. He knew very well that his role in Bucharest was to hide the truth, to lie to the Rumanian people, and to patch up the situation enough to permit recognition of the Groza government and to close the "Rumanian dossier." He did not doubt for a moment that that was his mission, which—besides—he fulfilled very well, for he was an honest man who did not at all enjoy the role he had to play.

For his sincerity in saying in his last sentence that he "thanked God he had not been born a Rumanian," he is likeable. He knew that Groza was dishonest, that he would not stick to his word; that Tatarescu was a cheat, that the elections would be falsified, that not one of the provisions made would be respected by the government, that Groza would not get out of the clutches of Vishinsky who operated in Rumania as if it were a Soviet province. He knew all that—even before going to Bucharest. In spite of all this, he forced the king's hand by flattery and threats, and Maniu and Bratianu to accept "a constitutional patchwork," i.e., to oblige them to dig their own graves alongside the wide grave of the entire Rumanian people. He knew it all before going to Bucharest. But, as he had been charged *with that mission, he fulfilled it*, but with regret, with repugnance, with sadness.

But here I must note the grave responsibility of the British govern-ment in the misfortune that has befallen the Rumanian people. Churchill and Eden promised—and gave us—to the Russians. Their successors, in turn—Clement Attlee and Ernest Bevin—lied to the Rumanian people about the spheres of influence. This was a great sin. Iuliu Maniu, Bratianu, His Majesty the King, asked to be told the truth, so that they should know how to proceed. They had all been consciously lied to, both by Churchill and Attlee. By those lies, the Rumanian nation has been tortured, ter-rorized, and decimated. What could Iuliu Maniu and Bratianu have done had they known the truth?

Certainly they could have prepared the country and thus reduced the suffering by a realist policy of resignation, but not one of "resistance," which with all its heroism and noble-mindedness, would have been a policy of collective national suicide.

I must say the same of Averell Harriman, American ambassador to Moscow. He too was aware of all of Churchill's arrangements with Stalin, in ceding Rumania on 9 October 1944, being Roosevelt's "observer" there, and kept informed daily by Eden. He was present also at Teheran and Yalta with Roosevelt, and with Truman at Potsdam. He knew the reality behind his mission to Rumania. He knew that the elections would be falsified, that the promises would not be kept.

But Harriman had a new president—Harry Truman—who did not wish to recognize the brigandish agreement in Moscow between Stalin and Churchill. Harriman's report could weigh more heavily and have different consequences than that of Ambassador Kerr. Averell Harriman knew that he would have to lie to the King and to Iuliu Maniu and Dinu Bratianu and he did so. They all implored him to tell the truth, i.e., whether Rumania had been handed over to Russian control. And Averell Harriman replied "*No.*" Why?

Harriman came from a very rich American family (American railways and banks) and had pro-Russian sentiments since his youth; he was an influential member of the Democratic Party; personal friend of Roosevelt, and founding member of the Committee for Foreign Affairs. According to some people (see *None Dare Call It Conspiracy*, by Garry Allen), Averell Harriman, i.e., his banks, financed Trotsky's revolution when the latter embarked with 275 revolutionaries for Leningrad on 27 March 1917 at New York, on the ship *Christiana*. Trotsky left with about ten million dollars (1917 exchange rate) borrowed in exchange for promises of rich mining concessions.

Harriman's case, therefore, is more serious, because he could have told the truth to his American people, but did not do so. He could—because of his material independence and authority, have told the Rumanian people the truth. But he did not do so. He could have reduced their suffering but he didn't want to. He did not express a word of regret or of sympathy for the Rumanian people unlike Kerr. He was proud and praised his own behaviour in Bucharest when he lied to everyone.

Thus, when Andrei Vishinsky died, the *New York Times* asked the former ambassador to Moscow—Averell Harriman—for an interview, as someone who had known Vishinsky well. As he was on the threshold of senility, believing that he was speaking about the "cynicism" of Vishinsky, he tells of an incident connected with him:

I was charged with a mission to go to Bucharest to arrange

225

things there and to convince the King and the Opposition Parties to hold free elections. We went by train and spent three days from Moscow to Bucharest. When I was invited into Vishinsky's carriage, I asked him:

"How many votes do you think the Communists would get if free elections are held in Rumania?"

"If free elections are held," replied Vishinsky, "the Communists will not get even 10%. But as we will arrange the elections, and they will not be free, the Rumanian Communists will get 90% and the others 10%."

But Averell Harriman, ambassador of the greatest power in the world; ambassador of the most noble, hard-working, honest, and generous people, who would never have accepted this reply—instead of getting out at the first station, banging the door and shouting the truth to everyone, went on peacefully drinking champagne in Vishinsky's company and reached Bucharest with him, to lie to everyone.

That is why Averell Harriman's sin is greater than that of Ambassador Kerr. Speaking of Vishinsky's cynicism, he forgot his own. He forgot that, knowing well what Vishinsky had said, he went to Bucharest and lied to the Rumanian people.

But we must recognize that each kept his word: Vishinsky to falsify the elections and Harriman to lie to the Rumanian people and to their leaders.

Churchill's wish—expressed in the Kremlin on 9 October 1944 was realized. The expression "spheres of influence" was not utilized by anyone, publicly or officially. But the Iron Curtain, forged by Churchill and Roosevelt, presses down on Rumania and the whole of Eastern Europe.

The farce of the three diplomats has been repeated in the same way in Poland, except that Molotov replaced Vishinsky.

But Kerr and Harriman were also the grave-diggers of Poland.

In the other countries, the same treacherous procedure was used as in Rumania.

In Bulgaria, considered as "the little sister of Russia," once the Red armies were in the country, and in their presence, Bulgarian Communists liquidated all the leaders of the traditional democratic parties, as well as those of the opposition, exactly as Tito had done in Yugoslavia.

In Bulgaria, always in the presence of the Red armies, and under their control, the Communists held elections, which they won, 100 percent.

Thus, in Bulgaria, the American "protest," and the Mark Ethridge Report on fraud went to the wall: the elections took place, and, according to Molotov, they were free elections.

But the comedy was played with the help of the American Secretary of State James Byrnes, and orchestrated by him.

"It was present in Molotov's demand, that governments wholly subservient to Russia should be maintained in Rumania, Bulgaria, and Hungary," writes Byrnes, on page 100 of his book *Speaking Frankly* and he adds, "Therefore I thought that if we could give them assurance on this score, perhaps the obstacle blocking the Peace Conference could be removed."

Thus, in turn, James Byrnes, President Truman's secretary of state, sold out too those countries, as Churchill and Roosevelt had done.

However, to spare President Truman who protested too loudly, and help him preserve appearances, Stalin agreed with Byrnes, as he did for Rumania, to advise the Bulgarians to include in their government two puppets of the so-called "Opposition," in order to enable the Americans to recognize the Bulgarian government, and to invite it at the Peace Conference in Paris to sign the treaties.

That was done, and no voice was raised to condemn the violation of the Yalta Declaration, the rigged elections. And nobody blushed for very shame in London or Washington.

CHAPTER 28

The Paris Peace Treaty

The mission of the "Great Three" was to save the face of President Truman—who had declared on innumerable occasions, both in the White House and at Potsdam, that he would never recognize the Groza government in Rumania. It was saved. The Opposition entered the government and so it was able to be recognized. The Ethridge Report, which had concluded that Groza's government was absolutely unrepresentative, arbitrary, abusive, servile, and altogether subordinate to the Soviet government—had been forgotten. It was not even published. Public opinion had to be kept further in ignorance.

The falsified elections were also soon forgotten; the very violent and just protests, which the United States and Britain had made in Bucharest in the votes of 27 May and 14 June 1946. Everything had been forgotten and this government, described by them as unrepresentative and abusive, was to represent Rumania and conclude the Peace Treaty in Paris.

It can be said that at least there, when the British and Americans had a word to say, the interests of Rumania could have been understood and defended. But this was not so. The Groza government, which had been installed by an ultimatum of two hours and five minutes on 6 March 1945, continued to be the faithful agent of Moscow.

Not much was to be expected from them at the Peace Conference. It was a struggle that had been lost beforehand.

Nonetheless, helped by a group of Rumanians in exile, Grigore Gafencu defended with patriotism, with ability and courage the interests of the absent country. He presented a memorandum that was excellent and well documented to the conference. But the results were nil.

Rumania was more severely treated than the others in the Axis. The conditions of the Peace Treaty were more severe than in that of the Armistice Convention. The Peace Treaty was the treaty of a vassal, completely subject to the Soviet Union. Everyone had forgotten the principles of the Atlantic Charter and the Declaration of Human Rights and other similar oratorical nonsense. The principles were thrown to the wastepaper basket. The right to self-determination of the Rumanian people was subordinated to the security interests of Russia and to her necessity to have "friendly governments along her frontiers."

"Co-belligerence"—which would have permitted Rumania to have more favourable treatment and which was expressly demanded in the armistice conditions, both on 12 April 1944, and in the Armistice Convention in Moscow on 12 September 1944—was not recognized. Co-belligerence was not recognized although twenty Rumanian divisions, the entire air force and fleet fought heroically alongside the Allies until the end, and although the Rumanian armies had had frightful losses, amounting to 50 percent of their total strength because they had been thrown into the front line all the time.

The fate of the Rumanian prisoners—over half a million—was not settled. It must not be left as a means of blackmail in the hands of the Russians.

In calculating the reparations, the desperate economic situation of Rumania was not considered nor any levies taken during two years by the Russians, nor the millions of dollars spent on the maintenance of the Russian armies and their units of officials in Rumania. The figure of three hundred million dollars "as reparations" was a gross falsification, because in reality—with all they had taken and received—the figure for the reparations approached two billion dollars, as the American delegate—Mr. Willard Thorp—had emphasized. The figures were even more false because the reparations (which were to have been paid in kind) were calculated not on the basis of their date of delivery, which would have been normal and just—but on the prices of 1938, which was an aberration and camouflage of the truth about the total figure.

Regarding the "political" clauses, the treaty spoke of Fascist-type organizations or punishment for war criminals or disaster to the country, without giving the slightest juridical definition or establishing any instance of supervision or recourse. These clauses were left to be applied by the Groza government, though denounced by the Allies as unrepresentative, arbitrary, and abusive only a few days before.

But the treaties had to be concluded and signed. The Iron Curtain—so odious to Winston Churchill—had to fall—and it did. "The Fascist" Iuliu Maniu, the "Fascist" Dinu Bratianu, the "Fascist" Titel Petrescu, and a great part of the Rumanian Democracy were liquidated as "Fascist."

The problem of Bessarabia and Rumanian Bucovina was not raised by anyone but only in Gafencu's memorandum. The Rumanian government did not dare to raise the question of the northern part of the country. So far as they were concerned, the problem was solved in 1924, when Ana Pauker's Communist Party Congress declared that "Bessarabia is a Russian land."

But the problem of Bessarabia, Bucovina, and Hertza must be seen under its various historical aspects.

To begin with, those territories were stolen by Russia on 26 June 1940, following an ultimatum by Stalin on the basis of the secret agreement made with Hitler on 23 August 1939. The theft of Rumanian ancestral earth was not only an act of military violence, which should normally have been considered null and void from a juridical point of view, but it was the direct result of a thieving agreement between Hitler and Stalin and therefore also from that point of view, must also be regarded as null and void.

Until President Roosevelt—over the heads of the State Department—gave his consent to this annexation, the official policy of the United States had been not to discuss and not to recognize *any annexation whatever since the beginning of the war by Hitler*. Bessarabia, Bucovina, Poland, Finland, and the Baltic countries all enter that category.

But even after the authoritarian and abusive president had promised Stalin these frontiers as a result of Hitler's aggression—recompense for a complicity without which Hitler *would never have dared to declare war*—the official policy of the State Department (Cordell Hull) was and remained non-recognition of Russian pretensions to Bucovina and Hertza.

In his *Memoirs*, the former secretary of state observes that Bessarabia had been Rumanian territory until 1812, when it was annexed by the Russians, and he also adds that Bucovina and Hertza had never been integrated into Russia, that they had always been Rumanian territory. Bucovina had been occupied by Austria in 1775 and so, as far as she is concerned, there can be no question of a Russian claim. Hertza was always Rumanian land, neither occupied nor annexed by anyone.

On 8 February 1944, the State Department (document number R 2835) decided to oppose the Russians regarding the annexation of those

Rumanian territories, telling them that their military occupation could not in any way prejudice the territorial arrangements made at the Peace Treaty. A postscript was added to the Bessarabian clause to the effect that, in case of necessity, it might eventually be recognized, because neither the United States nor the Soviet government had recognized its incorporation into Rumania.

But that document of 8 February 1944 recognizes clearly and categorically that Bucovina had never been Russian territory and that the matter must therefore be left for the Peace Conference.

In view of the discussion of these questions, the State Department—through George Kennan in Moscow—sought the advice and agreement of the British.

But here too, British generosity on the back of unhappy Rumanians was demonstrated pitifully. Sir O. Sargent (document 43992 of the same day, 8 February 1944) opposed the raising of such a question. He was afraid the Americans should "burn their fingers and those of the English" by raising it, especially as they were then discussing the cession of a good slice of Eastern Poland to Russia.

But it will be remembered that frontier problems, which were to be left for the peace treaties, had been regulated already in the Armistice Convention. This was done on the advice of Churchill in Moscow in October 1944 and on that of Stalin and Alger Hiss, member of the American Communist Party and delegate at Yalta. *The agreements had to be made between the heads of governments* and by the Armistice Convention, so as to find themselves in the face of a *fait accompli*, so as not to give the parliaments the possibility of discussing them and eventually to reject them. Parliament and the people had to be deceived.

So that is why the problem was not raised, either of Bessarabia or of northern Bucovina. That is why no one mentioned Molotov's reply at the conference in June 1940 when he was asked why he was taking Bucovina, which had never belonged to Russia:

> That patch of earth represents the booty due for twenty years' domination of Bessarabia and its retention will have a temporary character of equal duration.

Why did the servile Groza government not raise this question when the peace treaties were being discussed?

The puppet foreign minister then was George Tatarescu, who had been prime minister of sad memory on 26 June 1940. He knew of Molotov's declaration. He knew that Bucovina was the soul of the Rumanian nation where her glorious Stephen the Great rests and where their ancestral Faith has built—with ardour, tears, and soul the most beautiful monasteries in the world: Voronetz, Sucevitza, Moldovitza, Humor, and Arbore and where, from the shepherd's lament to the singing mountain streams, only the Rumanian tongue is heard.

But the Hertza region? That has always been Rumanian land and happy not to have known foreign occupation. It was a small province in the county of Dorohoi. It did not form part of Bucovina when the latter was annexed by Austria. The population were entirely Rumanian. There was no justification, either historical or ethnical, to annex it. Certainly the supplementary theft of those twenty purely Rumanian localities that form Hertza was carried out for military necessity. It was a strategic stopping place for the Soviet hordes in their advance towards the Carpathians.

But no one among the Rumanian delegates at the conference raised the matter. It had been transacted earlier, in 1940, when Hitler and Stalin divided up Europe. The Anglo-Americans respected scrupulously all the territorial advantages and spheres of influence granted by Hitler to Stalin. This was the reward to Stalin for his complicity in unleashing the war.

Why did Tatarescu—this lackey of all foreign interests—not show Rumanian courage to atone for his odious sins committed against the Rumanian nation, by speaking of Bucovina and Hertza?

How well Sir Archibald Kerr summed him up when he wrote in his report that Tatarescu was a liar, a hypocrite, and dishonest to the very marrow of his bones.

In these circumstances, Rumania lost 51,000 square kilometres of her ancestral Bessarabian and Moldavian land, leaving four million of their blood-brothers of the same Faith in the hands of the Russian intruders.

At the Peace Conference, also the confession of Karl Marx could have been evoked in the question of Rumanian Bessarabia. In a letter to Engels in 1854—speaking of Russian imperialism—Karl Marx denounced the annexation of Bessarabia "Rumanian earth; inhabited by Rumanians" as an act of brigandage and pillage.

In a series of articles, published in 1953, in the *New York Herald Tribune*, the patron of Leniu wrote:

The Russian frontiers have progressed from the time of Peter the Great, towards Berlin, Dresden and Vienna—about 1,100 kilometres; or towards Teheran, about 1,600 kilometres; towards Stockholm. Any annexation invites another annexation. In the conquest of Turkey, the frontier advanced about 1,000 kilometres and towards Constantinople, 750 kilometres. [While in another article] Russia will only be a prelude to the annexation of Hungary, Prussia and Galicia, [Karl Marx concludes] and the realization of the great Slav Empire, the fantastic dream of some philosophers of Panslavism. *To stop this policy of annexation is of the most urgent and greatest importance.*

But no one mentioned Karl Marx at the Peace Conference.

The treaties with Hungary, Bulgaria and Finland were concluded and signed the same way: at Moscow's command.

In Hungary, which fought to the end alongside the Germans, Anthony Eden thought that it was not even necessary to sign an armistice: "The Red Army is master of the country, so it can do everything it wants," said he.

But an armistice was signed, all the same, in Moscow, on the same pattern as the Rumanian and Bulgarian ones. Only the Russian Marshall signed it and only the Russian Armistice Commission were the master. The American and the British were only puppets, passive observers. They acted as figurants for the Russians who always like to give the impression of playing fair, and respecting the forms.

At the Peace Conference, Hungary had to pay, as Rumania, 300 million dollars USA, Bulgaria only 125 million dollars.

According to Byrnes, the Peace Conference was a success.

Everybody forgot that Stalin used to send telegrams of congratulations to Hitler, after every big victory of his, and that it was with his aid that London was bombed and the British soldiers killed.

The Katyn massacres were also forgotten, as was Stalin's attitude when he deliberately allowed Hitler to annihilate the Warsaw Ghetto, in 1944. Stalin accepted a Polish election "in a month's time," Ambassadors Kerr and Harriman were sent to "enlarge the Lublin Government and guarantee free elections in Poland."

Thus half of Poland's territory was annexed to Russia, and the whole of Poland—in spite of the seven million Poles in the USA—went under

Russian Communist rule. Roosevelt had kept his Teheran promise to Stalin.

This Poland that Churchill had—so much—in his heart and mind, Poland for whose independence and sovereignty he went to war.

CHAPTER 29

America Begins to Glimpse
the Tragedy of Yalta

After President Roosevelt's speech on his return from Yalta, the American people began to believe in a new era of harmony, prosperity, and social justice. These were the fundamental principles on which their democratic life and existence were based, and for which they had fought in two wars.

But soon after the death of their president, the American people began to get a hint of the truth. The Communization of the whole of Eastern Europe and the Communization of China, were attributed to the mistakes made at Yalta. Tongues began to wag, critics seized their pens. From his naiveté to his idealism, from Communist infiltration to betrayal, Roosevelt was responsible. By a personal, authoritarian, secret policy, he "sold" Poland, he "sold" China.

Instead of a new epoch of peace and understanding, a Cold War—which at any moment could become a hot one—broke out. Politicians began to cry out and to write: we won the war, but we have lost the peace. Historians and critics began to analyze the mistakes made and to establish the responsibility.

The American president had no positive political aim in the period following the war, or, more precisely, did not introduce any political element into the military operations. It was a question of victory at any price, devoid of any political consideration.

This criticism is aimed only at the government's policy with regard to military matters. It is not true that they had not a political plan for the end of the war. The State Department, in agreement with Congress, had formulated a clear, intelligent plan, *but it was discarded and trampled on personally by an abusive president.*

The extraordinary error of ''unconditional surrender'' was not made by the American people nor by their government; it was a personal error on the part of President Roosevelt. The same thing with the Morgenthau Plan.

His first victims were, and are, the American people, who must not be accused of their president's faults. The American people wished to have a just and generous peace, based on the Atlantic Charter, on the Declaration of Human Rights. They believed in an international organ for collective security, which would have ensured peace in the world and the settling of international conflicts by peaceful means. What was the result?

1. Eastern Europe was ceded to the Russians and the Communists, without the knowledge of the people or of Congress, or of the American government.
2. Poland—for whom Great Britain and France had entered the war—was given to the Russians. It had been promised to Stalin already at Teheran, by a sick president and a perfidious president.

Abandoning the fundamental principles of the honest, open, and fair politics of the American people, the president had promised him (Stalin)—by himself and in secret—territories and spheres of influence, without any constriction whatever, without any valid motive, either military or political. The arrangement was made orally for electoral reasons and they were respected. Even if the division of the world between those two great powers was not made by drawing a red line on the terrestrial globe, and by written documents, it achieved, by its spirit, a whole, with the same consequences.

What could Rumania have expected from Roosevelt who could only think in terms of votes for his election, when the seven million Poles in the U.S.A. were unable to do anything to save their country of origin? Rumanian votes in the U.S.A. were few. The same thing with other Eastern European countries. The Polish armies not only opposed Hitler, but fought alongside the Americans at Cassino, after having fought heroically in Libya and at Tobruk. The Poles fought too with their valorous air force to defend London.

But that did not prevent Churchill from accepting the division of Poland—the Curzon Line—nor giving it into Russian hands, by accepting a Communist government, servile to Moscow. Hitler demanded only

236

Danzig, but Churchill refused and made war, making Stalin master of Europe by giving him the whole of Poland.

Eight million Germans east of the Oder-Neisse Line fled or were deported to make room for "the new Poland."

Churchill did not cease to eulogize Stalin. On his return from Yalta, he made a speech in the House of Commons in which he said:

> The impression I brought back from the Crimea . . . is that Marshal Stalin and the Soviet leaders wish to live in honourable friendship and equality with the Western democracies. I also feel that their word is their bond. . . . I decline absolutely to embark here on a discussion about Russian good faith.

Put to the vote, the motion of the opposition on the question of Poland was rejected. But twenty-five Conservative members—disgusted by the question of Poland—voted against the government, and eleven members of his own Government abstained from the vote. They felt dishonoured.

How Winston Churchill must have bitten his tongue when—only a year later—he made his famous speech at Fulton!

Also at Yalta, both Churchill and Stalin had agreed to repatriate, forcibly, all Soviet prisoners. Over two million were, in that way, exterminated by Stalin. In their memory—and as a permanent reproach for that crime—the British people raised a monument, by public subscription—a fountain in Thurloe Square, in London.

It was claimed—and still is—that Roosevelt thought he could control Stalin through their personal relationship. Such an idea is an aberration. Peace cannot be built—after the most cruel war in the history of mankind—on a foundation of personal confidence. Roosevelt was ill and dying. But even had he not been ill, how could he consider himself to be immortal? Even if he were able to believe in the personal friendship of Stalin, the latter could have died. Can a greater aberration be imagined as the foundation for a durable peace?

All historians and critics agree that Roosevelt underestimated the Russian military potentiality, as Hitler too did. This is certain. But that was not his greatest mistake. That he did not realize the military potential of Russia can be explained by the mistakes in his Secret Services information. But can one forgive a president of the U.S. his total ignorance of *Russian imperialism* and of *Communist imperialism*? The most elementary treatise on universal history gives information on the aggressive, imperialist expansionist politics of Russia. No, Roosevelt did not cede Eastern Europe to the Russians out of ignorance, although his ignorance was obvious when he spoke of Rumanian Bessarabia, as if it had always "belonged to Russia." His ignorance was plain when he conceived the idea of the division of the globe into spheres of influence, as we have seen in the evidence of Cardinal Spellman and the books and articles of Walter Lippman. He did not realize that once those spheres were in possession of the Russians, the latter would realize their expansionist dream—the Testament of Peter the Great, and would, in the long run, dominate the whole world.

Also, Roosevelt knew nothing about the Marxist doctrine, its revolutionary dynamism, its oppressive and imperialist universalism. By these capital errors, Roosevelt prepared the ground for the situation that we have today in the world.

Roosevelt believed in the United Nations (although he had created spheres of influence for the Russians). But even there, he allowed himself to be deceived by Stalin and on this basis, he lied again to the American people.

When in the founding of the United Nations the Americans proposed a vote for every country, the Russians protested and demanded, to begin with, a vote for each of their republics, but in the end, were content with three votes (one for the Ukraine and one for Byelorussia). As the American Senate opposed such a proposal (even though Roosevelt had been against it in the beginning, saying that in that case, he wanted forty-eight votes, one for each of the states of the U.S.) and as Roosevelt *had agreed at Yalta to give the Russians three votes*, he asked Byrnes *not to mention anything about this in his report on the conference, and not, by any means, to discuss the question even privately* (James Byrnes, *Yalta*, p. 41). So the U.S.A. has only one vote.

The division of Germany into zones also favoured Russia by giving her 40 percent of the whole territory and 36 percent of the entire population. Berlin, in an exclusively Russian zone, remained—also due to Roosevelt—without any way of access by the Anglo-Americans and French. It has remained an abcess, which can, at any moment lead (as

238

almost happened in 1948 on the occasion of the Blockade), to an armed conflict.

The American critics reproached Roosevelt for the cession of Eastern Europe to the Russians, the unconditional surrender clause, for the three votes in the United Nations, for Poland, for the forced repatriation of prisoners and refugees. But they could not forgive him for his having asked for Russian help in the war against Japan. That was the capital error.

As I have said, a secret agreement was made in thirty minutes, between 15.30 and 16.00, on Thursday 8 February 1945. When it had been edited, it was signed on 11 February by the two participants as well as Churchill, who had not taken part in the discussion.

Roosevelt had been assisted by Harriman and the interpreter, Charles Bohlen. His Secretary of State *was not present*, nor did he *know anything* about it until after the death of the president when Truman found it in one of the safes in the White House.

By this written agreement (signed also by Churchill on 11 February), Roosevelt opened the gates to Asiatic Communism and Russian domination, and accelerated the Communization of China.

We must remember that, in 1943, in October, in Moscow, Stalin had offered his help in the war against Japan to Cordell Hull, without any conditions and unsolicited.

In those thirty minutes of *tête-à-tête*, Roosevelt ceded the Manchurian railways, as well as the harbours of Darien and Port Arthur, the southern part of the Sakhalin Islands, and the 800 kilometer-long Kurile Islands to Stalin. The "fist," as Roosevelt said to Cardinal Spellman, which should never have entered the hands of an enemy of America, because it is aimed directly at the heart of the country, passed into the hands of the president's personal friend—of Stalin—without anyone's knowledge—neither the American people, nor Congress, nor his own Secretary of State, who was with him at Yalta—Stettinius.

In five days of war, Stalin had become master of Asia. Indeed, the Iron Road permitted him to control the whole of China. Port Arthur and Port Darien had given him control of the seas.

The Sakhalin and Kurile Islands allowed him to control Korea, the Philippines, and to open the way to Hawaii, Australia, and the United States.

The betrayal of China (America's most faithfull ally) was, as in the case of Poland, not only a crime, but an unforgivable political error, which directly threatened the security of the United States.

For those five days of war, over two billion dollars worth of factories and equipment were taken by the Russians in Manchuria, which led to the complete lack of industrial progress in China.

But, by entering Manchuria—the most industrialized part of China—the Russians were able to equip and arm the armies of Mao and by so doing, the latter was able to Communize China.

In the same way, by assuring Stalin, in those thirty minutes, that he did not intend to send troops to Korea, Roosevelt invited the aggression of 1950. Condemning the presence of France in Indo-China, the president—also within those thirty minutes—invited the war in Vietnam.

But was Stalin's aid necessary in the war against Japan? The historian, William Chamberlain—in his *Second American Crusade*, believes that there was no military necessity to ask this help. In this connection, he cites the message in forty pages, of General MacArthur, of 21 January 1945, in which the latter informed Roosevelt of five attempts on the part of the Japanese to sign an armistice, on conditions which implied unconditional surrender. MacArthur believed in Japan's surrender without the necessity to land troops. Admiral Leahy was of the same opinion.

In his book *Secret Mission*, the naval expert, Ellis Zacharias, also writes that Japan was on the point of surrendering at the time of the Yalta Conference and therefore there was absolutely no need of the Russians.

The *New York Times* (Arthur Krock, Military Correspondent) published later, after Yalta, an article revealing how an American Air Force general informed the participants of Yalta about the true situation in Japan—that it was on the verge of surrender.

Moreover, President Roosevelt knew that the American atom bomb was almost ready for use.

In spite of that, he signed the secret agreement in those thirty minutes. Many have asked whether he did that because of his physical and mental debility. They were trying to find some excuse; some explanation. But the American historian—Sherwood—writes categorically that the president was ready long before the Conference at Teheran, in 1943, to accept almost all the Russian demands in the Far East. Therefore, even the excuse of physical incapacity could no longer be invoked, unless Roosevelt had been seriously ill since 1942, which might have been possible.

That is why, in the opinion of the former ambassador to Moscow—William Bullitt:

No more unnecessary, disgraceful and potentially disastrous document has ever been signed by a President of the United States.

What was more disgusting was the fact that the Russians were offered and given them, not that they could have taken them. By this act, Roosevelt gave the Russians moral justification for what followed. His action had forbidden the American people to protest any further. They had become prisoners of his errors, crimes, and turpitude committed in their honourable and guiltless name.

It is said that Roosevelt believed that—apart from his charm and smiles to keep Stalin yoked (after all he had given him!), he would have an ally in economic and financial aid, of which Stalin would be in need for reconstruction. He believed that this need for help on Stalin's part would limit him to a national policy and that he would renounce international Communism.

He put the idea into the heads of the American businessmen who foresaw a true El Dorado in Europe, Japan, and the U.S.S.R. after the war.

In this connection, one of the great capitalists, Donald M. Nelson, made contact with Stalin in 1943, and was given a list of priorities for post-war materials. Roosevelt himself believed that, in order to avoid a crisis, America would have to continue a dynamic policy of export.

But in this too, Roosevelt was badly deceived. Russia was rebuilt by the blood, the work, and the intelligence of the peoples of Eastern Europe and by the plunder committed in their countries. Stalin had no longer need of that ten billion dollars proposed by Donald Nelson. He had 120 million slaves, chattels who were more profitable.

The declaration—assurances—made by Roosevelt to Stalin, that immediately after the war, he would demobilize and "bring the boys back home" is considered too to be one of the capital mistakes committed at Yalta. It left *carte blanche* for Russian domination.

That is why the agreements called "Yalta" must be regarded as cynical, immoral, disastrous for the freedom and fate of mankind, as well as that of the U.S. That is why they must be denounced, strictly, and considered null and void with all the others made during the war. The mistakes should have been repaired by every means. But this has not been done up to today, although—as we have seen—the United States have been aware—since 1948—of the need to review and correct the enormous errors.

CHAPTER 30

Communist Infiltration? Treason?

One of the most important members of the American delegation at Yalta was Alger Hiss, a top counselor in the State Department.

At the State Department, Alger Hiss, special counselor, was in charge of coordinating the whole American external policy, and with the preparation of special files (dossiers) for the big and important international conferences, a planning and advisory role of the utmost importance for Americas's external policy, as we can see.

In our case, Alger Hiss was the man in charge with the study and preparation of all the Yalta problems and dossiers for the entire American delegation in Yalta. All these dossiers and material were in his exclusive custody.

As a special task, Alger Hiss had to prepare the dossier for the founding of the United Nations Organization, upon which was based the entire post-war American policy for peace in the world. Or, at least this should have been the role of this organization.

Alger Hiss was an important—clandestine—member of the American Communist Party.

Notwithstanding this, he was sent to Yalta as one of the most important members of the American delegation, to deal with Stalin.

At Yalta, the Russians reserved for him a room next door to the Roosevelt suite. He had telephone number four, after number one given to Roosevelt, number two to Harry Hopkins, and number three to Admiral Leahy, special counselor at the White House.

Alger Hiss's telephone number had priority over that of Chief of Staff General Marshall, and over that of Secretary of State of the United States Mr. Stettinius.

Alger Hiss travelled from Washington to Yalta with President Roosevelt, keeping in his custody, as I have already mentioned, all the American material for the Yalta Conference prepared by all the agencies in Washington.

At Yalta, whereas the Chief of Staff of the Army General Marshall, or Stettinius, or even Admiral Leahy, had problems in seeing their ailing president, Alger Hiss was conferring with Roosevelt every day, unhindered.

As is common knowledge now, in spite of the strong opposition from the State Department and the American Congress, Roosevelt gave Stalin three votes for the USSR in the new organization of the United Nations. The United States received only one.

Critics of the Yalta agreements held Alger Hiss responsible for these absurd and unthinkable concessions to Stalin, and even more so, that Alger Hiss was the American special delegate, in charge of the United Nations matters.

Great American men, astounded at what the Russians got at Yalta (and before Yalta), endeavoured to find some explanation for this "sell out," and all Roosevelt's errors.

Former President Richard Nixon, the great Senator Knowland, Senator Hickenlooper or Senator Ferguson, to mention but a few, publicly accused Alger Hiss of this disaster.

They asked themselves how far the Communist infiltration in the White House had gone? In the State Department? And all other American agencies? Was it treason?

Or just clever policy by the Russians, who took advantage of the physical and mental decline of an ailing, moribund president, to get all those incredible and irresponsible concessions?

From different parts of the United States, we started to hear:

"The United States were sold at Yalta."
"Sold out at Yalta."
"Eastern Europe sold out at Yalta."
"Poland sold out at Yalta."
"China sold out at Yalta."

Who sold them all? And why?

What is certain is that Alger Hiss was a member of the American Communist Party, and that he played a very important role at Yalta. The importance and the role played by Alger Hiss is not only revealed by the

243

proximity of his room to Roosevelt's, or by his phone number, but by his participation in every one of the meetings, even the smallest one.

The minutes of the Yalta Conference show how Alger Hiss interfered in the discussions at the highest level, and how he publicly advised President Roosevelt on what to do. For instance, during the Plenary Conference of the Big Three, when Roosevelt, in the act of selling out Poland, spoke about its new frontiers, it was Alger Hiss who suggested to him to avoid the "treaty" formula, and to use instead the "accord procedure," not between the three nations, but between the three heads of government of those countries.

As we have seen, Churchill proposed the same procedure to Stalin at the Moscow meeting of October 1944, in order to avoid the vote and the legal censure of the American Senate. The treaties, according to the American Constitution, must be ratified by the Senate. The "accords," administrative acts, escape such procedure. (The same procedure was adopted at Helsinki: we have "accords" mentioned, not "treaties."

To reward him for his valuable services, Alger Hiss was elected president of the first United Nations Organization; and this despite the accusations made in 1939, that he was a Communist.

Alger Hiss had the full confidence not only of Roosevelt, but even of Dean Acheson, whose "protégé" he was.

Under investigation by the Committee on Un-American Activities, under Richard Nixon, Alger Hiss denied that he was a member of the Communist Party. The Committee sent him to court. He underwent a thorough investigation, and got a very fair trial.

American justice (the jury) convicted Alger Hiss of perjury, and five years imprisonment, in 1950.

He served forty-four months, and he tried in vain to have his case re-opened and revised.

The part played at Yalta by Alger Hiss came up again in the American Senate debate, in 1963, on the occasion of the confirmation of Charles Bohlen as ambassador to Moscow. As the latter had been the interpreter of Roosevelt at Teheran and Yalta, at all the secret meetings between Stalin and Roosevelt, some senators thought he would speak up. But he avoided all the slippery questions, and he was confirmed in his post.

There is no doubt that Alger Hiss played a very big role in all the decisions made by Roosevelt, during the war and at Yalta. He was in a position to prepare the reports in a "special" way, and to influence the decisions to be made.

It was all the more easily done as President Roosevelt, as we have seen, was fascinated by Stalin, and very strongly inclined to give him everything.

Still, it was better for Stalin to have his own man in the place, as his eyes and ears in the State Department and the White House.

Un homme averti en vaut deux.

Besides Alger Hiss, Stalin had another man of his in the White House: Michael Whitney Straight, President Roosevelt's speech writer.

M.W. Straight had been a member of the American Communist party, and a Russian spy since 1937. He belonged to the spy-ring of Anthony Blunt (Her Majesty's Paintings Counsellor). Blunt recruited him from Trinity College, in Cambridge, as he likewise recruited Leo Long, Guy Burgess, Donald Maclean, and Kim Philby. (See Whitney Straight: *After a Long Silence*).

All these men infiltrated the Intelligence Department at the highest levels, while Straight spied in the White House.

Certainly many more of that kind are still at large, active, and as yet, uncovered.

If we add to this Communist infiltration Roosevelt's personal sympathy for Stalin, one can easily understand why the Red Czar got everything he wanted from the ailing American president, and from Churchill.

This chapter would not be complete if we did not add a parallel account of the Communist infiltration and betrayals in Great Britain before, during and after the war.

Readers will thus have the opportunity to learn about the immense spider's web that was spread from the White House and the State Department to the Foreign Office, and the Secret Services of M15 and M16 in London, led and manoeuvred by Moscow.

Through their spies—recruited from raw youths on the benches of the elite universities of Great Britain, the Kremlin learned everything and influenced everything.

Treason dined with the King.

A great part of the leading elite of Great Britain—students in Oxford and Cambridge—formed the basis for the Kremlin's Fifth Column, but these people were also the backbone of the British Empire.

Let us see of whom it was composed; how they were infiltrated, and especially in what important political events they took part, what role they played, and with what consequences.

245

Litvinov, who had been a "refugee" in England before the Revolution (married actually to an English woman, Mrs. Lowe), became foreign secretary of the USSR and soon realized that Britain would not be brought to her knees by the formation of a Communist Party there, and that this must be achieved by infiltration and treason on the highest level.

Great Britain—led by the feudal aristocracy—must be suppressed by her own elite: the aristocracy. Communist recruitment must start in the universities, preferably among the cream of the British aristocracy. Sons of dukes, barons, and lords must be inoculated with the Marxist virus from early youth on the university benches. Especially among the more intelligent and homosexually inclined, as they would be the future leaders of the British Empire.

Towards this end, Litvinov cast his eye on a "talent spotter"—one who could do the recruiting: Anthony Blunt, son of a priest, intellectually brilliant and a known homosexual. He remained in Trinity College, Cambridge, for eleven years and recruited—under the name of "The Apostles"—the notorious Guy Burgess, Donald Maclean, James Klugman, Allen Nunn May, Harold Philby, and certainly many others, unidentified even now.

A rich bibliography is at the disposal of those who are curious, but I do not intend to re-edit the "espionage adventures" of the latter.

What I wish to do—and to emphasize—is to reveal the role played by each of these youths in the great historical events of that period. Let us see how, and to what extent, these "Apostles" (among whom was the writer Michael Whitney Straight, who, as we have seen, wrote Roosevelt's discourses) were able to place themselves in strategic positions from which they could influence political decisions and load them in Russia's favour.

To begin with: the personalities:

1. *Anthony Frederick Blunt*, appointed by Moscow to seek out recruits. He entered the Secret Service of M15 as an officer as early as 1939. In 1945, he became "Surveyor of the King's Pictures"—Director of the Picture Gallery of the King of England and then of Her Majesty the Queen—a post in which he remained until 1979 when he was unmasked.

He was appointed Director—as an expert on paintings—of the famous Courtauld Institute in London.

He was knighted by the Queen in 1956. In Cambridge, Anthony

Blunt was a known member of the British Communist Party and marched through the streets of Cambridge, along with the other "Apostles," whose Communism and sexual deviations were public knowledge.

2. *Guy Burgess* was the son of a naval commander, colleague and friend of Victor Rothschild, where he was received as one of the family. Mrs. Rothschild even gave him a considerable sum of money monthly as supplementary pocket money. Victor Rothschild—today Lord Rothschild—is one of the world's and Britain's greatest bankers.

All the doors of this illustrious and powerful family, as well as those of the whole British aristocracy, were open also to Guy Burgess. Manipulated by the Comintern Chief—Samuel Borisovici Cahan—since 1934, Guy Burgess occupied a series of posts suggested by the latter from which the Russians had need of information: personal assistant to the powerful Conservative Member of the Parliament, Macnamara, President of the Anglo-German Association, then as an employee in the BBC propaganda section.

In 1938, Burgess entered the War Ministry as an expert in the propaganda office, without having been checked in any way before his appointment.

His personal—and certainly intimate—friend was Sir Harold Nicolson—one of the pillars of the Conservative Party and one of the closest friends of Sir Winston Churchill. Guy Burgess was appointed Assistant Principal Adviser to Sir Hector McNeil in 1945 when the latter became Under-Secretary of State for Foreign Affairs under Bevin. He remained in this post in the Ministry of Foreign Affairs also under Kenneth Younger.

Both of these ministers—as well as Sir Harold Nicolson—were assiduous guests at Guy Burgess's parties in his flat in Bond Street.

3. *Donald Maclean*. His father was Sir Donald Maclean, President of the Board of Education, i.e., the Ministry of Education.

Maclean was appointed in 1938 to a post in the British Embassy in Paris.

In March 1944, he was appointed First Secretary in the British Embassy in Washington, where he had access to absolutely every Anglo-American document, including atomic ones.

In May 1951, Maclean defected with Guy Burgess to Russia.

4. *Harold Philby*—Kim to his intimates, son of the counselor of King Saud of Arabia. In 1933 he went to Vienna where he married

247

Litzi—a militant Communist like himself. The British Secret Service could easily have been aware of the Marxist sentiments of Kim, as they had been informed already in 1933 by their representative in Vienna—Eric Gedye—that Kim was a Communist.

Philby was sent as special correspondent of the *Daily Telegraph* to cover the Spanish Civil War, camouflaged, naturally, like Guy Burgess, as an element of the Right.

Then Kim was engaged by M16—the counter-espionage service—where he advanced and became head of the entire Service. When the special Section D9 was founded after the war in order to counteract the propaganda machine of Moscow, the wolf was appointed to guard the sheep: Kim became head of the Russian sector (1945) of British MIG.

Kim Philby was later honoured by the decoration of the O.B.E. (Order of the British Empire).

In 1950 Philby was sent to Washington as representative of SIS, i.e., head of the British Secret Services in the USA, in order to co-ordinate the British and American Secret Services. The Cold War had begun.

Suspected already since 1951—after the flight of Guy Burgess and Maclean—Kim Philby was nonetheless declared innocent by Prime Minister Macmillan on 7 November 1955 in Parliament. He continued in the Intelligence Service in the Middle East until 23 January 1963 when he too fled to the USSR.

Today Kim Philby is a Russian citizen, Major-General in the KGB. He wrote a book, *My Silent War*, which sold like hot cakes, shamelessly, in Great Britain.

5. Regarding another of the "Apostles": *Allen Nunn May*, the celebrated specialist in nuclear physics who gave the Russians the atomic secrets, along with Fuchs, was, like the latter, later arrested and condemned by British justice. Another "Apostle," *George Blake*, arrested and convicted, was helped to escape, and is today in Russia.

And let us not forget James Klugman, personal representative of Sir Winston Churchill to Tito in Jugoslavia.

It would be useful, in this study, to add that Sir Anthony Blunt, who was suspected—indeed from the beginning of the scandal in 1951 confessed, i.e., owned up to his treason since 1964—was guaranteed immunity from penal conviction, and what is more surprising, even immunity from publicity. Everyone was silent.

Sir Anthony Blunt, ennobled in 1956, remained Sir Anthony until his public denunciation by Mrs. Thatcher in 1979 and, of course remained, until that date "Surveyor of the Pictures of Her Majesty the Queen."

Before examining the role of the "Apostles" in connection with the great historical events, it must be emphasized that Trinity College in Cambridge was not the only Communist cell of the British elite. They were to be found also in other universities, e.g., in Oxford, where a famous debate took place on 9 February 1933 when it was voted by an overwhelming majority that: "This house in no circumstances will fight for King and Country."

The Marxist virus—certainly introduced there by Litvinov—had spread. The aristocratic elite of Great Britain had been—also in Oxford—undermined totally and surely many of the Marxists of that university of the elite have occupied since then, and up to today, key jobs in the administration of England. But they have not yet been unmasked, as have those of Cambridge.

Let us now see in chronological order the events in which the "Apostles" were present and where they could influence a certain kind of politics and how they were able to inform the Russians.

1. *Degeneration of Anglo-German Relations*. Before Guy Burgess became first assistant to the President of the Association, a great part of British public opinion and of the aristocracy, including even King Edward, was in favour of better relations with Germany—even with Hitler. The president was a Conservative Member of Parliament—Macnamara. Certainly the Communist agent undermined the continuation of good relations, which deteriorated and led to war.

2. *When Hitler occupied the Ruhr in 1936, Great Britain did not make the slightest protest*. Why? Because Guy Burgess was informed by Edward Pfeiffer—a Communist homosexual like Burgess—Principal Private Secretary of Prime Minister Daladier, that the French had voted against military intervention by a majority of one vote. So the British made no move, thus permitting Hitler to make further conquests.

3. *The Parachuting of Rudolf Hess into Great Britain in view of concluding a peace with England*. Both in the espionage service M15 and in that of M16 for counter-espionage "Apostles" turned up—Blunt and Kim Philby. Even if they did not appear personally at the inquiry, they had all the information, which they certainly passed on to the Russians.

4. *The Attack on Pearl Harbor*. The Yugoslav double agent, Duska

Popov, German and British agent, informed the British Secret Service in June 1941 about the preparation for a Japanese attack. The information was not passed on to the Americans, either by M15 or by M16. The "Apostles" were present and kept watch. Their interest was to see America attacked so that she would enter the war. So they kept silent.

5. *The Battle of Stalingrad.* Like the German spy, Sorge, Anthony Blunt found out about the decision of the Japanese War Council not to attack the Soviet Union and, like Sorge, he informed Stalin. That fact allowed Stalin to withdraw 180 divisions from the Far East frontier. These, fresh and well equipped, were hurled into the Battle of Stalingrad.

6. *The Promotion of Tito.* Although the King of Yugoslavia was in London and had a government-in-Exile and his war minister—General Mihailovic—was fighting heroically against the German armies, the "Apostle" Klugman was sent as Churchill's personal representative to Tito.

"The Apostle" Maclean, who had been entrusted with the Yugoslav problems, took care that all provisions of armaments, munitions, and food should go to Tito, thus sabotaging General Mihailovic.

7. *German Attempts to make peace with Britain* in 1943 by the so-called *Schwarze Capelle*, led by Admiral Canaris, were sabotaged by the deputy chief of the Intelligence Service M16, Kim Philby.

The reports of the emissaries of Canaris, through Hans Bernd Gisevius, then by Fritz Kolbe, were simply suppressed by Kim Philby and did not even reach Churchill's office nor that of the General Staff.

The German lawyer, Otto John, tried in vain to make contact with the British agents in his capacity as emissary of Canaris. Kim Philby simply ordered his agents in Lisbon and Madrid not even to meet them. Naturally Philby informed the Russians of the efforts of Otto John. The proposal of Admiral Canaris—in which Himmler was included—to meet the chief of the Military Secret Service personally, in order to discuss a peace, was also sabotaged by the "Apostle" Kim Philby, although the proposal was so serious that it was raised finally in the White House in May 1943, but rejected by Roosevelt.

8. *The Manhattan Plan and Construction of the Atom Bomb.* The German refugees, Dr. Rudolf Peierle of Berlin and Dr. Otto Frisch of the Bohr Institute in Copenhagen both worked in Britain on atomic research. They were assisted by Allen Nunn May, "Apostle" of Cambridge and Klaus Fuchs, a Communist interned in Canada, without either of the latter having been checked as to their past.

They were all sent later to the U.S. to collaborate in the fabrication of the atomic bomb in the project "Manhattan."

Naturally, both Nunn May and Klaus Fuchs informed the Russians of the project and supplied all the technical information from the beginning. Rosenberg—later—gave them uranium, which was necessary for the fabrication of the first Russian atomic bombs.

That is why Stalin showed no surprise whatever at Potsdam when Truman informed him of the new and terrible weapon. He knew everything, was working on it himself, and did not allow himself to be intimidated. On the contrary, Stalin became even more exacting.

9. *Preparation for the Sale of East Europe to Stalin*. All information from that zone came through the M15 services of the "Apostles" Anthony Blunt and Kim Philby. The reports were drawn up by the third "Apostle," Donald Maclean, the golden boy of the Foreign Office. Thus is explained the fact that American Secretary of State Cordell Hull found out about Roosevelt's agreement to sell East Europe only by chance, and from the British ambassador in Ankara, eight days after this agreement. "The Apostles" were awake and watching.

10. *The Interpretation of the Yalta Agreements*. When President Truman, who succeeded Roosevelt in the White House, asked the Russians to keep their word regarding the Yalta agreements (free elections), the person who interpreted the agreements for Britain was none other than the "Apostle" Donald Maclean.

No comment.

11. *Free Elections in Rumania and Recognition of the Groza Government*. The architect of this mystification was Byrnes, Truman's Secretary of State. Ernest Bevin was in complete agreement with him. But Bevin's right-hand man was Hector McNeil, while *his* right-hand man was Guy Burgess, "Apostle" of the orgies in Bond Street.

That is how the Rumanian people were gulled and crucified.

12. *Beginning of the Cold War*. When, in 1947, the United States and Great Britain decided to form an agency to counter Russian propaganda, called IRD, the chosen head for this purpose—in which writers, journalists, and politicians from behind the Iron Curtain were recruited—was none other than Guy Burgess. That is how the Russians were informed, and the families of these writers were exterminated.

"Apostle" Burgess was keeping watch.

13. *Mao's China*. At that time, Guy Burgess was in the Far East Section of the Foreign Office, in charge of the Chinese problems.

Let us not forget that the first Western Power to recognize Communist China was Great Britain.

14. *The War in Korea.* "Apostle" Blake was appointed Consul in South Korea—a strategic position. At that time, "Apostle" Maclean was head of the American Section of the Foreign Office. Both knew everything and both informed the Russians.

We must recall that on 4 December 1950, Prime Minister Clement Attlee flew to Washington to convince President Truman not to use the atomic bomb and not to allow General MacArthur to cross the Thirty-Eighth Parallel. Naturally, both the Consul and the head of the American Section in the Foreign Office in London were aware of this. They informed the Russians and the Chinese. General MacArthur had to fight until he was dismissed—as he said—with his hands tied behind his back: he could not use the atomic bomb, nor cross the Thirty-Eighth Parallel.

15. *When the United States, through Wiesner, wished to carry out the recommendations of the National Security Council* (of which I speak in Chapter 33), to launch a political offensive to free Eastern Europe and planned to drop parachutists in the Ukraine and Albania, "apostle" Kim Philby was among those who organized the plan. This explains how the parachutists were picked up on landing by the militia, as were those Rumanians who had been dropped in the Fagaras Mountains. They were awaited by the police, for Kim Philby had announced their approach to the Russians.

16. *The same thing happened with the Revolution in Hungary.* When the American, Wiesner, asked at the time of the Revolution that the Hungarians be supplied massively with armaments, munitions, and food by air-lifts, "apostle" Kim Philby refused and nothing was done. The heroic Hungarian people were isolated and had to fight with their fists against the Russian tanks.

17. *The Marshall Plan; The Atlantic Alliance; NATO.* It would be useless to add that all the preparations and negotiations of those capital events in international life were known by the Russians, down to the smallest detail.

Because the "Apostles" were vigilant.

18. *Some of the "Apostles" of Trinity College fled to Russia.* Some died. Others spent several years in prison or escaped from it, like Blake (with whose help?). Others are now citizens of the free world, honoured and decorated.

But treason continues.

Other "Apostles" have been recruited and other *elites* will be leaders of tomorrow's Britain.

The danger is all the greater in that the "Apostles" now have the support of the man in the street—the proletariat.

It is enough to mention the case of Geoffrey Prime of the Headquarters of the Intelligence Service HQ in Cheltenham.

Paid monthly by the Russians, he was able to photocopy thousands of ultra-secret documents and send them to Moscow for eleven years, without even having been checked or hindered in any way.

And even so, Geoffrey Prime was only an ordinary married man without any convictions. He was neither a Cambridge nor Oxford don; nor an aristocrat, nor a homosexual, nor an expert on painting. Prime had not even been decorated like Kim Philby, nor ennobled like Blunt. Nonetheless, Geoffrey Prime committed treason for eleven years in complete silence and security.

Why?

In the Philby and Blunt time, I can understand. It was easy. One led the espionage service, M15. The other belonged to M16 counter-espionage service. But today?

This is why; that extraordinary woman; that providential woman—Margaret Thatcher, prime minister of Great Britain—decided to take these services into her own hands and to be personally responsible for them. To put a stop to treason. (See Boyle Andrew: *The Climate of Treason*. Coronet Books, 1983.)

CHAPTER 31

America Awakens, But Not Enough

Truman, the new president, soon realized the errors of Yalta. He was beginning to see the truth—at least partly. I say "partly" because the agreements made by Roosevelt were in some cases verbal, in others, written, and in general, secret. They had not been communicated to the State Department, so Truman tried to reconstruct them from the papers he had found in the safe at the White House, and by questioning those who had accompanied Roosevelt to the conferences.

The historian, Daniel Yergin, in *The Shattered Peace*, shows up the chaos in Roosevelt's papers when he speaks of *The Clifford Report*, demanded by Truman concerning the policies regarding Russia. Truman accuses Byrnes—the secretary of state—of incoherence and lack of clarity in those policies. Byrnes excuses himself by explaining that Roosevelt had made secret arrangements with Stalin and therefore he had been unable to carry out any clear, well-defined policy regarding Russia, not knowing what Roosevelt had arranged.

In view of his report, Clifford asked President Truman what had been agreed at Cairo, Teheran, Yalta, and Potsdam; who had been present, and what had been decided, because he had not the respective papers. The reply—Clifford writes—

> was very vague. Truman knew nothing about those meetings, with the exception of that at Potsdam.

Truman had a horror of "spheres of influence" and would not admit them. This is why, initially, he rejected them in protest votes, as in the cases of Rumania and Bulgaria. Truman did not know that Roosevelt had two languages: one for speaking to Stalin; the other, for the American public. He could not believe that Roosevelt went so far, because on 23 April 1945, he (Truman) had shown a pugnacious attitude when he had received Molotov at the White House:

> From now on, the Russians must respect their undertakings as they are interpreted by Washington. Our relations will no longer be "up a one-way street" for the exclusive benefit of the Russians.

This was a new, welcome language.

However, in the case of Rumania, Clifford began to reconstruct the secret agreements made by Roosevelt. Thus, Harriman, as one of the participants both at Yalta and Moscow (Churchill-Stalin), demanded in 1945 *recognition of the Russian government installed by Vishinsky in Bucharest*. That is why no Rumanian can forgive that millionaire American (heir to the Union Pacific Railroads, who financed the Russian Revolution by gigantic contracts for manganese, signed by Trotsky)—his behaviour towards Rumania. When he went to Bucharest in 1946, it was not to "reconcile" and "smoothe" things, but to convince the Rumanian people to accept Russian domination. How many tens of thousands of innocent Rumanians filled the prisons and cemeteries because of those lies!

Likewise, the new secretary of state under Truman, viewed the situation in the same light. As Roosevelt's collaborator, he respected what the latter had arranged.

In a speech on 31 October 1945, referring to Eastern Europe, Byrnes said:

> The United States understands the special security interests of the Soviet Union in the countries of Eastern Europe. It is evident that Russia will no longer tolerate, in those countries, a policy directed—intentionally—against Russia and against her political system.

James Byrnes too did much harm to Rumania. He did not even publish the Ethridge Report, which had denounced Russia's abuses. A member of the Democratic Party, with presidential ambitions, he strongly defended all Roosevelt's mistakes. After the Potsdam Conference—where Truman had raised the question of the Vishinsky government in Bucharest and of free elections—Byrnes also "sold" Rumania and again at the

255

conference that followed in Moscow, in December 1945, when he sent Kerr, Harriman, and Vishinsky to Bucharest.

In Byrnes's two interviews with Stalin, he proposed that they should go to Bucharest to arrange for the inclusion of two Opposition members in the government "in order for the pill to be swallowed more easily." Stalin accepted immediately.

On hearing of this mystification and comedy, the American Armistice Commission—to their credit—wished to resign *en bloc* (*Yergin*, page 152).

But the situation in Rumania could not be changed. Her fate was sealed, as well as that of all the other East European States.

The awakening of America took the form of realizing the Russian Communist danger. This happened relatively quickly in spite of the fact that Roosevelt's influence was still powerful, and that Eleanor Roosevelt was again asking for discussions between Truman and Stalin.

Admiral Leahy was retained at the White House by Truman. The former was against Roosevelt's policy of abandonment, maintaining that it was making the Russians masters of Europe and that it would lead to another war.

Navy Secretary James Forrestal demanded an immediate confrontation, which, according to him, would be inevitable.

Likewise, Dulles—the spokesman on foreign policy of the Republican Party—was against any sort of compromise with the Russians.

> Principles and morality must be re-established in international politics and in the world, [he said, adding: that] peace is one and indivisible.

But that protest, especially as it was from the Opposition—didn't go too far. The problem for the Americans (who now saw that the Russians "have a global policy to conquer and Communize the world"), was how to stop the Russians—not how to liberate Eastern Europe.

The Americans had begun to see—as Churchill said at Fulton on 5 March 1946—that "the Russians are swallowing countries one after another," and that they must be stopped; that the Russians would not withdraw from Iran of their own free will and that Truman must give them an ultimatum to leave the country. Then they saw the *coup* in Czechoslovakia—which had not been on Roosevelt's programme. Seeing all these things, the Americans awoke and wished to stem the Russian advance.

According to the *Truman Doctrine* and *the Marshall Plan*, a luckless policy of ''containment,'' of checking Russian expansion was formed. This theory—of sad memory—of George Kennan, caused so much harm and allowed Russian expansion to continue. Instead of a doctrine of ''roll back'' of Russian expansion and *to force her to retire behind her own so vast frontiers*, the pro-Communists advocated a defensive policy of ''containment.''

Let us now look at an ultra-secret document now declassified in which a new American policy was formulated. This was the report of the National Security Council of the United States, number 7, of 30 March 1948.

In it can be seen the speed with which the American government realized both the danger of Russian expansion and imperialism, and the danger of the Communist Fifth Column as well as the need to face all these.

But let us leave this sensational document to speak for itself, for it is very eloquent and to the point.

ULTRA SECRET

The position of the USA with regard to World Communism directed by Russia

NSC7   *30 March 1948*

1. As well as the problem of relations with the Soviet Union herself, the Washington Government must take into account the connections of this country with the international Communist Movement. The Meeting of the National Security Council 7, prepared by the members of this Council, by the State Department, in consultation with representatives of the Army, Navy and Air Force, the National Resources Board and C.I.A. represents the first attempt to be made by the Government to examine this problem as a whole and in depth. This document is significant in the premises pointing out the solidarity of the international Communist Movement; in regard to China and on the fact that it insists on the internal danger of Communism which approaches, in importance, the threat of external Communism.

2. The final objective of world Communism—directed by the

Soviets—is domination of the whole world. Towards this end, international Communism, directed from Moscow, uses politico-military pressure against her victims and subversion and internal revolution from inside. But these instruments are supported by the immense material power of the U.S.S.R. and their use has been facilitated by the chaotic state of the world after the war.

3. The conquest of the Axis Powers left only two great genres of national power in the world—the United States and the U.S.S.R. The U.S.S.R. is the principal source of the power of international Communism and it is only from that source that the threat to the free nations comes.

On the other hand, the United States are the only Power capable of organizing a successful opposition to that Communist objective. Between the U.S.A. and the U.S.S.R. are Europe and Asia, continents of great potential which, if added to that of Russia would allow the latter to become so superior in manpower, resources and territories that the *chances of the U.S.A. to remain free would be very reduced.*

In this situation, the Soviet Union have forced the United States to enter a power struggle—cold war—in which our national security is at stake and *from which we cannot withdraw without committing suicide.*

4. International Communism directed from Moscow has already achieved alarming success on its road to world domination. It has established satellite police states in Poland, Yugoslavia, Albania, Hungary, Bulgaria and Czechoslovakia; it also threatens Italy, Greece, Finland, Korea, the Scandinavian countries and other countries. The Soviet Union have obstructed the concluding of Peace Treaties with Germany, Austria and Japan. They have made the control of the atom-bomb impossible, as well as the effective functioning of the United Nations. Today, Russia is on the point of realizing what Hitler had attempted in vain. The Soviet World today stretches from the Elbe to the Adriatic and to Manchuria and comprises one-fifth of the world's surface.

[It must be noted that this report was made in March 1948. Did Henry Kissinger read it before going to greet Breznev? What a triumphal march the Soviets and world Communism have made from 1948 until today! And all because of the faults of Roosevelt and Churchill made during the war and at Yalta (*Author's note*].

5 Moreover, the Communist International has something new in the history of Mankind to say to the non-Communist world: i.e., *The Fifth Column.* It is used to falsify foreign politics, to divide

258

and confuse people; to plant the seeds of national disunion in the event of a war. In a word, its role is to destroy the freedom of the democratic countries.

6. Until now the Soviet Union have avoided direct military conflict with us. *Time is on the side of the Soviet Union in this postponement of confrontation, so long as she can continue to increase her power and continue her policy of indirect aggression and internal subversion.*

7. All this being the case, *a defensive policy on our side cannot be considered valid for the halting of Communism or for convincing the Kremlin to renounce her aggressive aims*, because we should only dissipate our resources and allow the Kremlin to choose the time and place to attack. Such a policy would only permit her to hold on to what she has already taken. As an alternative to a defensive policy, the United States have the possibility to launch a *Counter Offensive* over the whole planet. This would imply the strengthening of the military potential of the U.S.A. and in addition, the mobilization and strengthening of the whole non-Communist world.

8. *The Conclusions:*

Defeat [not peaceful co-existence, Mr. Kissinger] of the world Communist forces directed from Moscow is vital—*indispensable*—*for the security of the United States.*

9. This objective cannot be reached by a defensive policy.

10. The United States must therefore take the initiative for a counter-offensive in the whole world, with the aim of mobilizing and strengthening the anti-Communist Front, both in Europe and in the rest of the world so as to undermine the Communist force in the sphere of the U.S.A. itself.

As immediate measures, the report provides for the strengthening of the military potential of the United States; the eventual institution of obligatory military service; the reconstruction of the armament industry; atomic superiority; the suppression of the American Communist Party. In addition, the mobilization of both State and civilians in a vigorous campaign of information to ensure the bipartisan support in American foreign policy.

1. On the external plane: in the counter-offensive, our priority must be given to Western Europe, without neglecting the other countries of Europe and the Middle East.

2. Acceleration of the Marshall Plan.

3. Vigorous promotion of the Union of the West European countries.

4. (not reproduced because not relevant)

5. (not reproduced—not relevant)

6. (not reproduced—not relevant)

7. Intensification of the anti-Communist programme on the Radio.

8. The formulation of an effective ideological campaign.

9. *Formulation of a co-ordinated programme to help the Resistance Movements both behind the Iron Curtain and in the U.S.S.R. herself,* when the time will be opportune.

10. The creation of a large fund—urgently—to combat international Communism.

11. To point out clearly and categorically to the Kremlin the decision of the United States to resist Soviet Communist aggression—direct or indirect—in order to avoid the possibility of a war provoked by "accident" by the Soviets in the face of the reaction of the Western Powers.

I have allowed this extraordinary document of March 1948 to speak for itself. From it we can see that the American government was aware of the mortal danger that international Communism represented and for the need to face up to it at once by every means.

It is a true general mobilization of America and of the free world, which was advocated thirty-four years ago; military, political, ideological, economic, and information mobilization.

The entire internal and external policies of the United States had to be reviewed.

Funds were to have been allocated for a general counter-offensive, forming, encouraging, and financing resistance behind the Iron Curtain and in Russia.

For this purpose, the "National Committee for a Free Europe" was set up with "Radio Free Europe," and visas for the United States for political refugees of importance—or of less importance—were issued.

It should be remembered that this was in March 1948, before the Berlin Blockade, the war in Korea, the Tito-Stalin conflict and Mao's victory in China.

As can be seen, this report of the National Security Council speaks of International Communism directed by monolithic Moscow as the one and only in existence. The report does not foresee the ulterior schisms that took place in Yugoslavia and later in China.

260

But several months later, the same council re-examined the problem in the light of Tito's exclusion from Muscovite Communism (the Cominform) in July 1948, and they (the Council) came to extraordinary conclusions regarding the satellite countries. Let us see what they are and examine them. Here is this ultra-secret document of 14 September 1948 (number NSC 58) declassified also. It is entitled:

THE POLICY OF THE UNITED STATES
WITH REGARD TO THE SOVIET
SATELLITE COUNTRIES OF EASTERN EUROPE

Reviewing different matters relating to Yugoslavia—but which, if discussed here, would considerably lengthen this book—the Security Council passed on to the other Satellite countries.

28. In order to eliminate Soviet power in the Satellite countries, only two solutions can be conceived: one, a war; the other, measures to be taken without going to war.

29. Recourse to war is mentioned here in order to emphasize that war is out of the question and therefore other means must be found.

30. In trying to eliminate Soviet control in those countries, we must ask what kind of Governments will follow when Soviet control no longer exists: it must be our aim to replace—immediately—Governments friendly to us or to any Government—even Communist, but not under the control of Moscow—which might be acceptable.

31. Our final aim, of course, must be the establishment in Europe of non-totalitarian administrations, anxious to participate in the communities of the free world. However, very strong tactical considerations are against recommending this course for the moment. Not one of the countries of Eastern Europe with the exception of Czechoslovakia has ever known anything but an authoritarian regime. Democracy, as we know it in the West has been foreign to their cultures and traditions. Moreover, the leaders of Parties which could have become really democratic, were systematically divided and crushed and so have never had a chance to come to power except by armed intervention from the West.

32. But if we are ready, as a first step, to permit heretical—schismatic—Communist regimes to replace the present Stalinist Governments, we may have a better chance of success. Of

261

course it would be a very difficult task to try to break relations between the Kremlin and the Satellite countries. But it would not be so difficult as to try, from the beginning, to overthrow the Communist regime in power, with its complexity of ideology and methods and a long tradition of authoritative government.

33. *Therefore—for the immediate moment—the easiest possible cause is to encourage and sustain an ideologico-heretic (schism) break on the part of the Satellite countries*, for, however weak they may appear at present, there are potential chances of ideological schism.

We can contribute to that schism or extend it without assuming responsibility, while, where the final break would be accomplished, that would not entail loss of prestige on the part of the U.S.S.R. It would seem to be a quarrel between the Kremlin and the respective heretical Communist Party.

35. Regarding the above, let us see what would be the best road to follow.

Certainly the most important and most urgent step would be to succeed in removing the Soviet troops from the Satellite countries. The conclusion of a Peace Treaty with Austria would eliminate the justification of keeping those troops in Hungary and Rumania, the same would apply to the Peace Treaty with Germany. But of course there is absolutely no guarantee that—in case of a break with Moscow on the part of those countries—the U.S.S.R. would not resort to the conclusion of direct treaties with them, in order to maintain troops or even to incorporate some—or all—of those Satellite countries into the Soviet Union.

36. A second means would be for us to attack the weak points of the Stalinist Governments in the Satellite Countries and the mass organisations. Nor would that be easy, but weak points do exist. The Stalinist elements in those countries, especially the Party members, must be identified and isolated, as a first step towards their elimination from power.

This kind of action is closely bound up with a front-line attack on the doctrinaire level, specially aimed at dogma in the Satellite Countries, emphasizing their dependence and servility to Moscow. That Satellite doctrine—the cornerstone of the whole operation—ought to be ceaselessly attacked on the whole political, economic and cultural front and in all its applications. On the other hand, the opposite to the dogma of Stalinist Nationalism must be encouraged. The offensive must not be carried out openly only; it must be also camouflaged.

262

38. The political and cultural grounds offer us possibilities of exercising our influence. But the most fertile ground is the economic one; here we have a concrete, effective influence.

42. In encouraging Communist heresy in the Satellite countries we must not forget that our final objective is the installation of regimes in those countries which would be truly democratic. Therefore, we must increase our help and support to the refugee leaders of those pro-Western Parties.

45. The situation of each Satellite country must be taken into consideration, according to her degree of vulnerability, by a flexible policy from case to case.

In conclusion, [the document ends]:

46. Our objective regarding the Satellite countries must be the gradual reduction—and eventual total elimination—of the preponderance of Soviet power in Eastern Europe, without recourse to war. We must encourage the heretics among the members of the Communist Party in those countries to form non-Stalinist regimes as a first step—even if they are still Communist.

A massive attack against the Stalinist doctrine in the Satellite countries; the promotion of Communist Nationalism and the utilization—to the maximum—of our economic strength towards that end.

Both these extraordinary documents were compiled in 1948, *during the Truman Administration.*

CHAPTER 32

Hope Is Reborn and Dies

In spite of all the diplomats' lies, of all the falsified elections, in spite of the fact that Marshal Antonescu was assassinated following a fake trial, although Iuliu Maniu was arrested and sentenced together with other leaders as "Fascists" in spite of the abolishment of the democratic parties, of the arrest and imprisonment of their leaders, the Rumanian people still hoped. They could not—because they did not want to—believe the truth. The same hope of other people from behind the Iron Curtain.

They could not believe that they had been sold, that they had been betrayed.

Radio programmes contributed much to this attitude. The Voice of America and the BBC began to broadcast about events behind the Iron Curtain. The Truman Doctrine, the Marshall Plan, instead of being interpreted as failures on the part of the West and as defensive measures against new Soviet attacks, were wrongly interpreted as offensives to force the Russians to return to their own home. The Prague *coup*, the Berlin Blockade, and then the Korean War were—for these peoples—not proofs of Western inferiority and weakness, but a hope that they would have a chance to repair the mistakes made during the war and force the Russians to leave.

Their tortured souls, their racked bodies did not allow these peoples to see the cruel truth.

On the basis of the two documents quoted, a U.S. programme was quickly put into application. A National Committee for a Free Europe was formed with Radio Free Europe in New York for people behind the Iron Curtain. The Rumanian section was headed by the great patriot and leader, Mihail Farcasanu. General Nicolae Radescu—the last legal prime minister of Rumania—organized the League of Free Rumanians and was ready to organize a "Rumanian Army of Liberation." The other exiles took the same steps. Encouraging signs. The American people were conscious that the war won heroically by them on the battlefield, had been lost by Roosevelt by his pledges given to Stalin and Churchill. The American people had realized that—because of those mistakes—they risked to lose their own freedom. For that reason, they were ready to fight again.

But the American government did not want confrontation with the Russians. They wanted only to bar the road to the Soviet hordes, to halt them.

The whole policy of the government (not that recommended by the Security Council) *was without any ideological basis, any doctrine of liberty that could stand up to Marxist ideology. They had no plans to repudiate the agreements made by Roosevelt before, and at, Yalta. They had no policy to liberate the countries behind the Iron Curtain.*

Their entire policy was one of "containment," of stopping any Russian advance. That was a fundamental, tragic mistake.

By a counter-offensive policy, by diplomatic and economic pressure and a show of military strength, the countries behind the Iron Curtain could and should have been liberated. That should have been done in order to prevent the Russians consolidating their positions and creating new bases from which to launch the final assault on the Western world.

But what could have been expected from the Truman Administration in material for liberation when even Secretary of State Dean Acheson declared in 1947:

It will be silly to believe that we can do anything for Rumania, Bulgaria or Poland. We can do nothing. Those countries are in the sphere of Russia's military strength.

It is hard to believe that the same liberal-democratic strength that sustained Roosevelt's policies is still at work and that it hinders a radical change of policy.

The Fifth Column was in full swing, although the president had enforced a "loyalty oath" to oblige organizations with Left-wing views to subscribe to it, and they were put on the list of suspects.

There was a great deal of treachery in that period. The atomic bomb was given to the Russians by the Rosenberg couple. In the war in Korea, the team of British diplomats—Guy Burgess and Donald MacLean—passed all the secrets to the Russians and Chinese.

But in 1952, hope was born again among the exiles in New York. A new wind was blowing, which announced a change.

But let us pause a little and ponder on this change of American public opinion in 1952 on the eve of the presidential elections, when General Eisenhower, the Republican candidate, was elected president.

This was seven years after Yalta. The American public had looked on, indignant and incensed at the devouring of Eastern Europe and the destruction of those unhappy peoples. They had come to realize the aggressive intentions of Russia by the Berlin Blockade and the war in Korea.

Public opinion was gradually assessing the danger of the Communist imperialism and beginning to learn the full extent of the mistakes made by their great hero—Roosevelt.

That is why we find the following in the platform of the Republican Party:

> In the seven years of our Democratic Administration, more than half a billion non-Russian people—belonging to fifteen different countries—have been absorbed into the Communist sphere of influence of Russia who continues to aim at the conquest of the whole world.
>
> Our initiatives and moral aims as well as our hopes for a better world have been betrayed; deceived. This has given Russia a propaganda advantage in her military affairs, which, if we do not oppose it, will destroy us.
>
> The Democrats have abandoned to the Russians, friendly nations like Latvia, Lithuania, Esthonia, Poland and Czechoslovakia to struggle alone against the Communist aggression which was soon to swallow them.
>
> The Democratic Administration trampled on the obligations undertaken by us to ensure peace—and mocked them—like the Atlantic Charter. They did this to the advantage of tyrants who consider that assassination, terror, slavery, concentration camps—as well as the suppression of every human right—to be legitimate in the carrying out of their objectives.
>
> Teheran, Yalta and Potsdam were the theatres of these tragedies.

266

The Leaders of the Democratic Administration committed these mistakes without the knowledge or consent of Congress or of the American people.

They sold our great victory for a new enemy and for new oppression and new wars which have already begun.

What more ruthless criticisms could anyone make than that text against the enormous and tragic faults committed by Roosevelt?

It should be noted that this platform was that announced by the Republican Party; that public opinion adopted it because on its basis were chosen Eisenhower and Vice President Nixon.

But the platform of the Republican Party of 11 July 1952 in Chicago went much further:

The United States Government under Republican leadership will repudiate all the obligations contained in secret agreements like that of Yalta, which permitted Communist subjugation.

We will proclaim in the clearest possible manner and with the highest authority of the President and of Congress that one of our principal pacific aims is to see the dawn of a happy day when those captured peoples will obtain true independence.

Speaking, in continuation of Communism and of the danger it represents, the platform of the Republican Party in Chicago said:

By the weak policy of our Democratic Party with regard to Communism both in our country and outside it, the Communists and "fellow-travellers" were able to serve in ministerial posts and to infiltrate our everyday lives. We have always denounced this as part of a world conspiracy against freedom and religion, etc. etc.

What was the result of this platform?

Nothing. Once in power, Eisenhower forgot all about his own party's plan. The resolution introduced in the Senate for the denunciation of secret agreements was postponed on his request—*sine die*.

The fund of a hundred million dollars voted by the Congress—to help refugees from behind the Iron Curtain to fight for the freedom of their countries, remained unused. General Eisenhower did not wish to spend that amount and Congress was unable to persuade him.

General Eisenhower had forgotten his own message to the American Congress on 4 January 1953, in which he said:

> *The new Administration will not recognize any obligations contained in the secret agreements of the past which would allow the enslavement of any nation.*

Nothing could have been more in conformity with the opinion of the American public who had elected Eisenhower president. Nothing could have been clearer. It was not a question of "abusive interpretation made by Russian bad faith," but of the repudiation of "all obligations contained in recent agreements in the past," i.e., he attacked the cause and not the effect. He promised repudiation of the *consent* given by the Anglo-Americans to the enslavement of those peoples, but not of the hypocritical declarations like that of Yalta referring to the liberation of Europe, which were nothing but an obituary notice, a necrology of Eastern Europe.

Evidently this message was what the American people desired. It was drawn up by John Foster Dulles, the new Secretary of State.

In the meantime Stalin died on 5 March 1953. Eisenhower no longer wanted to raise his fist. Probably he wished to avoid provocation of the new leaders in the Kremlin. For that reason he ordered the liberation of Eastern Europe to be "soft-peddled" as well as the policy of "roll back" by the Russians, which had been advocated by Dulles. From a glorified general of victorious armies, Eisenhower had transformed himself into a village parson who believed in miracles and prayers.

After Stalin's death—(on the incredible occasion when the question arose of righting the mistakes made by Roosevelt)—Eisenhower made visible efforts to reconcile himself with the Russians.* Until Dulles—this admirable politician who was deeply conscious of the Russian peril and who had advocated the policy of "roll back" of the Russians, which had been inscribed in the Republican platform in Chicago—was obliged to climb down and accept Eisenhower's policy of capitulation.

---

*Eisenhower was, beyond all doubt, deeply influenced by Churchill and by the British policy of appeasement at all costs toward the successors of Stalin; that went against all policy of encouragement to the Eastern nations to shake off the Muscovite yoke. (See documents from the British Cabinet meetings of 1953. Released December 1983.)

On 17 September 1953—in his speech at the United Nations—Dulles began his talk with the celebrated phrase of Yalta: "the United States understands the need of the Soviet Government to be surrounded by friendly nations."

Instead of the resolution repudiating "secret agreements of the past" another resolution—*pro forma* and as a mystification—was voted, condemning only "the perversion of those agreements" in their application.

It was clear to anyone that President Eisenhower had decided to respect all the secret agreements made by Roosevelt and Churchill with Stalin.

As a consequence, Eastern Europe had to go on existing under a "friendly government" as Stalin had demanded in 1941.

Having seen already in March 1952 the truth concerning the sell-out of Eastern Europe by Roosevelt and churchill, I wrote, at that time, an article in the Rumanian newspaper *Romanul* (of General Radescu) about it.

In this article I was writing that the so-called "National Committees of Representation," of enslaved countries—formed in Washington—must be completely changed as to policy and personnel.

A "representative committee" was an aberration. Whom could the exile represent, and to whom, when the British and American had their ministers in capitals of their Communist countries, and the Communist government had theirs in Washington and London?

Therefore I suggested that the exiles form themselves a Committee for action and struggle. President Eisenhower was elected by the American people to carry out a certain policy. He didn't. He renounced it. Therefore, it is in the midst of the American people that the exile's action and struggle should be carried out, and the necessary allies found.

It was wrong for the exiles to become salaried persons of the Secret Services.

At that time, in 1953, I went even further. I wrote to my King a Memorandum in which I stressed that the Eisenhower Administration had decided to leave the Eastern European countries in the Soviet zone of influence, in spite of the American people's vote and desire to see them free.

Therefore, I respectfully suggested a complete change of policy: the abandoning of a National Committee for Representation, paid by the American Secret Services, and its replacement with a Rumanian Committee for Action and Struggle, directly in the midst of the American people. Only the American people could have forced the Eisenhower

269

Administration to change its mind, and keep the electoral promises.

It is thirty years since I wrote that Memorandum. Nothing was changed. And the National Committee were paid by the American Secret Services during all those years.

Even now—the exiles do not realize the need for a change.

But they still pretend to represent their country and their people.

CHAPTER 33

Instead of Conclusions

In the presentation and discussion of the errors made by Churchill and Roosevelt during the war, I have emphasized that the first victims of these tragic errors have been the British and American people. Committed in their name and without their knowledge or consent, these mistakes cannot in any way be attributed to these noble, generous, and democratic nations.

Two of their leaders—in the graver moments of their history—assumed personal powers to which they had no right and in so doing, determined the fate of so many innocent people by their personal, dictatorial, and abusive behaviour.

These two leaders desired to confront Hitler's tyranny to defend their individual and national freedom. Both were courageous and inspired leaders who led their heroic peoples to victory. Both won the fights against Hitler on the field of battle when World War II left thirty million dead.

But both these leaders—giants of history—lost, tragically, the battle for freedom for which they had made war. For the Hitlerite tyranny threatening Europe, they substituted an equally tyrannical and barbarous regime—if not even more savage and more dangerous—the tyranny of Russo-Communism. By their errors, they created the conditions for Soviet world domination and led us to the threshold of a third world war.

The distinguished Rumanian diplomat—Grigore Gafencu, formerly foreign minister of Rumania comments—in a prophetic article in the *Journal de Génève* of 25 July 1945—on the creation of spheres of influence in Europe:

But there are today factual situations which seem to prevail over theories. Closed zones exist. That should not be so. But it is.

So long as that will be so, the peoples will neither be democratic nor free and their union will seem to be fancy.

This situation can only be a consequence of the war; its prolongation will always be dangerous for we see *the principle of division appearing again. It is gaining ground even in England.*

Speaking of the ideological demarcation line (of the Iron Curtain that fell on Europe), he continues prophetically:

But we must not deceive ourselves—such a line, enveloped in mystery and silence, does not mark a frontier, *but a fighting-front.* Division in a sphere of influence is war.

With how much moral authority and subtlety does Grigore Gafencu reproach Winston Churchill for trampling on his own principles—in the sale of Eastern Europe—when he reminds him of what he had told him on 9 May 1939, when they met in London. Gafencu told Churchill that he visited Berlin and it had given him the impression that Hitler wanted to have an understanding with Britain and not a war and Churchill told him:

We were advised not to worry about all the countries of Central Europe; not to bother to observe the Pact of the United Nations; to recognize that all that is nothing but stupidity and vanity, in order to conclude a special Pact of Friendship with Germany. But I ask to know what this Pact would be and at whose expense it would be made? Of course our Government could come to some agreement with Germany; there is no doubt. It would be enough . . . to give *carte blanche* to Hitler, authorizing him to expand his Nazi dominance as far as he pleases in Central Europe. In my opinion, such a pact would be shameful and disastrous. To begin with, it would lead us straight into war.

As you see, Churchill—recognizing that for them it would be easy to come to an understanding with Hitler in order to avoid a war, by making concessions behind the backs of the countries of Central Europe—preferred war than to cede them. But in the end, he gave them all to Stalin; he fought a war in which thirty million men died and he lost the British Empire. Where is Winston Churchill's genial vision? Where is his morality, which on 9 May 1939 stopped him from avoiding a war?

His later speeches in Zurich and Fulton are only painful admissions of failure and of renunciation of the moral principles that ought to be at the base of men's actions and of international politics.

Churchill can be reproached today in the light of so many secret documents, at least for his four capital mistakes in connection with Germany.

First of all, for the rise to power of Adolf Hitler. This could have been avoided by a different British policy towards Germany.

Lloyd-George had understood the aggressive, unjust, and potentially dangerous Treaty of Versailles and struggled, as best he could, to improve it. He was put in the minority by Clemenceau and by President Wilson. But he saw the danger and advocated a realist policy towards Germany, but no one listened.

With foresight, "which surpassed that of Churchill," says Lord Boothby, Lloyd-George told him what he would do to ameliorate the Treaty of Versailles:

1. To review the Polish frontier in Silesia.
2. Abolish the Polish Corridor between East and West Germany, which is a running sore.

(The population in Danzig was almost entirely made up of Germans. This town, which had always been German, was declared an Open City after Germany lost the war. It was governed by a high commissary appointed by the League of Nations. The Poles had the administration of the Customs, and looked after business affairs outside of the city.

It stretched between Germany, properly speaking, and East Prussia, thus dividing in two the Reich. The Germans were obliged to cross Polish ground—the Polish corridor—[in armour-plated] locked railway-carriages, which was "really unbearable," as Leonard Mosley wrote in his book, *The Great Reprieve*.

Hitler asked Colonel Beck for the return of Danzig, pledging free access of the town to the Poles, as well as their right of access to the port.

He also asked permission to build a six-lane highway, and a railroad that would cross over the "Corridor" in order to link the two Germanies that would be—with a thin strip of land on each side—German territory.

Poland refused, and World War II started.)

3. Abolish reparations and with them, all inter-Allied debts.
4. Form a good international monetary system.

> Only after that [said Lloyd George], can we get a steady and agreed disarmament and close European co-operation.

Such a policy was not formed. Certainly it would not have permitted a demagogue like Hitler to come to power. That could have been avoided. But Winston Churchill, with Neville Chamberlain, carried out another policy that permitted demagogy and the ascent of Hitler.

In the second place, Winston Churchill can be reproached because he did nothing to stop Hitler once the latter had come to power. He did nothing when Hitler occupied Rhenania, nor when he annexed Austria—when he awoke, it was already too late, and Chamberlain was on the way to Munich. . . .

Hitler's bluff was such that General Gamelin set forth as a preliminary condition for an intervention, a general mobilization in France.

But we know today, from secret documents, that the German troops, on entering Rhénania, had received the express order to retreat at the smallest French military reaction.

Another mistake—the third—is equally important and needs more ample discussion. It is a question of the plot made by the German Resistance against Hitler in 1938, before Munich.

The attempt made by Colonel Count von Stauffenberg on 20 July 1944 was not an isolated act. It was only part of the continual resistance and plans to plot, from Hitler's rise to power, right up to his death.

It is now known—from the secret documents—that General Beck, Hitler's Commander-in-Chief, had adopted a hostile attitude to Hitler's military actions—Rhenania, Austria, Czechoslovakia, and Poland—as disastrous, leading to World War II and the collapse of Germany.

The resistance group led by General Beck sent, in mid-August 1938, a first civil-emissary: von Kleist; at the beginning of September, another one, a military, followed by a German diplomat from the German Embassy in London, to inform the British government of their plot to seize power, arrest Hitler, and bring him to court. They asked Chamberlain not to yield to Hitler's pretensions, and not to go to Munich.

It would have meant the end of Nazism, and the fate of Europe and of the world would have been different.

But Chamberlain went, first to Bad-Götesberg on September 22, and to Munich on the 29th, in order to "settle" the fate of Czechoslovakia, without a single representative from that country having been heard.

In order to grasp the scope and gravity of the conspiracy, one must bear in mind the discontent of the German Army at the time: the war minister, Field-Marshal von Blomber, was forced to resign for having married Eva Gruhn, a young girl with a bad reputation; although Hitler and Göring attended the marriage. Gernal von Fritsch, Commander-in-Chief of the German Army, dismissed for homosexual activity with a so-called Schmidt, lies concocted by the Gestapo to overthrow him, and get hold of the army.

As well as the war minister, and the commander-in-chief, thirteen generals were released from their command, forty-four others either transferred or pensioned off, as well as several other high-ranking officers.

Furthermore, the Chief of Staff General Beck himself, disenchanted, was at the head of the conspiracy to overthrow Hitler. What a lost opportunity!

General Beck was replaced—and for a long time no one knew about this—by General Halder. But he too was opposed to Hitler's plans.

Together with General Beck, General Halder planned a military *coup d'état* to overthrow Hitler; to arrest and bring him before a military tribunal.

Also in the plot was General Witzleben, Military Commandant of Berlin, General von Stulpnagel, commander of the Berlin Police, Count Hellendorf, General von Brockdorff, and many others, together with a large group of civilians like Geordeler and Hjalmas Schacht.

It should be noted that General Canaris was alongside the plotters against Hitler until the latter's end.

In August 1938, the preparations of the plotters were very advanced. They were only waiting for a firm Anglo-French attitude to arrest and bring Hitler to trial.

Both William Shirer, in his *The Rise and Fall of the Third Reich*, and Paul Berben in his book, *L'Attentat contre Hitler*, give us the frightful details:

.... and this group kept the British informed about the progress of their plot, asking their co-operation, [writes Shirer on page 368, and continues]

On 5th September Thodore Kordt, Counsellor at the German

275

Embassy and member of the conspiracy, communicated a secret to Lord Halifax about the date fixed by Hitler for his attack on Czechoslovakia and begged Great Britain and France to resist Hitler's threats until the planned revolt could be launched and Hitler arrested.

The Secretary of the Foreign Office also spoke of the affair with Chamberlain who appeared sceptical. Neither one nor the other breathed a word to their French ally.

The French prime minister heard of this plot only in 1964 when he read William Shirer's book.

On page 17 of his volume, Paul Berben implicates Winston Churchill directly:

> The act to exterminate is led by foreign businessmen who have contacts in England with Churchill and Lord Vansittart.

What did Churchill do? Nothing. He did not even inform the French, nor encourage the plotters.

When Chamberlain went to Munich and accepted Hitler's proposals, he strengthened Hitler's hand and the plot could no longer succeed. But it was a splendid and unique occasion in 1938 to avoid the war.

The fourth great mistake for which Churchill is responsible concerning Germany is his refusal to discuss a separate peace with Hitler's opposition.

In 1942, Geordeler, with the whole team, and with Canaris, tried to make contact with Churchill through Raoul Wallenberg, the Swedish banker. Churchill refused to discuss the matter. The same, in May 1942, at a Church Congress in Stockholm, the friend of General Oster (Adjutant of Admiral Canaris) was asked by Pastor Bonhoeffer to send information to Churchill about the opposition to Hitler and about their intention of making a separate peace. The message, sent by the Reverend Bell of Chichester, was rejected by Eden on 12 July 1942 in a letter, in which he affirms that "it would be against British interests" to give a reply to the opposition—the plotters against Hitler.

The same negative attitude as in the case of Rudolf Hess.

Every attempt on the part of Admiral Canaris and the Vatican to make a separate peace was squashed by the negative reply of Churchill.

The proclamation of the doctrine of "unconditional surrender" of Roosevelt at Casablanca in January 1943, prolonged the world war—with all its horrors—for two years. It discouraged any plot against Hitler and strengthened his position, which, at that time, was so shaky.

Is that procedure to be called "vision," "genius"?

Historians today are asking themselves—in view of the effects of the war—whether it would not have been better to avoid the war by coming to an understanding with a Germany rid of Hitler?

A. J. P. TAYLOR

One of the greatest English historians asks himself seriously:

In 1938, Czechoslovakia was "betrayed," and in 1939, Poland was "saved." Less than a hundred thousand Czechs died in the war, but almost seven million Poles perished in this war for their "salvation."

What is better—to be a "betrayed" Czech or a "saved" Pole?

I am happy that Germany was beaten and Hitler destroyed, *but I know the price that others have had to pay for that and I acknowledge the honesty of those who consider that the price was too high.*

Here is the great question: would it not have been better to have come to an understanding with a Germany, which was rid of Hitler—or even with him—than a war leaving the situation as it is today? Europe would have remained on her feet. The equilibrium of world power would have been little changed; the Jewish people would not have been liquidated in crematoria; civilized Christian countries would not have been thrown into the hands of atheist savages. Out of the thirty million dead, many would today have been alive. Western civilization and democracy would have been strengthened, not forced to their knees and threatened with destruction.

In view of this question, the political genius of Churchill must be judged. I am not a historian, but I ask the question just as the great English historian—A.J.P. Taylor—did.

* * *

Franklin Delano Roosevelt must also be judged in the same historical perspective. Because he too wanted confrontation with Hitler and with Japan and there are serious historians who claim that the United States could not only have avoided entering the war, but could have even prevented it both in Europe and in the Pacific.

Roosevelt was elected president on the basis of a pacific programme, because he had promised not to involve America in war. The American people did not want it; they wanted to remain neutral in the case of a conflict.

Roosevelt was accused first of all, because he didn't try by a firm, decided attitude, to convince Hitler and Mussolini to renounce war. The critics claim that, by mediating, war could have been avoided. But he did not try.

Historians accuse him in that—once the war had begun—he did everything, not only to help one of the belligerents—Britain—by trampling unashamedly on the Neutrality Act of the United States, but did all he could to involve America in the war.

The controversy over the attack on Pearl Harbor is not yet over. Many critics claim that, he, Roosevelt "pushed the Japanese up against the wall," i.e., that he forced them by his exaggerated demands, to enter the war. I am not at all competent to discuss this question, which is still under discussion. I only mention it. Moreover, it is claimed that the Americans who had the Japanese code—could have known that the Japanese were preparing to attack. But, as Washington had not put the garrisons in a state of alarm and thus the attack on Pearl Harbor was possible, that attack caused the entry automatically of the United States into the war against the American people, who did not want it. After the attack, however, it was a question of honour and of legitimate national defence.

So far, neither Roosevelt nor Churchill have been brought to the bar of history to stand a fair and serious trial.

Some timid endeavours were made concerning Franklin Delano Roosevelt, but it was too soon.

J. Brooks B. Parker, a Philadelphia millionaire, left in his will an important grant for "a contemporary appraisement of Roosevelt."

The executors of Parker's will selected Professor Edgar Eugene Robinson, of Stanford University, for this difficult and delicate job.

Professor Robinson's opinion was rendered in the book: *The Roosevelt Leadership: 1933–1945*, published in January 1955.

One must keep in mind that Professor Robinson had at his disposal but a few of the secret documents related to World War II, such as the Yalta Conference papers released at the time.

But all the others were unavailable to him. They were released only in 1972, as well as the British ones.

278

All the material concerning President Roosevelt's health conditions were published later. Professor Robinson did not have the opportunity to examine this aspect of Roosevelt's personality, and to judge, appraise, and assess his accomplishments or his failures in that light.

Notwithstanding those handicaps, Professor Robinson draws a grave, a tragic indictment.

Among the errors and mistakes of Roosevelt, this study quotes:

a) the liaison with the Soviet Union starting in 1933, failing to realize the malignant nature of Communism.
b) The casual diplomacy and slovenly management, which permitted the disaster at Pear Harbor;
c) The unpremeditated and thoughtless announcement of "Unconditional Surrender";
d) The approval of the Morgenthau Plan, which, with the "unconditional surrender" clause, permitted the Soviets to set up their power in the heart of Europe, and finally;
e) The "unbelievable" surrender at Yalta, which resulted in the loss of Asia to Communism.

What would have been Professor Robinson's appraisal with all the documents available today?

As in the case of Churchill also, the historians are asking what use did the war serve? Would it not have been better to avoid it by some form of compromise with mutual serious guarantees? This is the great question that the historians of tomorrow will have to solve, coldly and objectively.

But whatever the reply, their mistakes, made when the war had begun, were unforgivable and tragic.

Their great guilt was not only what errors they committed. That could have been due to lack of political perspective, to errors of judgment, or even to diminished intellect because of the superhuman efforts both men were obliged to make, to overwork, or to the diseases from which both were suffering.

What, however, can not be forgiven them is that they committed these mistakes by undertaking personal, dictatorial, and secret policies. Roosevelt especially ruled over the heads of his collaborators, over the official policies of the United States, and hid the truth about this from the American people.

By his secret, authoritarian politics and by his cession of free peoples

279

to Soviet barbarism, Roosevelt trampled underfoot everything that stood at the basis of democracy and of the American state. The moral principles that formed the basis of the Declaration of Independence of Philadelphia, proclaimed on 4 July 1776, were abandoned by Roosevelt. They guaranteed life, liberty, and the pursuit of happiness *to all men*, and therefore *to all nations*. Those principles, which form the foundation of the very existence of the American people, were betrayed and corrupted by Roosevelt. For them, he substituted compromise, dishonesty, and profiteering in international relations. By secret agreements he departed slowly, slowly from those moral and noble principles until he arrived at the window-dressing politics of Henry Kissinger, or the ''Doctrine of Organic Integration'' of his assistant, Sonnenfeld. After having abandoned those basic, holy principles, the rest followed easily in a cascade. Once the moral dam was broken by Roosevelt, the tide flowed smoothly for his successors.

But the American people, whose roots were deeply implanted in those moral principles, are finding themselves again, are awakening. They know that for a long time to come, the destiny of mankind is still in their honest, powerful hands, and that if there be any hope, it will come from there.

That is why I quote a series of my articles published in *Europa & Neamul Romanesc (Europe and the Rumanian Nation)* thus:

> On this occasion, the new *platform of external politics* must proclaim the renunciation of isolationism; the tightening of relations with the Allies; the re-arming of Japan and the rebirth of the Doctrine of the *Liberation of Eastern Europe*, by the application of a dynamic and wise policy of encouragement and support for the tendencies towards national independence of those countries and their helpers, by a true Marshall Plan.
>
> This platform must proclaim the right of the Free World to oil and all prime necessities without which the Free World would become asphyxiated and die. These prime necessities must not be left—by any plan of political influences—in the hands of Moscow, to create inflation, unemployment, recessions and therefore, political revolutions.
>
> . . . a new *Declaration of Freedom and International Independence* of all countries on the globe should have been proclaimed. Once done, this new policy should have been courageously and imaginatively carried out by a strong hand and *with every means* at the disposal of the great power of America.

The theory of "détente" in one direction must be renounced. Moscow must be asked to agree that, in the interests of world peace, the countries of Eastern Europe will be independent; to renounce her ideological fight on a world scale; to cease the export of Bolshevism and territorial expansion. She must renounce the starvation of the peoples of the Soviet Union in order to arm to the teeth, and the supplying of arms and propaganda to undermine the order of the Western world.

As individual liberty is one and indivisible, the enemies of man's freedom and of that of nations must be forced to renounce tyranny and despotism both internally and externally. The great American people—who landed on the moon—have the means to apply such a policy once it has been formulated and adopted. Her strength—her immense strength—is intact. America is passing through a crisis of leadership which will be momentary. The new leader, the new Messiah, must place his hand on the whip if necessary, in order to put the infamous in their place. She must use her colossal strength—given by God—not only to enrich traders, but in her external politics in defence of the freedom of nations and of herself.

There is no need for conventional or for atomic war. On the contrary, just to avoid war, every pacific weapon must be used which America and the Free World have at their disposal: *cereals*; technology; economy; capital; investments and "know-how; commercial and cultural exchanges, etc.

As the planet is a single unit, even the great countries—the "Super Powers"—have become interdependent. All great or small countries need each other. As the Soviet Union has great need of the United States and the Free World, the latter must force Moscow to change her baleful politics and collaborate, peacefully and honestly, in an international forum for peace and freedom.

The destiny of Mankind is—and remains—for a long time, in the honest, reliable hands of the great American people. . . .

N. Baciu

As far as Rumania is concerned, what could she have done to change her sad, unjust fate once the war had begun?

General Ion Antonescu? Had he not proclaimed himself dictator in 1940, another would have come forward, and *he* would have been appointed by Hitler. Antonescu, at least, was a soldier of great valour and prestige, and a great patriot. By his prestige and authority, he was able

281

to stand up to Hitler, both in saving Rumanian lives by not sending all his Rumanian soldiers to the front, as well as by obstructing the pillage committed by Hitler in the Rumanian economy. Marshal Antonescu did not order general mobilization because he was sparing with Rumanian blood. He sent only a minimal army to the front. The same applied to the country's resources. In that way too, he was able to save the Jewish population from being exterminated as can be seen in Filderman's letter.

As regards the total reversal of alliance between Rumania and the Axis Powers, some essential points should be remembered:

1. Rumania had been completely abandoned by her former Anglo-French-American Allies;
2. After the infamous agreement between Hitler and Stalin of 23 August 1939—when the non-agression pact between these two offered spheres of influence to Russia in Rumania, the Rumanian frontiers were no longer guaranteed by anyone. Marshal Antonescu asked Hitler to guarantee them—the only thing he could do.
3. This guarantee was all the more urgent and necessary because (today the secret documents show why) the Russians had asked Hitler not to oppose their ulterior demand for the cession of *Southern Bucovina* (see *Speaking Frankly*, by James F. Byrnes, p. 287).

   Moreover, it is now known that the Russians wanted also part of southern Moldavia and complete control of the mouths of the Danube so as to have a corridor through Bulgaria to Yugoslavia.

   But who could doubt today that, had Marshal Antonescu not made a change of alliance, the Germans would have imposed a government of their own choosing on Rumania with whom they could have done what they wanted? Were they not then masters of the whole of Europe?
4. Although pro-British and pro-French, Marshal Antonescu had every reason to believe in the victory of the German armies.

General Eisenhower in his *Crusade in Europe*, on p. 49, speaks of the opinion of superior American officers regarding a German victory:

Col. John P. Ratay, who, at the beginning of the war had been our Military Attache in Rumania, was an extremely energetic officer and one of our best Military Attaches.

He was thoroughly convinced that the German military power had not yet been fully exerted and that it was so great that Russia and Great Britain would most certainly be defeated before the United States could intervene effectively.

He believed that the Germans then had 40,000 Combat Airplanes in reserve, ready with trained crews to operate at any moment.

With regard to that change of alliance, Marshal Antonescu took upon himself the responsibility both to the Rumanian nation and to history. He made no secret of it.

At the Nuremberg Trials, the Russian General Zorya—at the sitting of 11 February 1946–used the statements made by Marshal Antonescu and Mihai Antonescu in Russia to emphasize Hitler's aggressive intentions regarding the Soviet Union and their beginning.

The Russian procurator spoke of the personal papers of the Marshal "captured" by the victorious Russian armies that "conquered" Bucharest in which he had found a personal note of the latter:

> Without hesitation, I stressed the point that, as early as 6th September 1940, when I took over the Government of the country, supported only by Mr. Mihai Antonescu, I declared without asking the opinion of my people, that we must follow a policy of adherence to the Axis Powers. I said that this was the only example in history of nations when two persons dare to make an open declaration and to call upon their people to follow a policy which, no doubt, could only appear odious.

With all the moral and physical torture suffered by the two Antonescus in Russian prisons, in 1944–1946, I do not doubt that the quotation above is correct. Except that it was not written—as the procurator supposed—so as to remain secret, but on the contrary, to become public; historical. The marshal was conscious of the affection of the Rumanian people for her Allies in World War I and of the hatred of the entire nation for the German armies, which had invaded and bled Rumania in that way, and who had divided and mutilated the frontiers by the Hitler-Stalin Pact. The marshal knew this and wished to take the responsibility for severing those alliances before history and before God. Why?

Because he believed, like the best American Military Attaché Colonel John Ratay—that the German armies would be victorious, that Rumania therefore would recover her brothers in Bessarabia and Bucovina and the eastern frontiers as they had been agreed by the Allies after World War I.

Only the eastern frontiers?

No. Something more. Marshal Antonescu hoped to recover at least part of Transylvania, taken by the Hungarians by the Treaty of Vienna, dictated by Hitler and Mussolini.

All the secret archives of the Nuremberg Trial concerning the complicity of Hitler and Stalin, who were missing from the war criminals dock—without whom the war would never have begun—explain for us Marshal Antonescu's hopes regarding Transylvania:

> The first meeting with Hitler took place in November 1940 in Berlin. In reply to my assurances of loyalty to the pact with Germany, Hitler declared that the German soldiers would guarantee the frontiers of Rumania.
>
> At the same time, Hitler told me that the Vienna Arbitration should not be considered as final and thus gave me to understand that Rumania could count on a revision of the decision previously taken in Vienna on the question of Transylvania [Page 59–62, document book U.S.S.R.].

Mihai Antonescu also makes these revelations concerning Transylvania in his statement used in the Nuremberg Trial, on page 68 of the same dossier.

Therefore, in 1940—like the most able American attaché—Marshal Antonescu believed in a German victory. But in order not to render the whole Rumanian nation entirely responsible, as well as the Opposition, he took the responsibility alone just so as to leave the alternative of an Anglo-French-American alliance to the Opposition. It was rather an act of foresight of a statesman, than an act of defiance.

Regarding the sending of the Rumanian armies across the Dniester—against the advice and contrary demands of the Rumanian Opposition—the explanation can be found in Hitler's promise to restore part of Transylvania. The Hungarian armies were fighting alongside the Germans, and for him it would have been difficult to halt on the Dniester.

A mistake? Perhaps, but I do not believe that it changed the fate of Rumania in any way, except in a case where the whole country from the King to Iuliu Maniu, to Marshal Antonescu—and to the best peasant—would

284

have been united in a single block, unitary and solid. But this was not so.

To Marshal Antonescu's credit, we must state the fact that he had recognized in the approach to Stalingrad—(where he was to have commanded the mixed Rumanian-German units in the place where—later—Field Marshal von Mannstein took command)—that Germany had lost the war.

With all the rigidity of his conception of military honour, which hindered him, a soldier, from fighting against his war comrades, Marshal Antonescu initiated—from that date—the action for Rumania's withdrawal from the war.

And more, he conceived a collective action on the part of the Axis satellites, led by Italy, i.e., by Mussolini with whom he had made contact towards that end.

Winston Churchill's nightmare—of which his doctor, Lord Moran speaks—when he dreamt in the spring and summer of 1944, how Communism "is spreading like a cancer all over Europe" was foreseen by the Marshal in 1943.

This is what Count Ciano—son-in-law of Mussolini, and his foreign minister—noted in his diary on 10 January 1943, p. 543:

> I think the Germans would do well to watch the Rumanians. I see a reversal of attitude in the words of Mihai Antonescu. The sudden will for reconciliation with Hungary is suspicious to me.

And Count Ciano was right, because Mihai Antonescu, certainly on the Marshal's order, went much further. This is what he noted on 19 January 1943, on page 548 of the same diary:

> Bova Scoppa [the Italian Ambassador in Bucharest] has made a report on his long conference with young Antonescu who has returned from German Headquarters. The latter was very explicit about the tragic condition of Germany and foresees the need for Rumania and Italy to make contact with the Allies in order to establish a defence against *the Bolshevization of Europe. I shall take the report to the Duce and shall make it the subject of conversation which I have been planning for some time.*

Thus could Europe and mankind have been saved from the "Communist cancer" of Winston Churchill, by the withdrawal of the Axis satellites and of Italy from the war in 1943.

How did Churchill reply? With the clause of "unconditional surrender," which permitted the crowning of Josef Stalin and the prolongation of the war by two years.

Was that political genius? Vision of a genius?

After the triumph of Peter the Great, through Stalin, at Yalta, the
Red Tzar Leonid Breznev triumphed at Helsinki.

This conference was the confirmation of all the understandings and
secret agreements made between Roosevelt-Churchill-Stalin, this time by
thirty-four heads of state of Europe, the USA, and Canada.

Considering this conference a terrible political mistake, I wrote President Ford of United States the following letter:

Mr. President,

I write this letter in my dual role as an American citizen and
a Rumanian political refugee since I was honoured by a special visa
from the Government of the United States in 1951 on my arrival
in your welcoming country.

Having lived for many years among the industrious and generous American people, I have learnt what true democracy means
with its rights, but also with its obligations. Thus I have learnt that
every citizen *ought* to take part in formulating the policies of his
Government, expressing his opinion openly and honestly. That is
what I do here.

In my situation as a political refugee that it is my honourable
duty and an obligation to speak my mind out of gratitude to the
American people, especially in the present moment when the Government is called upon to participate in a conference—in an action—which not only is outside the usual line of procedure and
against her principles, but which is in contradiction with the vital
interests of the United States and which—tomorrow—may even
threaten the foundations of her very existence.

*It is a question of the Conference of European Security at
Helsinki.*

Demanded insistently in 1954 already by Molotov, the idea of
this Conference was accepted—with some reservation—by your
predecessor, President Nixon. It was a goodwill gesture in view of
the policy of détente which had been sketched.

But the long-awaited détente has not materialized. The Russians have continued their aggressive politics by proxy in Vietnam, in the Middle East, everywhere. And moreover they provoked for us hotbeds of trouble in Cyprus and Portugal through the local Communist Parties under their control and are only waiting for a chance to launch an attack on the democratic Governments in Italy and France.

Leonid Breznev was in a very great hurry for this Conference—for which they had been waiting for twenty years—to be held. He claimed that that was the most important act in his political life—and I, for one, can believe it. Because for the Russians, that Conference was to be the solemn and unequivocal recognition of all the territorial and political conquests made by Moscow during and after the Second World War—from Karelia to Rumanian Bessarabia.

For the Russians the Helsinki Conference was meant to amplify the advantages obtained at Yalta by the declarations of Churchill and Roosevelt by the signing, this time of some real treaties, with thirty-five Heads of European States (from Andorra to San Marino), and of the United States and Canada so that it could not be said that these advantages were obtained without the knowledge and agreement of the American people and of the European States. They wished to procure a document to engulf the Eastern half of Europe in legal form.

The haste and insistence of the Russians in the holding of this Conference is also explained by: the Soviet Policy of Aggression; the situation in the Middle East; the tragedy of Asia; the oil crisis; the events in Portugal, Turkey and Greece—all of which meant that Western Europe was passing through a grave military political, economic and financial crisis like the United States. The Russians naturally wished to profit by the weakness of the latter and to force their hand by holding this Conference.

Everyone agrees with this interpretation. Everyone—in Europe—is aware that by the Helsinki Conference, Moscow follows not only the guarantee of her territorial conquests but also for her zones of influence, exclusively and in perpetuity in the countries subordinated to her at Yalta but—as well—the right to interfere in the affairs of Western Europe by her direct, active presence in the permanent organs which would be set up at Helsinki: Moscow wishes—and is ready to obtain—a free hand in the whole of Europe.

The editorial in the *Washington Post* newspaper of 3rd March 1975, entitled so suggestively "The Unhappy European Conference" sums up the general opinion about the Helsinki Conference.

In the face of such important problems when the American people are called upon to confirm the enslavement of the East European countries to Moscow; when Russia is given the right to mingle in the affairs of the chief ally of the United States—Western Europe—thus directly threatening the defence and interests of the United States, the *American People*, Mr. President must be *informed and consulted*, and until then, that Conference must be *postponed*.

The secret diplomacy of Yalta must be replaced by open diplomacy. The secret Committees in the corridors and salons of Geneva must be replaced by public, democratic debates.

The American Congress must debate the question of this Conference as a preliminary, according to the usual procedure. The debates in Congress should be held with open doors and with the convocation—so as to make their depositions—of all representatives of Americans of Rumanian, Hungarian, Czech, etc., origin.

All sides must be listened to according to American democratic procedure.

The American Congress—when the debates and surveys are made—must express their opinion by a *resolution* to which the representatives of the American people at Helsinki must pay attention. Even more, I believe that Republican and Democrat representatives of Congress ought to accompany your Excellency to Helsini.

In that way, the American Delegation will be backed up not only by their executive power but by the whole American people. And not to make concessions to the Soviet Union in her suppression of the innocent peoples of Eastern Europe, but, on the contrary, to demand—pointedly—the right to the complete freedom and independence of those peoples, in conformity with the generous ideals and principles of life of the great emigrant people—the Americans.

At Yalta—in order to hide the truth from the American people—President Roosevelt, on the suggestion of his chief Counsellor, Alger Hiss (member of the Communist Party, later sentenced to five years' prison by the American Courts) did not avail himself of the procedure *to be utilized between the participating countries which would have had to be satisfied by the American Congress* (Senate) and that of *"Communications"* and *"Declarations"* *by the Heads* of State—not by the States themselves—so as to avoid, in this way, ratification of what he had done.

The procedure and tragedy of Yalta must not be repeated at Helsinki, Mr. President. On the contrary, if a Conference must be held at Helsinki, it must be in the interests of peace and justice to atone for the mistakes and tragedy of Yalta.

Please accept, Mr. President, the assurance of my respect and the most sincere sentiments which I have for you.

Nicolae Baciu

I will end this book (this act of faith) with my conclusions of four articles I wrote in *E.N.R.* in August 1981, with the title: "FROM DE-TENTE TO A PLANETARY YALTA?"

After the miscarriage of the risings in Budapest and Prague, the West helped the Soviet Empire, by discouraging any discussion about liberalization. These were her satellites and must remain so, helpless victims on the altar of détente. That being the situation, the West accepted the Soviet hegemony without question as a necessity for world peace. But after the events in Poland, it was clear that the latter no longer wanted to accept the *status-quo*. The same thing, in the whole of Eastern Europe.

As regards Washington, they too had to adapt themselves to the new reality: that Eastern Europe was refusing to accept the *status quo* even if the West wanted it. In other words, Eastern Europe had become a zone of insecurity both for the Soviet Union and for the United States—a fact that demanded new solutions on both sides.

It must be understood that a new solution will have to be found. The solution of Soviet tanks to maintain the influence of the Kremlin is full of dynamite. It must be replaced by something else: the Finlandization of Eastern Europe as a first step; its neutralization in a second phase, its embodiment in Europe—the *alma mater*, as the third phase.

When America will be in search of a new, coherent policy, this problem must be put before to her; to the European Allies, and to NATO. Let the diplomats—who were invited by Churchill on that infamous night of 9 October 1944 in the Kremlin, where we saw half of Europe handed over to Stalin—to cover up what he did, to "find a formula," together with the American people, and the other free nations, to Finlandize and neutralize those countries, enslaved in that night.

289

The idea of a Russian sphere of influence in Eastern Europe as a stabilizing element was an illusion. On the contrary, *Realpolitik* demands their retreat from that sphere. The new American policy must proclaim that openly. Communist leaders of satellite countries must be encouraged to become dissidents, on condition of gradual liberalization of the regime through commercial exchanges and economic aid. The dissidents must be encouraged, sustained, and rewarded. The detachment of the respective countries from Moscow must be one of the chief objectives.

THE FINLANDIZATION OF EUROPE
AND HER NEUTRALIZATION

The exiles from Eastern Europe must contribute to influence public opinion for the best. By writing, by speaking every day, finding in every country journalists, senators, members of Parliament, men who are influential in politics or science, in order to plead the cause of the revision of Yalta. In this way, we may persuade the State Department and the White House to set to work, especially as arguments are not lacking.

It is not only a question of elementary respect for the right of peoples to organize their own lives. It is not a question of repairing certain historical injustices inflicted by men who are soulless. It is a question of righting certain political mistakes, which led to the present situation, which, if not amended, will continue to be a factor of instability, crisis, and danger of war. Any future treaties must be based on the rectification of Yalta.

The heroic struggle of the Polish people against the Kremlin tyranny has shown that the wind of freedom is beginning to blow in Eastern Europe. The sacred fire of the right to live in freedom—lit in Gdansk, by the courageous hand of Lech Walesa may—from one day to another spread all over Eastern Europe and even to Russia. No one has wanted to fan the flames. Everything has been done to prevent it spreading.

The interests of peace, of stability, of detente demand the emancipation of those countries. Otherwise, they will remain permanently as a hotbed of instability. The triumph of Gdansk must be the first step towards the revision of Yalta. "Communism with a human face" made its first appearance in Belgrade, then in Prague, and in triumph at Gdansk. Its example must be followed by the Communist leaders in the countries neighbouring on Russia. Gradually, gradually, the fetters must be loos-

290

ened, the prisons emptied, people treated as decent human beings. These reforms are necessary in the interests of those leaders themselves. They must become the chief dissidents of the Kremlin in the evolution of reforms and in the affirmation of freedoms.

But, to that end, a *Reagan Doctrine* must be proclaimed urgently, in forming a new American policy. That is an absolute necessity.

WAR OR PEACE?

If the chances of absolute military superiority in America and their monopoly of the conquest of space are almost a certainty, the utilization of these priorities to organize world politics is less certain.

I do not believe in a preventive Soviet war to hinder American military superiority nor in an American space war once they have become masters of the skies. America is aiming *to avoid war*.

I am afraid of a new world agreement. I am afraid of all the problems I have evoked, so as not to oblige the Reagan Administration to become compromised in some planetary agreements, in some new Yalta with disastrous effects. I am afraid that extraordinary prophecy of the sociologist, Alexis de Tocqueville—who wrote in *La Democratic en Amérique*, in 1840—could be fulfilled:

> There are today in the world two great peoples who, setting out from different points, seem to advance towards the same end: these are the Russians and the Anglo-Americans. Both have grown up in obscurity while men's eyes were fixed elsewhere; they have suddenly come forward to the front ranks of the nations and the world has learnt at the same time about their birth and their greatness. . . .
>
> Their point of departure was different; their ways are varied; nevertheless, each of them seems to be called by a secret design on the part of Providence to hold the fate of half of the world in their hands one day.

One can only pray and fight that this hallucinatory prophecy may not be fulfilled. Russia must be stopped and forced to retire behind her legitimate frontiers. Otherwise, when she becomes leader with the con-

291

tract in her hand for half of the world, she alone would be ruler of the entire planet, because, unlike America, she has no scruples. Russia must be stopped now, while there is time. And by every means.

New York
November 1983

Select Bibliography

As I explained in the Preface, I used for this book, primarily, the secret documents from State Archives in London, Washington, and the Library of Congress. Also the top secret documents from military archives such as the Pentagon Papers, and the Military Library of Kings College in London.

But, of course, many other books, magazines, newspapers, and articles have contributed to this book. These are some of them:

Accoce, Pierre and Dr. Rentchnick. *Ces malades qui nous gouvernent.* Geneva.

Accoce, Pierre and Quet, Pierre. *La Guerre a été gagne en Suisse.* Press Pocket Books, 1966.

Aldea, General. *Curierul* from Oct. 13, 1944. London, Public Records.

Ardemagni, Mirko. *Proceso el Churchill.* Negard, 1977.

Aron, Raymond. *Pledoyer pour l'Europe decadente.* Lafayette, 1977.

Berben Paul. *L'Attentat contra Hitler.* J'ai Lu.

Bergier, Jacques. *La grande conspiration russo-américaine.* Albin Michel, 1978.

Bohlen, Charles. *The Transformation of American Foreign Policy.* Norton, 1969.

———. *Teheran Files.* Hull. Mss. Box 52 and letter to James C. Dunn.

Boothby, Lord. "Vision Which Exceeded Churchill's." *Daily Telegraph,* 1982.

Boyle, Andrew. *The Climate of Treason.* Coronet Books, 1983.

Buchheit, Gert. *Hitler chef de la guerre,* 2 vols. J'ai Lu, 1961.

Bullitt, Orville H. *For the President, Personal and Secret.* Boston: Houghton-Mifflin, 1972.

———. Three articles in *Life Magazine,* 1945.

Cartier, Raymond. *Les Dessous de la Guerre Hitlerienne*. Fayard.

Chamberlain, William. *Second American Crusade*. New York.

Chicago Tribune, July 10, 1952.

Churchill, Winston. *The Second World War*, 6 vols. Boston: Houghton-Mifflin, 1953.

──────. *Secret Session Speeches*. London. British Library.

Ciano, Comte, Galeazo. *Journal Politique*, 2 vols. Bacounniere, 1946.

Cioranesco, Filiti, G,G., Floresco, R., Cherman, D., Gorjiu, A., Korne, M., and Neculce, N. *Aspects des rélations russo-roumains*. Paris: Minard, 1967.

Clemens, Diana Shaver. *Yalta*. New York.

Clifford, Clark. *Files and Papers*. Truman Library, Independence, Missouri.

Conte, Arthur. *Yalta*. Robert Lafont, 1964.

──────. *Apres Yalta*. *Plon,* 1982.

Cretzeanu, Alexandru. *La politique de la paix de la Roumania*, 1954.

──────. *The Lost Opportunity*. Cape, 1957.

Decaux, Alain. *Dossier sécrets de l'histoire*. Perrin, 1966.

Dedijer, Vladimir. *Le defi de Tito*. Gallimard, 1970.

De Gaulle, Charles. *War Memoirs*, 3 vols. New York: Simon & Schuster, 1964.

De Launnay, Jacques. *Miroir de l'histoire: Soviet-Roumainie Armistice*.

Djilas, Milovan. *Conversations with Stalin*. New York: Pelican Books, 1969.

Dreptetes, (Rumanian newspaper, 1946) British Library, London, MF 669 M.

Duca, I.G. *Amintiri Politics,* 3 vols. Munchen: Jon Dumitru.

Dulles, Allen. *Secret Testimony in Congressional Committee*. 1947.

──────. *The Secret Surrender*.

Eden, Anthony. *The Reckoning*. Cassel, 1965.

Eisenhower, Dwight. *Crusade in Europe*. Garden City: Doubleday.

Espionage Revise.

Ethridge, Mark. *Negotiating on the Balkans*. Dauwett & Johnson.

──────. Secret Report on Roumania, 1945.

Farago Ladisles. *La guerre des grandes espiones*. Stork, 1971.

Fois, Herbert. *Churchill-Roosevelt-Stalin*. Princeton: Princeton University Press, 1957.

————. *The Potsdam Conference*. Princeton: Princeton Univ. Press, 1960.

Fontaine, Andre. *The History of the Cold War*. New York: Knopf, 1968.

Foreign Office & Cabinet Papers. Public Record Office, London, 1938–1948.

Foreign Relations of the United States: Yalta Papers.

Frederik, Pierre. *Washington ou Moscou*. Hachette, 1948.

Fuchaer, Larry W. *Neville Chamberlain and Appeasement*. Norton, 1982.

Gafencu, Gregoire. *Derniers Jours de l'Europe*, 1946.

————. *Preliminaires de la guerre Mondial*. Muller, 1945.

————. *Memoir for the Paris Peace Conference*, 1946.

Gannon, Robert. *The Cardinal Spellman Story*. New York: Doubleday, 1962.

Gardner, Schlesinger, et. al. *The Origins of the Cold War*. Waltham, 1970.

Geddis, John Lewis. *The US and the Origins of the Cold War*. New York: Columbia University Press, 1972.

Gilbert, Martin. *Churchill: Official Biography*. New York: Oxford University Press.

————. *Strategy of Containment*. New York: Oxford University Press.

Glees, Anthony. *Exile Politics during the Second World War*. Oxford, 1982.

Grasset, Philipe. *La drôle de détente*. Vokeer, 1979.

Gray, Allen, and Abraham, Larry. *None Dare Call It Conspiracy*. Concord, 1971.

Harriman, Averell. *America and Russia in a Changing World*. New York: Doubleday, 1971.

————. *Special Envoy to Churchill and Stalin*. New York: Random House, 1975.

Hickok, Lorena. *Letters from Eleanor Roosevelt*. Roosevelt Library, Hyde Park, NY.

L'histoire pour tous. December 1962.

Historama Review.

Hull, Cordell. *Memoirs*, 2 Vols. New York.

L'Internationale des Traîtres: Les Communists démasqués. Sociéte Roumain d'Editions, 1953.

Iorga, Nicolas. *Istoria Romanilor*, British Library, London.

Ismay, Hasting. *Papers*, Liddel–Hart Military Library Archives, Kings College, London.

Journal de Génève, 1945.
Journal of Central European Affairs, Oct. 1951 with:
    Alexandru Cretzeanu, "The Rumanian Armistice Negotiations, Cairo 1944." Fred Nano, "The First Soviet Double Cross" (Stockholm Negotiation.)
Jurnalul de Diminests, 13 Mei 1946, British Library, London.

Kennan, George. *Memoirs, 1925–1950,* New York: Bantam, 1969.
————. *1950–1963.* Boston: Atlantic-Little-Brown, 1975.
————. *Russia and the West under Lenin and Stalin.* New York: New American Library, 1961.
Kissinger, Henry. *A la Maison Blanche.* Fayard, 1979.

Lash, Joseph P. *Eleanor Roosevelt and Her Friends.* New York, 1982.
Leahy, William. *I Was There.* Whittlesly House, 1950.
Lee, A. Stanley Gould. *Crown Against Sickle.* Hutchinson, 1950.
Leuchtenburg, W. *Franklin D. Roosevelt and the New Deal.* New York.
Library of Congress, Washington, DC:
    Congressional Papers.
    Herbert Feis Papers.
    Hoyt Vandenberg Papers.
Lippman Walter. *U.S. Foreign Policy,* New York: Pocket Books, 1943.
————. *U.S. War Aims.* London: Hamilton, 1944.
Loftus, John. *The Belarus Secret.* Nathan Miller, 1982.
Luce, Alfred Fabre. *L'histoire demaquillés.* Lafont, 1967.

MacArthur, Douglas: *Memoirs and Personal Papers.*
MacIntire, Ross. *White House Physician.* New York: Putnam, 1944.
McNeil, Hector. *America, Britain, Russia.* Oxford University Press, 1953.
Mander, John. *Berlin, Hostage for the West.* New York: Penguin Books, 1962.
Markham, Reuben. *La Roumania sous le Joug Sovietique.* Calman Levy, 1949.
Marx, Karl. *Letters to Engels* and articles in Herald Tribune, 1863.
Massis, Henry. *Défense de l'Occident.* Plon, 1927.
Massu, General. *Baden 1968.* Plon, 1983.
Moran, Lord. *Churchill, The Struggle for Survival.* Boston: Houghton-Mifflin, 1966.

Mordal, Chevallez, Gerysen & Launnay. *Dosiers de la guerre froide*. Maraubout Universite, 1969.

Morgan, Ted. *Churchill, Young Man in a Hurry*. New York: Simon and Schuster, 1982.

Moseley, Philip. *Face to Face with Russia*, New York.

National Archives USA, Washington, DC: State Department Papers.
　　　National Security Papers
　　　Pentagon Papers, declassified.

New York Times, newspaper, N.Y.

Nixon, Edgar. *F. D. Roosevelt and Foreign Affairs*, 3 Vols. Cambridge: Harvard University Press, 1969.

Nixon, Richard. *Memoirs*.

————. *La vraie guerre*. Albin Michel, 1980.

————. *The Six Crises*. New York.

Nuremburg Trials of Major War Criminals. Archives at Memorial War Museum Library, London.

Penesco, Nicolas. *Le Roumania de la Democrates au totalitarisme*. 1980.

The Pentagon Papers, New York Times Edition. New York: Bantam, 1971.

Pompidou, Georges. *Pour rétablir une vérité*. Flamarion, 1982.

Reilly, Mike. *That Was Yalta*. New York.

Robinson, Edgar E. *The Roosevelt Leadership, 1933–1945*. Pens.

Romanul, Radescu, newspaper article, 1952.

Roosevelt, Eliott. *F. D. Roosevelt: His Personal Letters, 1928–1945*. Dull, Sloane, and Pearce, 1950.

Roosevelt Library, Hyde Park, NY: Map Room File and Official Files.

Rothwell, Victor. *Britain and the Cold War*. Cape, 1982.

Salinger, Pierre. *Avec Kennedy*. J'si Lu, 1974.

Schlessinger, Arthur. *The Imperial Presidency*. Boston: Houghton-Mifflin, 1973.

Scoppa, Bova. *Colloquio con duo dittatori*.

Seicaru, Pamfil. *Le Roumania dans la grand guerre*, Minard, 1968.

Shepard, Gordon. *Russia's Danubian Empire*. New York: Praeger.

Sherwood, Robert. *Roosevelt and Hopkins*. New York: Bantam, 1950.

Shirer, William. *Histoire du III Reich*. Stock.

Smith, F. Bradley. *The Shadow Warriors*. New York: 1983.

Solzenitsyn, Alex. *Lettre aux dirigente de l'Union Sovietique*. Seuil, 1974.

———. *Lenin in Zurich,* New York: Penguin Books, 1977.

———. *L'Archipel du Goulag,* 3 Vols. Seuil, 1974.

Der Spiegel, magazine, W. Germany.

Stettinius, Edward, Jr. *Roosevelt and the Russians*. New York: Doubleday, 1949.

———. Yalta and Stettinius papers.

Stindardul, Rumanian newspaper, München, W. Germany.

Straight, Whitney Michael. *After Long Silence*. New York: 1983

Sturza, Mihail. *Romania si sfarsitul Europsi,* Dacia, 1966.

Sulzberger, C.L. *Des derniers des géants*. Albin Michel, 1972.

———. *The Roast and Ashes of Yalta*. New York: Continuum, 1983.

Survey Magazine, 1976.

Tatu, Michel. *Le triangle Washington-Moscou-Pékin stiles deux Europes*. Casterman Poche.

Taylor, A.J.P. *Churchill Revised*. New York: Dial Press, 1969.

Tocqueville. *De la Democratie en Amérique*.

Tolstoi, Nicolai. *Victims of Yalta*. London: Corey.

Truman, Harry. *Years of Decision*. New York: Doubleday, 1955.

———. *Plain Speaking*. Berkeley: Medallion Books, 1973.

Vaizay, John. *The Squandered Peace*. London: Hodder, 1983.

Wilmot, Chester. *Stalin's Greatest Victory*. Heath, 1972.

Yargin, Daniel. *Shattered Peace*. Boston: Houghton-Mifflin, 1978.

Zacharias, Ellis. *Secret Mission*. New York.

About the Author

Nicolas Baciu was born in Rumania. He was a lawyer in Bucharest before proclamation of the Communist republic in Rumania. Purged from the bar, arrested by the Communists, the author succeeded in escaping, to swim across the Danube into Yugoslavia in September 1948.

Arrested by Tito's police, Nicolas Baciu experienced life in Communist prisons in Yugoslavia. Then he succeeded in escaping again to the free world—to Austria.

Arriving in Paris, the author wrote his first book: *Des Geôles de Ana Pauker aux prisons de Tito*, in 1951, in Paris. The book was published by the French newspaper *Le Monde* and by the Swiss *Gazette de Lausanne*, and Baciu was awarded the great *Silvio Pellico* Prize, which he shared with Henry Barraud.

Mr. Baciu collaborated after 1950 with the BBC radio station in London, where he gave a series of lectures, as well as with Radio Europa Libera in New York, where he edited the Rumanian programs.

Since then Mr. Baciu has written various articles that have appeared in the Western press to draw the attention of the West to the danger of Russian imperialism and of international communism. In *Le Monde*, the *New York Times*, the *Christian Science Monitor*, the *Herald Tribune*, *L'Aurure*, and *Gazette de Lausanne*, the author has constantly put the West on their guard and sought vigorous anti-Yalta action.

Although now a naturalized American, the author remains faithful to his Rumanian nation. He has written all this time in the Rumanian Press in exile, as in *Romanul* or *Europa* and the *Neamul Romanesc* as well as *Buletinul Europeen*, to help his countrymen in exile to preserve their identity and to sustain their morale and fighting spirit.

The present book will appear in a Rumanian edition with a series of annexes regarding—especially—Rumania and the author's direct experiences with its development.

De Lux

net = $2475

$1856.25

O Con